CN00951615

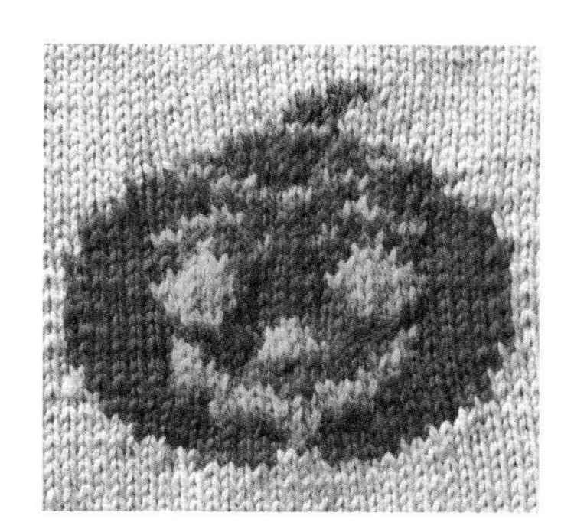

KNITS FOR ALL SEASONS

JEAN MOSS

KNITS FOR ALL SEASONS

JEAN MOSS

Happy Knitting Carmen!
With best wishes
Jean Moss

MITCHELL BEAZLEY

Editors: **Sally Harding, Jane McIntosh**

Executive Art Editors: **Larraine Lacey, Robin Whitecross**

Photography: **Simon Brown** (pages 1, 8-9, 10, 27, 44, 50-51, 52, 82-83, 84, 120-121, 123, 125, 129, 157)

Tessa Codrington (pages 2, 11, 12, 13, 16, 17, 22, 23, 34, 35, 110, 111, 116, 117, 122, 124, 128, 132, 133, 136, 142, 147)

Philip Mercer (page 6 and jacket back flap)

Pia Tryde (pages 4-5, 7, 26, 38, 39, 44, 45, 53, 54, 55, 58, 59, 66, 67, 72, 73, 78, 79, 81, 85, 86, 87, 90, 91, 96, 97, 99, 100, 101, 105, 106, 107, 137, 143, 146, 152, 153, 156, 159

Photographic Styling: **Alex Anderson**

Additional Styling: **Melanie Molesworth** (pages 8-9, 50-51, 82-83, 120-121)

Charts: **Textype Typesetters**

Production: **Fiona Wright**

First published in Great Britain in 1993 by Mitchell Beazley, an imprint of Reed Consumer Books, part of Reed International Books Limited, Michelin House, 81 Fulham Road, London SW3 6RB
and Auckland, Melbourne, Singapore and Toronto

ISBN 1 85732 256 8

A catalogue record for this book is available from the British Library.

Produced by Mandarin Offset
Printed in Hong Kong

ABBREVIATIONS

alt	alternate
approx	approximately
beg	begin(ning)
cm	centimetre(s)
cont	continu(e)(ing)
dec	decreas(e)(ing)
foll	follow(s)(ing)
g	gramme(s)
in	inch(es)
inc	increas(e)(ing)
k	knit
LH	left hand
m	metre(s)
mm	millimetre(s)
oz	ounce(s)
p	purl
patt(s)	pattern(s)
psso	pass slip stitch over
rem	remain(s)(ing)
rep	repeat(s)(ing)
rev st st	reverse stocking (stockinette) stitch
RH	right hand
RS	right side(s)
sl	slip
st(s)	stitch(es)
st st	stocking (stockinette) stitch
tbl	through back of loop(s)
tog	together
WS	wrong side(s)
yd	yard(s)
yo	yarn over

* Rep instructions after asterisk or between asterisks as many times as instructed.

() Rep instructions inside parentheses as many times as instructed.

COLOURWORK NOTE

When working the intarsia method, use short lengths of yarn approx 46cm (18in) long so that yarn does not become tangled.

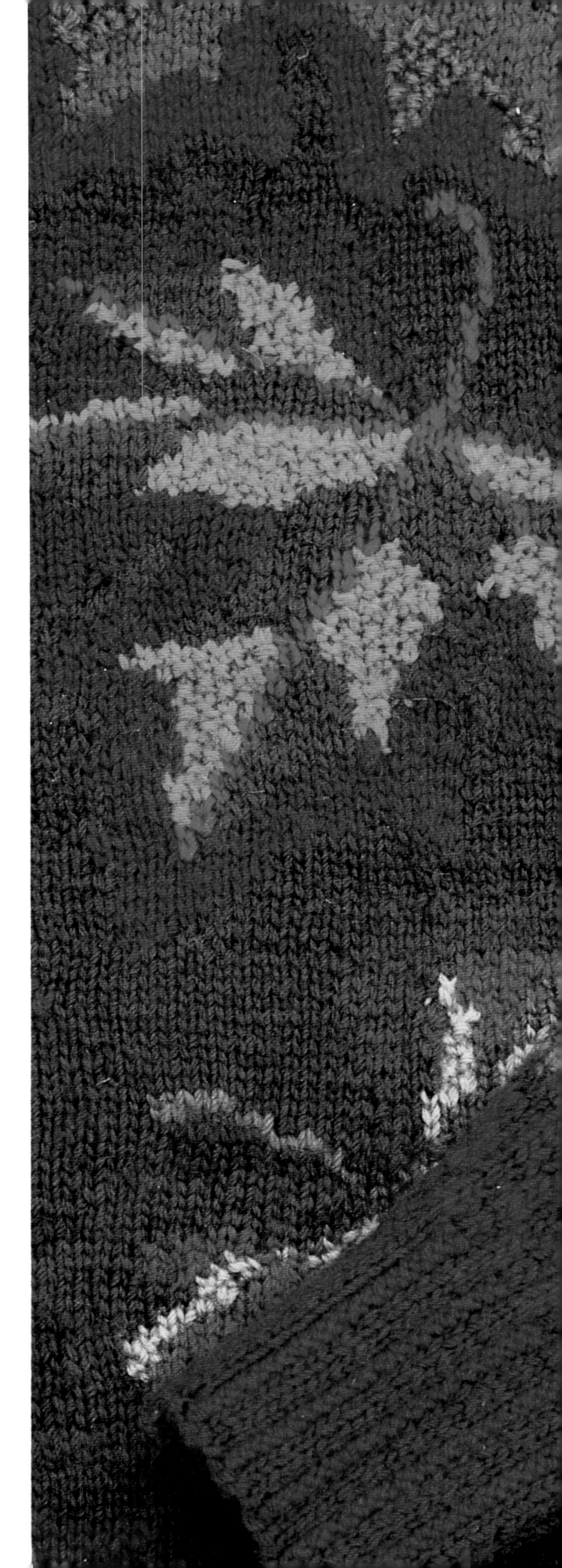

Contents

* Sweaters marked with an asterisk are available as kits. Please see leaflet inside cover of book for details and order form.

KNITTING NEEDLE SIZES

Metric	US	Old UK	Metric	US	Old UK
2mm	0	14	4½mm	7	7
2¼ mm	1	13	5mm	8	6
2¾ mm	2	12	5½mm	9	5
3mm		11	6mm	10	4
3¼mm	3	10	6½mm	10½	3
3½mm	4		7mm		2
3¾mm	5	9	7½mm		1
4mm	6	8	8mm	11	0

Introduction

I have always wanted to create a book of sweater designs that will fire the imaginations of knitters. Every design in this book is completely different and is capable of giving birth to a whole new collection of its own. So, not only will you be able to knit the sweaters from the patterns, you will also be able to use your own ideas to personalize them. Each sweater has its own particular knitting interest, to develop and expand your skills. There are four seasonal chapters, each with family members wearing sweaters which, for me, suggest a special seasonal activity, celebration or festival.

Don't feel you have to follow the patterns to the letter. Providing your tension is compatible and your graph centred, there are lots of ways you can adapt them. Simply by changing the buttons, adding new or unusual trimmings or altering the neckline, you can bring a sweater alive just for you. Try turning a winter woolly into a summer sweater by using cotton yarn of a similar weight. For instance, the ALMANAC sweater would look stunning in cotton. The EQUINOX and BIRTHDAY offer great opportunities for your creativity – just invent your own designs for the backs.

You don't have to be Matisse to make a sweater unique for you. Substitute your own motifs for mine, and remember that the motif shape is not the most important thing, as detail is dictated largely by yarn, tension and stitch. Don't worry about being realistic – the most attractive shapes are often naive or impressionist ones. Have confidence, trust your intuition and concentrate on choosing the colours that will make your design 'sing'.

I'm always thrilled to see people wearing my sweaters – it's such a compliment that someone will dedicate so much time and effort to knit my fantasies. But I hope in the future to notice a few sweaters in my workshops that look familiar, but which I can't quite identify. Then I'll be pleased to think that I might have helped you to achieve some of your own knitting fantasies.

WINTER

Winter

I have always relished the celebrations which for me mark the movement of the seasons through the calendar. The year is punctuated by events which give it rhythm and interest, making each season unique.

This is true no more so than of Winter, with its short days, long dark nights, bare trees, pale grey skies and thin, watery light. Winter holds its own attractions and beauty, but just as for nature it's generally a time of hibernation, so we humans need to occupy ourselves more indoors. It's probably the time when most of our knitting gets done – it certainly is for me.

In my family Winter is heralded by our preparations for *Yuletide* celebrations, a time for thinking about old friends and family. The choosing of gifts is important to us and we like to make as many as we can each year. Finding greenery to cheer up the house is something which gets us out into the countryside. I have fond memories of many long walks enjoyed after I had been winkled out from the warmth of the fireside. On our return, hot crumpets toasted on an open fire seem to be one of Winter's luxuries.

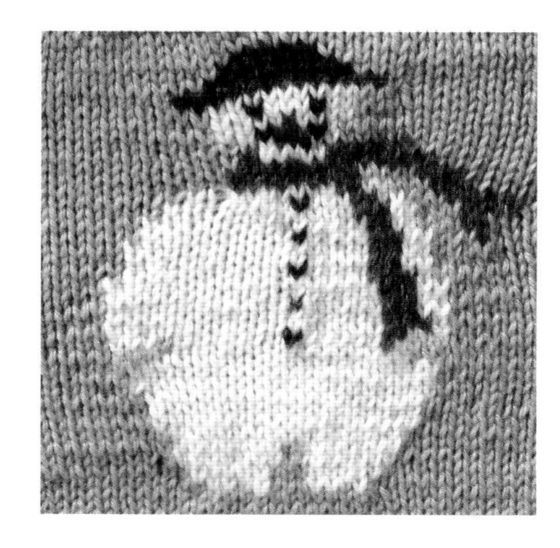

Another thing that always causes a flurry of excitement in our house is the first fall of snow. It's a magical surprise for children (of all ages!) to wake up to a blanket of snow. When we lived in the country, the kids would be out with their toboggans, sometimes before breakfast so as not to miss a moment. *Winter Sports* for me usually involves nothing more than tobogganing, snowballs and helping to make our snowman, but one day I'll get round to fulfilling a resolution by learning to ski!

I always feel that Spring is on the way with the approach of St Valentine's Day. In my view, there's no better way to spend a long Winter's evening than a romantic candlelit supper beside an open fire with your *Valentine*. The intrigue, mystery and excitement all appeal to my sense of drama and conspire to create a truly colourful climax to winter.

FRANKINCENSE

I ASSOCIATE THIS SWEATER WITH THE COLOURS AND SMELLS OF OUR MID-WINTER CELEBRATIONS: DARK BERRIES AND EVERGREENS AMIDST THE SCENT OF CANDLEWAX, INCENSE AND LOGSMOKE. USING AS ITS SOURCE THE BEAUTIFUL TRADITIONAL PATTERNS OF THE FISHERFOLK OF NORTHERN BRITAIN, EACH PART OF THIS SWEATER HOLDS ITS OWN KNITTING INTEREST AND HISTORY.

SIZE

One size only to fit 96–112cm/38–44in chest

See diagram for finished knitted measurements.

MATERIALS

Rowan *Botany* 25g/1oz hanks as foll:

A (no.659: aubergine) 10 hanks

B (no.420: Ascot green) 1 hank

Rowan *Donegal Lambswool Tweed* 25g/1oz hank as foll:

C (no.473: pepper) 1 hank

Rowan *Silkstones* 50g/1¾oz hank as foll:

D (no.25: dried rose) 1 hank

E (no.35: eau de nil) 1 hank

F (no.29: woad) 1 hank

G (no.26: chilli) 1 hank

Rowan *Silk and Wool* 20g/¾oz balls as foll:

H (no.848: rapid blue) 2 balls

Rowan *Wool and Cotton* 40g/1½oz balls as foll:

I (no.923: wedgewood) 1 ball

One pair each of 2¼ mm (US size 1) and 3¼mm (US size 3) knitting needles

Set of four 2¼mm (US size 1) double-pointed needles and set of four 3¼mm (US size 3) double-pointed needles for yoke

ALTERNATIVE COLOURWAY

This sweater can also be worked in the colourway shown below, where:

A = *Wool and Cotton* no.920: hazelnut

B = *Wool and Cotton* no.923: wedgewood

C = *Botany* no.602: burgundy

D = *Botany* no.80: chocolate

E = *Silkstones* no.826: chilli

F = *Donegal Lambswool Tweed* no.473: pepper

G = *Botany* no.9: gold

H = *Silkstones* no.829: woad (1 ball only)

I = *Botany* no.104: apricot

TENSION (GAUGE)

30 sts and 35 rows to 10cm/4in measured over diamond patt worked on 3¼mm (US size 3) needles

PLEASE CHECK YOUR TENSION (GAUGE) CAREFULLY AND CHANGE KNITTING NEEDLE SIZE IF NECESSARY

NOTES

When working Fair Isle borders, do not strand yarn across back of work for more than 3 sts, but weave the loose strands on every 4th st.

For back, front and sleeves read charts from right to left for the RS (odd-numbered) rows and from left to right for the WS (even-numbered) rows. For neckband and yoke (which are worked in rounds) read all rows from right to left.

BACK

Using smaller needles and A, cast on 190 sts and beg foll rib pattern chart as foll:

Chart rib row 1 (RS) K1, p1, k2, p1, k1, p1, ***k1, p1, *k2, p1, k next 2 sts tog leaving sts on LH needle, then insert RH needle from the front between the 2 sts just knitted tog and k the first st again, then slip both sts off LH needle tog – called *right twist* or *RT* –, *, rep from * to * twice more, k2, (p1, k1) twice, p1, **k2, with the RH needle behind the LH needle skip next st and k the 2nd st on LH needle through the back loop, then insert RH needle through backs of both the skipped st and the 2nd st and k2tog through back – called *left twist* or *LT* –, p1**, rep from ** to ** twice more, k2, p1, k1, p1***, rep 44-st repeat from *** to *** 3 times more, k1, p1, k2, p1, RT.

Beg with chart row 2, cont foll the chart for the rib patt (working RT and LT which are split at the beg of chart on rows 1 and 7 as a k st) until chart row 8 has been completed.

Rep first-8th chart rows 4 times more, so ending with a WS row.

Change to larger needles and beg foll diamond pattern chart as foll:

Diamond chart row 1 (RS) K7, ***k9, p1, RT, k19, LT, p1, k10***, rep 44-st repeat from ***

to *** 3 times more, k7.
Cont foll chart for diamond patt and rep 24-row repeat throughout, until back measures 47cm/18½in from cast-on edge, ending with WS row.

Armhole shaping

Keeping patt correct throughout, beg armhole shaping as foll:

Next row (dec row) (RS) K2, sl 1-k1-psso, work in patt to last 4 sts, k2tog, k2. 188 sts.

Work one row without shaping.
Dec one st at each end of next row and at each end of every foll alt row 15 times in all. 158 sts.
Work without shaping until back measures 64.5cm/25½in from cast-on edge, ending with a WS row.

Neck and shoulder shaping

Next row (RS) Work 54 sts in patt, turn leaving rem sts on spare needle.
Working first side of neck only, dec one st at beg of next row (neck edge), then at neck edge on every foll row 22 times in all. 32 sts.
Work without shaping until back measures 73cm/28¾in from cast-on edge, ending with a WS row.
Cast (bind) off 16 sts at beg of next row, work one row without shaping, cast (bind) off rem 16 sts.
Return to rem sts and with RS facing, slip centre 50 sts onto a st holder, rejoin yarn to rem sts and work in patt to end of row.
Complete 2nd side of neck to match first side, reversing shaping.

FRONT

Work as for back until front measures 42.5cm/16¾in from cast-on edge, ending with a WS row.

Neck and shoulder shaping

Keeping patt correct throughout, beg neck shaping as foll:

Next row (RS) Work 94 sts in patt, turn leaving rem sts on spare needle.
Working first side of neck only, dec one st at beg of next row (neck edge) and at neck edge on every foll alt row 38 times in all, then on every foll 3rd row 8 times *and at the same time* when there are same number of rows as back to armhole work armhole shaping at armhole edge as for back by dec one st (2 sts from edge) on next and every foll alt row 16 times in all.
When neck and armhole shaping have been completed, work without shaping on rem 32 sts until there are same number of rows as back to shoulder, ending with a WS row.
Cast (bind) off 16 sts at beg of next row, work one row without shaping, cast (bind) off rem 16 sts.
Return to rem sts and with RS facing, slip centre 2 sts onto a st holder, rejoin yarn to rem sts and work in patt to end of row.
Complete 2nd side of neck to match first side, reversing shaping.

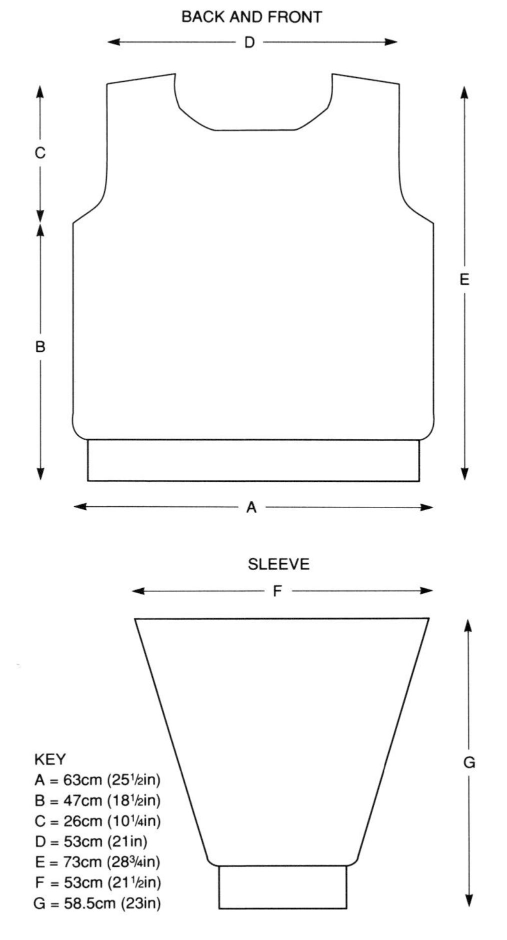

SLEEVES

Using smaller needles and A, cast on 72 sts and beg foll rib patt chart:

Chart rib row 1 (RS) K1, (LT, p1, k2) twice, (p1, k1) twice, p1, *k2, p1, RT*, rep from * to * twice more, k2, (p1, k1) twice, p1, **k2, LT, p1**, rep from ** to ** twice more, k2, (p1, k1) twice, p1, (k2, p1, RT) twice, k2.

Beg with chart row 2, cont foll chart for rib patt until chart row 8 has been completed.
Rep first-8th chart rows 4 times more, then rep first-2nd chart rows once more, so ending with WS row.
Change to larger needles and beg foll Fair Isle pattern chart as foll:

Chart row 1 (RS) Using D, knit.

Chart row 2 Work 24-st rep 3 times across row.

Cont foll chart for Fair Isle patt *and at the same time* inc one st at each end of next row and every foll 3rd row (working new sts into patt as indicated by edge sts on chart) until chart row 27 has been completed, so ending with a RS row. 90 sts.
Change to A. P one row.
Beg foll diamond patt chart as foll:

Chart row 1 (RS) K10, LT, p1, k19, p1, RT, k19, LT, p1, k19, p1, RT, k11.

Cont foll chart for diamond patt and rep 24-row repeat throughout *and at the same time* cont shaping sleeve by inc one st at each end of next row and every foll 3rd row 3 times in all, then every 4th row 32 times, working new sts into patt. 160 sts.
Cont without shaping in diamond patt until sleeve measures 58.5cm/23in from cast-on edge or desired length, ending with a WS row. Cast (bind) off.
Make 2nd sleeve in same way.

DIAMOND PATTERN CHART

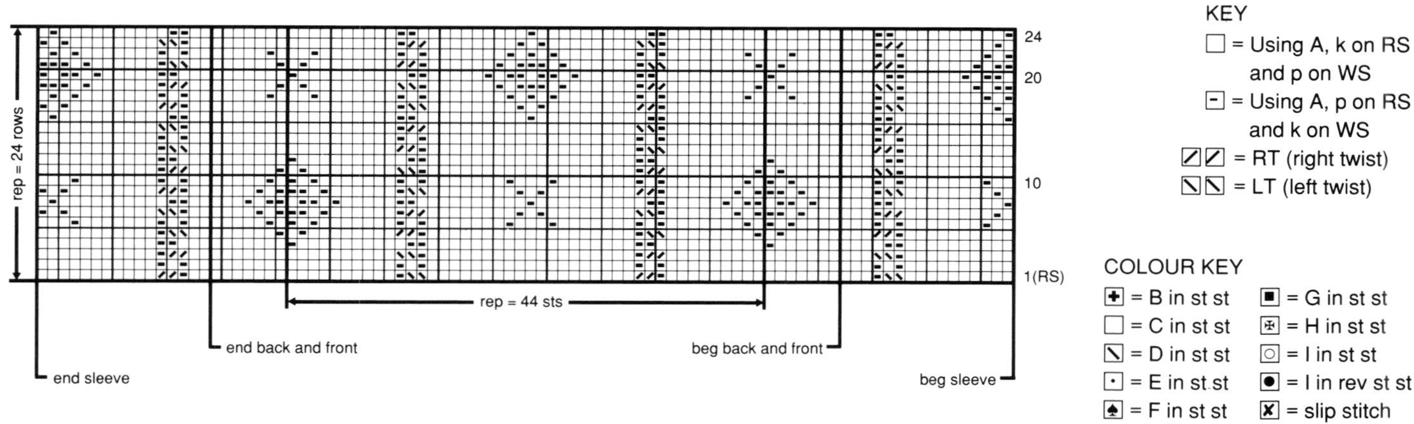

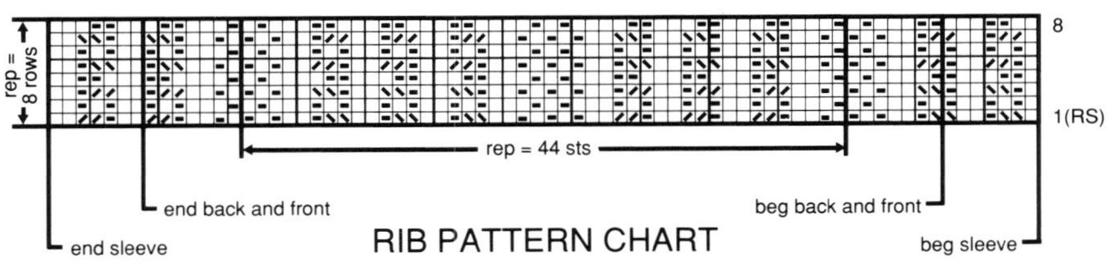

FAIR ISLE PATTERN CHART

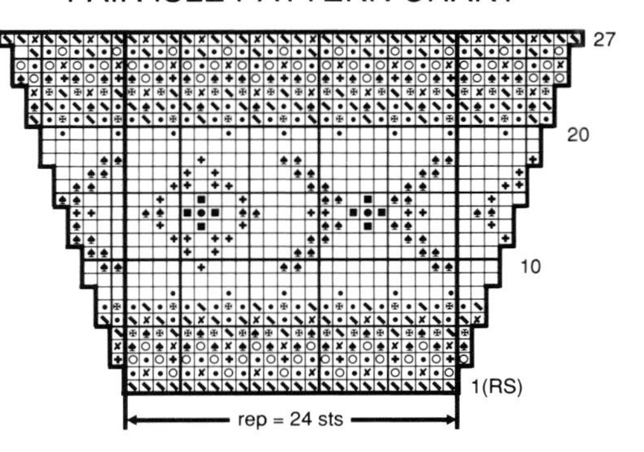

YOKE AND NECKBAND

Join shoulder seams.

Using set of larger double-pointed needles and A and with RS facing, beg at centre front and pick up and k106 sts up right front neck from 2 sts on holder to shoulder seam, 29 sts down right back neck, k50 sts from back neck st holder, pick up and k29 sts up left back neck, 106 sts down left front neck and k2 sts from front st holder. 322 sts.

Note: Remember to read all chart rows from right to left.

Beg working Fair Isle pattern in rounds (RS always facing) foll chart for patt as foll:

Round 1 Using D, k2tog, k to last 4 sts, sl 1-k1-psso, k2 centre sts. 320 sts.

Round 2 K2tog, work in patt to last 4 sts, sl 1-k1-psso, k2, *and at the same time* foll chart for colours by working 24-st repeat 13 times, then first 6 sts of patt rep, ending knit 2 centre sts in C.

Keeping patt correct, cont in this way foll chart for patt as set, keeping 2 centre front sts in C throughout Fair Isle chart and dec one st at each side of 2 centre sts on every round, until chart row 8 has been completed. 306 sts.

Round 9 Using C only (as indicated on chart), k2tog, k5, (k2tog, k6) 36 times (to last 11 sts), k2tog, k5, sl 1-k1-psso, k2. 267 sts.

Round 10 Using C k2tog, k4 in C, rep 24-st repeat 10 times, work first 13 sts of 24-st repeat, then using C k4, sl 1-k1-psso, k2. 265 sts.

Cont foll chart from row 11, working sts at beg and end of round in C, and dec one st on each side of 2 centre sts on every round, until chart row 18 has been completed. 249 sts.

Round 19 Using C only (as indicated on chart), k2tog, k10, k2tog, (k20, k2tog) 10 times (to last 15 sts), k11, sl 1-k1-psso, k2. 236 sts.

Round 20 K2tog, work in patt to last 4 sts, sl 1-k1-psso, k2, *and at the same time* foll chart for colours by working 24-st repeat 9 times, then first 18 sts of patt rep, ending knit 2 centre sts in C. 234 sts.

Keeping patt correct, cont in this way foll chart for patt as set and dec one st at each side of 2 centre sts on every round, until chart row 27 has been completed. 220 sts.

Change to set of smaller double-pointed needles and using A only, beg foll rib patt chart as foll:

Chart rib row 1 K2tog, work in patt to last 4 sts, sl 1-k1-psso, k2 *and at the same time* foll chart for patt working 44-st repeat across first 218 sts, then keep 2 centre sts k.

Keeping patt correct, cont foll rib pattern chart for patt and dec one st at each side of 2 centre sts on every round, until chart row 8 has been completed. 204 sts.

Cast (bind) off in rib, working decs.

FINISHING

Press pieces very lightly on WS with a warm iron, omitting ribbing.

Sew cast (bound) off edge of sleeves to armhole edge (including decreased edge). Join the side and the sleeve seams.

Press seams lightly on WS.

CHOO-CHOO

WHEN YOU FIRST LOOK AT THIS SWEATER IT SEEMS TO BE AN ABSTRACT FAIR ISLE DESIGN, BUT IF YOU LOOK CLOSER YOU'LL SEE THAT IT'S TWO LITTLE TRAINS – A PASSENGER TRAIN AND A GOODS TRAIN THAT I FOUND ON A NAVAJO BLANKET. THE CHOICE OF BUTTONS IS SO IMPORTANT AND I LOVE THESE BULL'S-EYE ONES WHICH ECHO THE COLOURS OF THE JACKET.

SIZES

To fit 2–3[4–5] yrs or 52–53[56–58]cm/20½–21[22–23]in

Figures for larger size are in brackets [ ]; where there is only one set of figures, it applies to both sizes.

See diagram for finished knitted measurements.

MATERIALS

Rowan *Lightweight DK* 25g/1oz hanks as foll:

A (no.625: dark grey) 8[11] hanks
B (no.146: taupe) 2[3] hanks
C (no.60: grey) 2[3] hanks
D (no.430: olive) 1 hank
E (no.71: dark brown) 1 hank
F (no.13: burgundy) 1 hank
G (no.141: blue) 1 hank
H (no.91: sea green) 1 hank
I (no.136: rust) 2 hanks
J (no.426: yellow gold) 2 hanks
L (no.45: red) 2 hanks
M (no.88: smokey blue) 2 hanks

One pair each of 3¼mm (US size 3) and 3¾mm (US size 5) knitting needles

Four 18mm/¾in buttons

ALTERNATIVE COLOURWAY

This jacket can also be worked in the colourway shown right, where:

A = no.73: green
B = no.655: teal
C = no.87: chocolate
D = no.45: red
E = no.71: dark brown
F = no.132: burgundy
G = no.151: dark blue
H = no.136: rust
I = no.99: purple
J = no.14: yellow
L = no.57: royal blue
M = no.88: smokey blue

TENSION (GAUGE)

25 sts and 29 rows to 10cm/4in measured over patt worked on 3¾mm (US size 5) needles

PLEASE CHECK YOUR TENSION (GAUGE) CAREFULLY AND CHANGE KNITTING NEEDLE SIZE IF NECESSARY

NOTES

When working the bicolour stripes in C and G and in J and L, strand the colours loosely across the back of the work when they are not in use. But when working all the other motifs use the intarsia method, using a separate length of yarn for each isolated area of colour, twisting the yarns together when changing

the colours in order to avoid making a hole.

Read charts from right to left for the RS (odd-numbered) rows and from left to right for the WS (even-numbered) rows.

BACK

Using smaller needles and A, cast on 90[96] sts and k1, p1 rib for hem as foll:

Rib row 1 (RS) *K1, p1, rep from * to end.

Rep last row 10 times more, so ending with a RS row.

K one row to form foldline for hem.

Change to larger needles and beg with chart row 1, work in st st foll chart until chart row 56[60] has been completed, so ending with a WS row.

Armhole shaping

Cont to foll chart for patt and keeping patt correct throughout, beg armhole shaping as foll:

Chart row 57[61] (dec row) (RS) K2, sl 1-k1-psso, work in patt to last 4 sts, k2tog, k2.

Work one row without shaping.

Working decs in same way as first dec row, dec one st at each end of next row and then every foll alt row 5[6] times in all. 78[82] sts.

Work without shaping until chart row 105[113] has been completed, so ending with a RS row.

Neck shaping

Chart row 106[114] (WS) Work first 23[25] sts in patt, turn leaving rem sts on a spare needle.

Working first side of neck only, dec one st at beg of next row (neck

edge), then at neck edge on foll row. 21[23] sts.
Work one row without shaping.
Cast (bind) off.
Return to rem sts and with WS facing, rejoin yarn to rem sts and cast (bind) off centre 32 sts, work in patt to end of row.
Dec one st at end of next row (neck edge), then at neck edge on foll row. 21[23] sts.
Cast (bind) off.

LEFT FRONT

**Before beg front, work pocket lining.

Pocket lining

Using larger needles and A, cast on 18 sts.
Beg with a k row, work 20 rows in st st, so ending with a WS row.
Break off yarn and slip sts onto a st holder.

Begin front

Using smaller needles and A, cast on 40[43] sts and beg k1, p1 rib for hem as foll:
Rib row 1 (RS) K0[1], *p1, k1, rep from * to end.
Rib row 2 *P1, k1, rep from *, ending p0[1].
Rep last 2 rows 4 times more, then rep row 1 once more, so ending with a RS row.**
Next row (WS) Cast on 18 sts, then K to end of row to form foldline for hem. 58[61] sts.
Change to larger needles and beg with chart row 1, work in st st foll chart until chart row 3 has been completed, so ending with a RS row.
Cont to foll chart for patt and keeping patt correct throughout, beg first pair of buttonholes as foll:
Chart row 4 (WS) Work first 3 sts in patt, cast (bind) off 3 sts, work 6 sts in patt (including st already on needle after cast (bind) off), cast (bind) off 3 sts, work in patt to end of row.
Chart row 5 Work in patt, casting on 3 sts over those cast (bound) off in last row.
Work without shaping until chart row 20 has been completed, so ending with a WS row.
Chart row 21 (RS) Work first 43[46] sts in patt, cast (bind) off 3 sts, work 6 sts in patt (including st already on needle after cast (bind) off), cast (bind) off 3 sts, work in patt to end of row.
Chart row 22 Work in patt, casting on 3 sts over those cast (bound) off in last row.
Work without shaping until chart row 32 has been completed, so ending with a WS row.

Insert pocket lining

Chart row 33 (RS) Work first 11[14] sts in patt, slip next 18 sts onto a st holder, then with RS of pocket lining facing work in patt across 18 sts of pocket lining, work rem 29 sts in patt.
Work in patt until chart row 56 has been completed, working buttonholes on chart rows 38 and 39 and rows 55 and 56 in the same way as before, and casting on 20 sts at beg of chart row 56. 78[81] sts.
Cont in patt until chart row 56[60] has been completed, so ending with a WS row.

Armhole shaping

Working decs as for back, dec one st at beg of next row (armhole edge) and at armhole edge on every foll alt row 6[7] times in all. 72[74] sts.
Work without shaping until chart row 108[116] has been completed, so ending with a WS row.

Shoulder shaping

Chart row 109[117] (RS) Cast (bind) off 21[23] sts, work in patt to end of row.

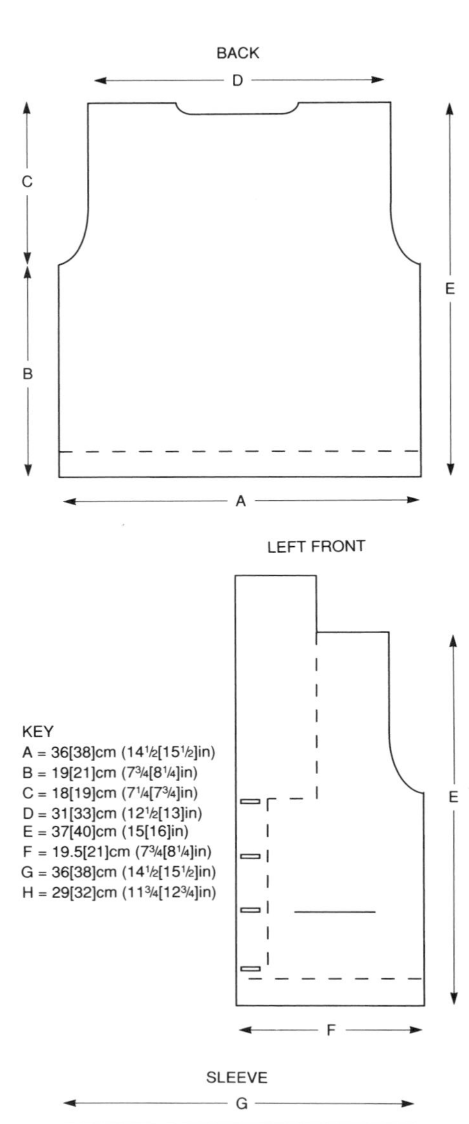

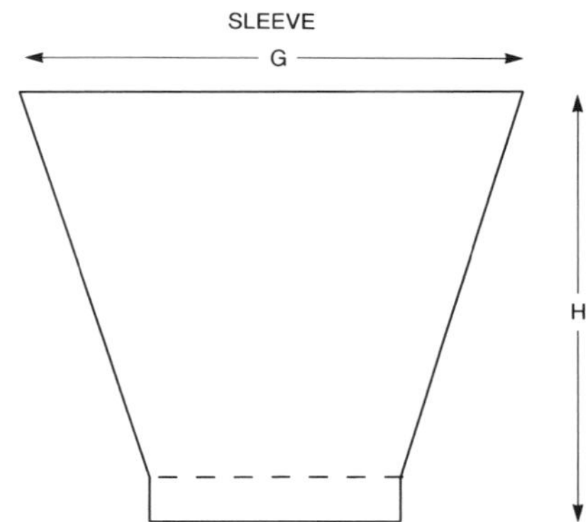

Collar extension

Work collar extension without shaping on rem 51 sts until chart row 132[140] has been completed, so ending with a WS row.
Cast (bind) off.

RIGHT FRONT

Work as for left front, but foll chart for right front and reversing all shaping and position of pocket.

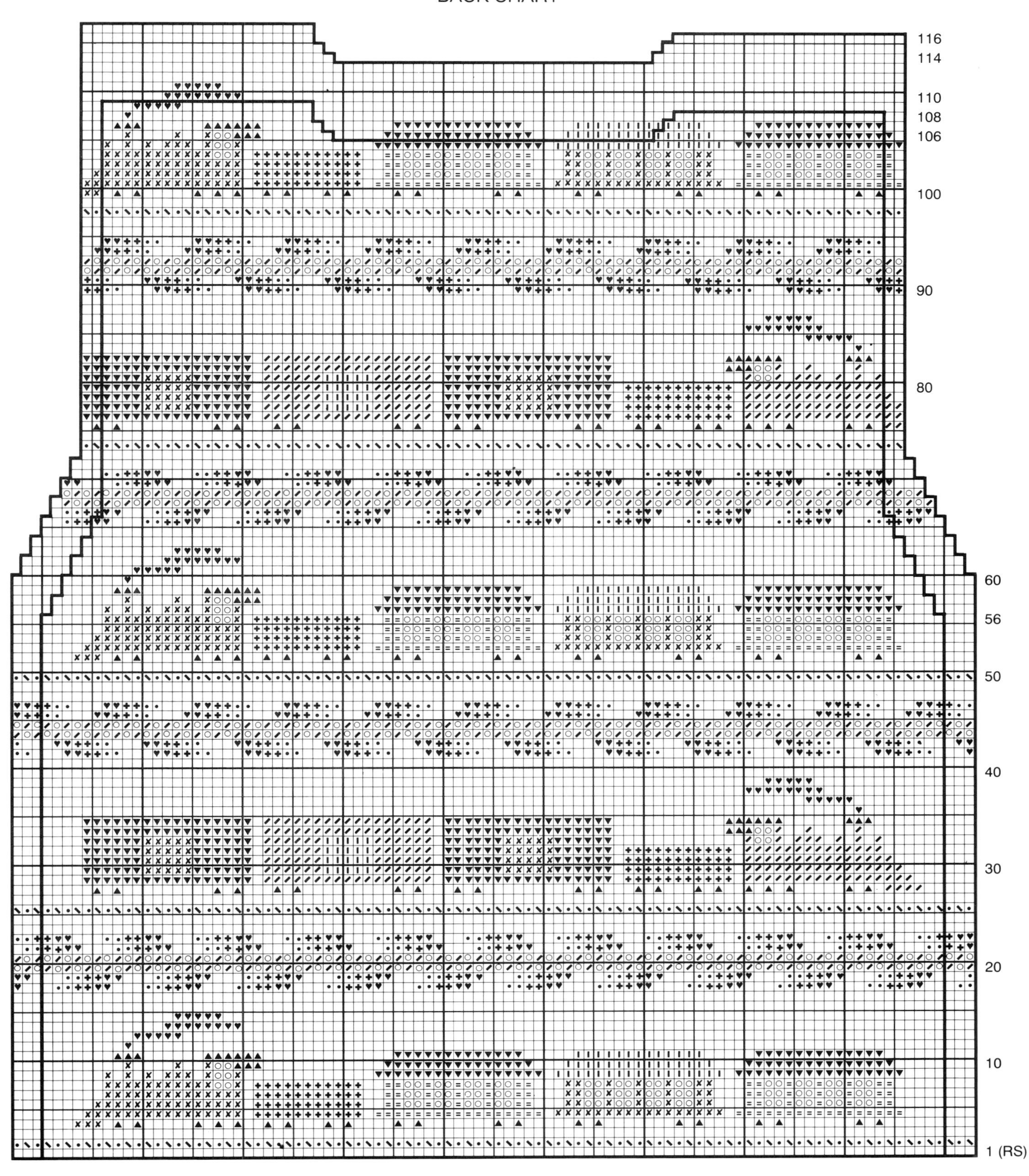

SLEEVES

Using smaller needles and A, cast on 42[46] sts and work 9 rows in k1, p1 rib as for back, so ending with a RS row.

K one row to form foldline for hem.

COLOUR KEY

☐ = A	☒ = D	◹ = G	◎ = J
✚ = B	▲ = E	▯ = H	⁄ = L
· = C	= = F	▼ = I	♥ = M

SLEEVE CHART

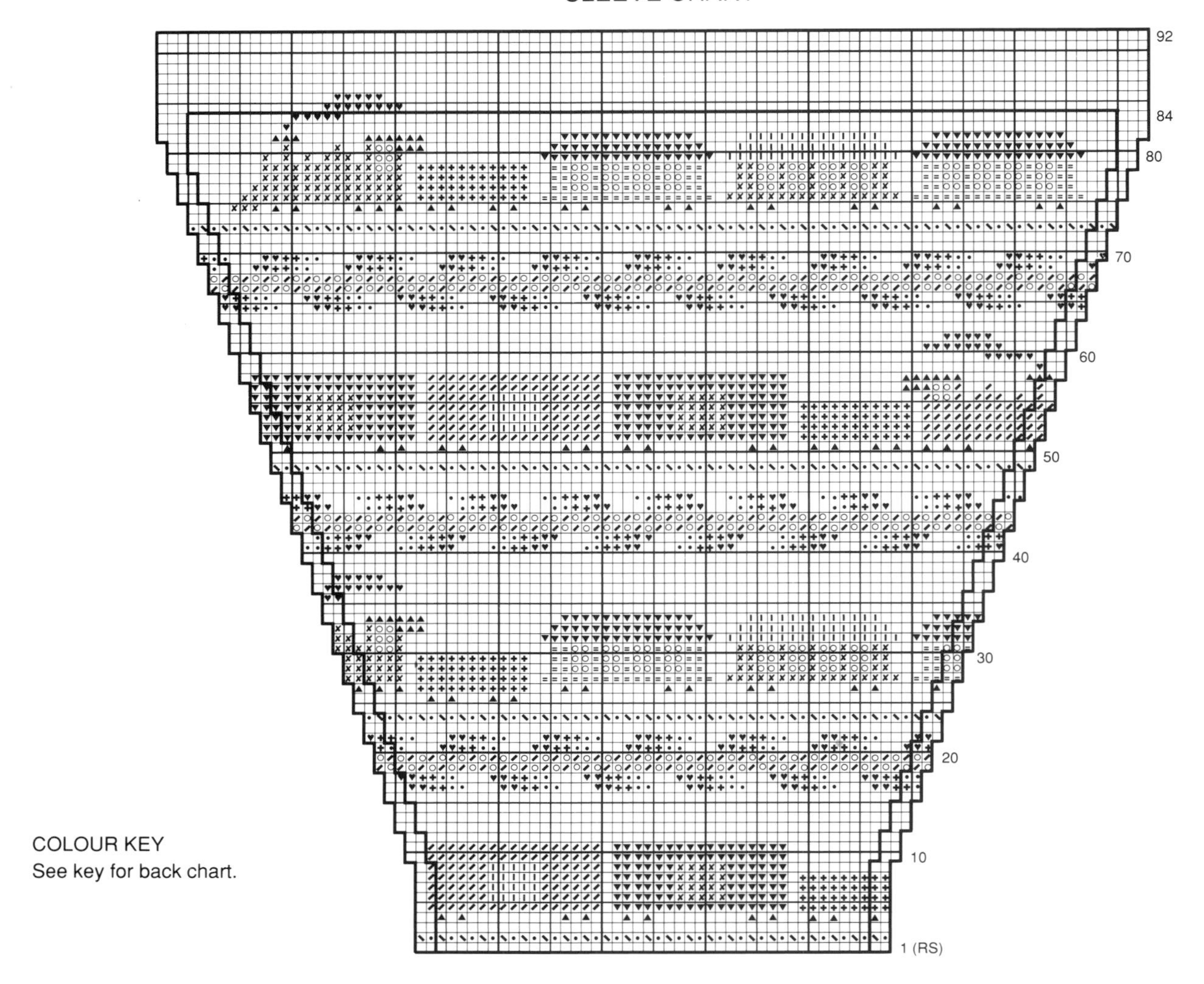

COLOUR KEY
See key for back chart.

Change to larger needles and beg with chart row 1, work in st st foll chart until chart row 9 has been completed, so ending with a RS row.
Cont to foll chart for patt and keeping patt correct throughout, inc one st at each end of next row and then at each end of every foll 3rd row until there are 90[96] sts.
Work in patt without shaping until chart row 84[92] has been completed, so ending with a WS row.
Cast (bind) off all sts.
Make the 2nd sleeve in the same way as the first sleeve.

FINISHING

Press pieces lightly on WS with a warm iron over a damp cloth, omitting ribbing.

Pocket hems

Using smaller needles and A and with RS facing, k across 24 sts of left front pocket. K one row to form hemline fold. Work 4 rows in k1, p1 rib.

Cast (bind) off loosely in rib.

Work hem at top of right front pocket in same way.

Turn pocket hems to WS of fronts and slip stitch in place.

Slip stitch pocket linings to WS of fronts.

Join seams using a small neat backstitch on very edge of work, except for ribbing – use an invisible overstitch (overcast st) on ribbing.

Join shoulder seams.

Placing centre of top of sleeve at shoulder seam, sew cast (bound) off edge of sleeves to armhole edge (including decreased edge).

Join side and sleeve seams.

Turn up hem on back and fronts to WS along p row above ribbing and slip stitch in place. Turn hem on sleeves to WS in same way and slip stitch in place.

Join cast (bound) off edges of collar extension. Then sew collar extension to back neck, easing in collar. Fold collar in half (WS sides tog) and fold front button band and buttonhole band facings to WS (9 sts from edge), and slip stitch in place.

Sew 2 layers of each buttonhole tog all around buttonhole edge.

Press seams lightly on WS.

Sew buttons to button band to correspond with buttonholes.

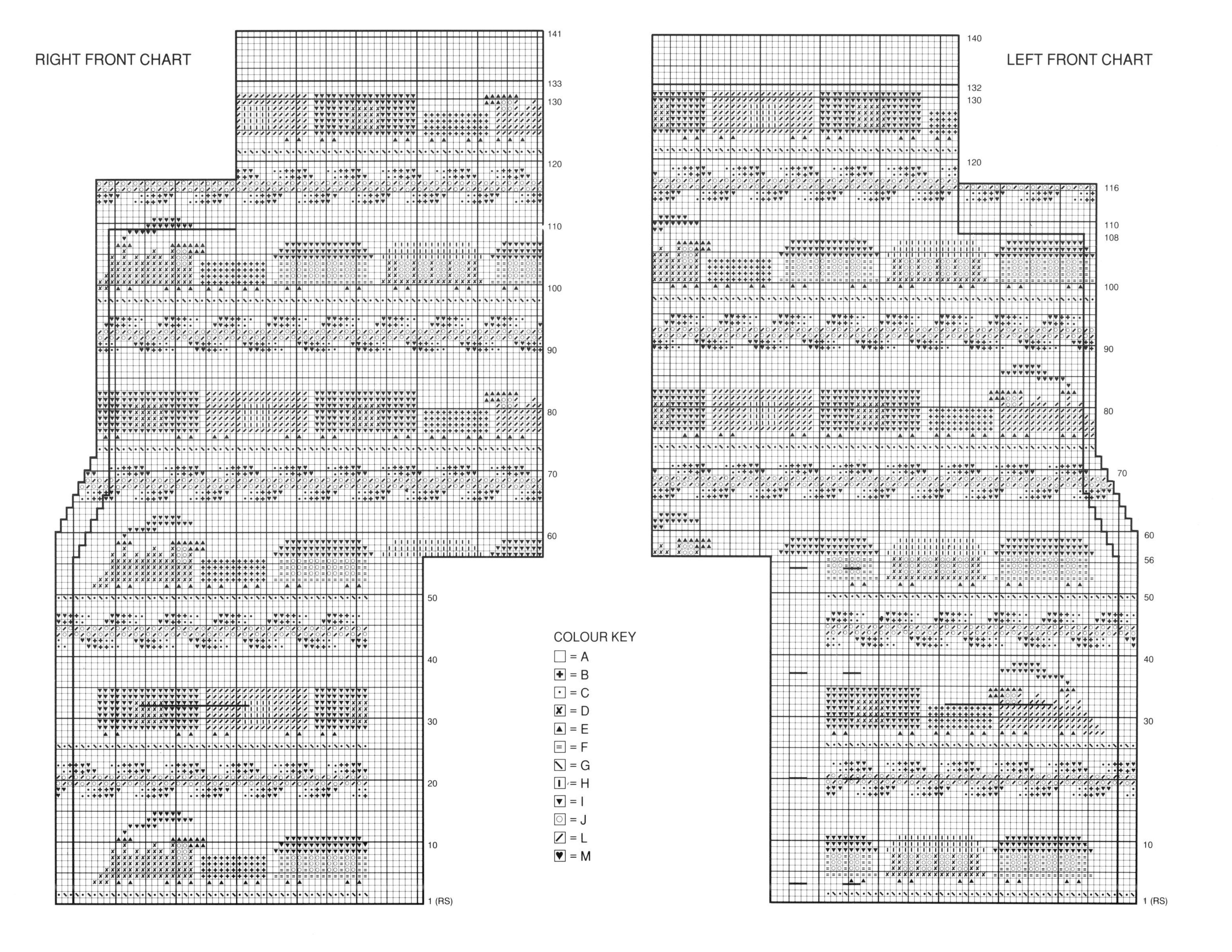
RIGHT FRONT CHART
141
133
130
120
110
100
90
80
70
60
50
40
30
20
10
1 (RS)
LEFT FRONT CHART
140
132
130
120
116
110
108
100
90
80
70
60
56
50
40
30
10
1 (RS)
COLOUR KEY
= A
= B
= C
= D
= E
= F
= G
= H
= I
= J
= L
= M

CAIRNGORM

THIS SWEATER IS INSPIRED BY THE CUT-PILE EMBROIDERIES OF THE SHOOWA PEOPLE OF ZAIRE. THE DESIGN LOOKS SO DIFFERENT WHEN THE COLOURS ARE CHANGED. THE MAIN COLOURWAY HAS AN ARGYLL SORT OF FEEL, BUT WHEN COLOURS OF A SIMILAR TONE ARE SUBSTITUTED IN THE ALTERNATIVE COLOURWAY, LOOK HOW THE BALANCE AND EMPHASIS CHANGE.

SIZE

One size only to fit 96–116cm/38–46in chest

See diagram for finished knitted measurements.

MATERIALS

Rowan *Magpie* 100g/3½oz hanks as foll:

A (no.450: dapple) 4 hanks
B (no.451: badger) 2 hanks
C (no.452: Welsh) 2 hanks
D (no.612: neptune) 1 hank
E (no.504: admiral) 1 hank

Rowan *Rowanspun Tweed* 100g/3½oz hanks as foll:

F (no.759: cedar) 2 hanks
G (no.753: cranberry) 2 hanks
H (no.761: fig) 2 hanks
I (no.752: tea) 2 hanks
J (no.764: grey) 1 hank
L (no.756: one a.m.) 1 hank
M (no.755: damson) 1 hank

One pair each of 3¾mm (US size 5) and 5mm (US size 8) knitting needles

ALTERNATIVE COLOURWAY

This sweater can also be worked in the colourway shown right, where:

A = *Rowanspun Tweed* no.764: grey
B = *Rowanspun Tweed* no.760: caviar
C = *Rowanspun Tweed* no.756: one a.m.
D = *Silkstones* no.836: mulberry
E = *Magpie* no.504: admiral
F = *Rowanspun Tweed* no.755: damson
G = *Rowanspun Tweed* no.757: iris
H = *Magpie* no.608: sealord
I = *Magpie* no.612: neptune
J = *Silkstones* no.825: dried rose
L = *Magpie* no.118: highland
M = *Magpie* no.451: badger

Note: Use *Silkstones* double.

TENSION (GAUGE)

18 sts and 23 rows to 10cm/4in measured over patt worked on 5mm (US size 8) needles

PLEASE CHECK YOUR TENSION (GAUGE) CAREFULLY AND CHANGE KNITTING NEEDLE SIZE IF NECESSARY

NOTES

When working the colourwork pattern, use the intarsia method, using a separate length of yarn for each isolated area of colour and twisting yarns together when changing colours to avoid making a hole.

Read charts from right to left for the RS (odd-numbered) rows and from left to right for the WS (even-numbered) rows.

BACK

Using smaller needles and I, cast on 100 sts and beg k2, p2 rib as foll:

Rib row 1 (RS) *P2, k2, rep from * to end.

Rep last row to form rib patt, work one row more in I, then work 2 rows in C.

Using A, work in rib until ribbing measures 8cm/3in from cast-on edge, ending with a RS row.

Keeping rib correct, inc 18 sts evenly across next row as foll:

Next row (inc row) (WS) Rib 3, work into front and back of next st – called *inc 1* –, *rib 5, inc 1 into next st, rib 4, inc 1 into next st*, rep from * to * 7 times more, rib 5, inc 1 into next st, rib 2. 118 sts.

Change to larger needles and beg foll patt chart in st st as foll:

Chart row 1 (RS) K first 7 sts of chart before patt repeat begins as indicated on chart, rep 52-st repeat twice, k last 7 sts of chart as indicated.

Cont in st st foll chart for patt and rep 96-row repeat throughout, until back measures 46cm/18in from cast-on edge, ending with a WS (p) row.***

Armhole shaping

Keeping patt correct throughout, beg armhole shaping as foll:

Next row (dec row) (RS) Work 2 sts in patt, sl 1-k1-psso, work in patt to last 4 sts, k2tog, work 2 sts in patt.

Work one row without shaping. Rep dec row once.

Rep from ** to ** 8 times more. 98 sts.

Work without shaping until back

measures 71cm/28in from cast-on edge, ending with a WS (p) row.

Neck and shoulder shaping

Next row (RS) Work first 37 sts in patt, turn leaving rem sts on a spare needle.

Working first side of neck only, dec one st at beg of next row (neck edge).

Next row (RS) Cast (bind) off 17 sts, work in patt to end, dec one st at end of row.

Dec one st at neck edge on next row.

Cast (bind) off rem 17 sts.

Return to rem sts and with RS facing, rejoin yarn and cast (bind) off centre 24 sts, work in patt to end of row.

Complete 2nd side of neck to match first side, reversing shaping.

FRONT

Work as for back to ***.

Armhole shaping

Keeping patt correct throughout, beg armhole shaping as foll:

Next row (dec row) (RS) Work 2 sts in patt, sl 1-k1-psso, work in patt to last 4 sts, k2tog, work 2 sts in patt.

**Work one row without shaping.

Rep dec row once.**

Rep from ** to ** 3 times more. 108 sts.

Work one row without shaping, so ending with a WS (p) row.

Divide for neck

Next row (RS) Work 2 sts in patt, sl 1-k1-psso, work next 59 sts, turn leaving 45 rem sts on a spare needle.

Next row Using F cast on 18 sts (neck edge), work in patt to end of row. 80 sts.

Next row Work 2 sts in patt, sl 1-k1-psso, work in patt to end, working patt over 18 new sts. 79 sts.

Work one row without shaping.

Next row Work 2 sts in patt, sl 1-k1-psso, work in patt to end, inc one st at end of row (neck edge). 79 sts.

Work one row without shaping.

Working decs at armhole edge as set and keeping neck edge straight, dec one st at armhole edge on next row and foll alt row. 77 sts.

This completes armhole shaping.

Work 3 rows without shaping, so ending with a WS (p) row.

Inc one st at neck edge on next row and on every foll 8th row 4 times in all. 81 sts.

Work without shaping until there are same number of rows as back to shoulder, ending with a WS row.

Shoulder shaping

Cast (bind) off 17 sts at beg of next row and foll alt row.

Collar extension

Work without shaping on rem 47 sts for 9cm/3½in more, ending with a WS (p) row.

Break off yarn and leave sts on a st holder.

2nd side of neck

Return to rem sts and with RS facing work as foll:

Next row (RS) Using F, cast on 36 sts onto RH needle, then work in patt to last 4 sts, k2tog, work 2 sts in patt. 80 sts.

Next row Extending patt over 36 new sts, work in patt to end of row.

Next row Work in patt to last 4 sts, k2tog, work 2 sts in patt. 79 sts.

Work one row without shaping.

Next row Inc one st at beg of row (neck edge) and work in patt to last 4 sts, k2tog, work 2 sts in patt. 79 sts.

Work one row without shaping.

Working decs at armhole edge as set and keeping neck edge straight, dec one st at armhole edge on next row and foll alt row. 77 sts.

This completes armhole shaping.

Work 3 rows without shaping, so ending with a WS (p) row.

Inc one st at neck edge on next row and on every foll 8th row 4 times in all. 81 sts.

Work without shaping until there are same number of rows as back to shoulder, ending with a RS (p) row.

Shoulder shaping

Cast (bind) off 17 sts at beg of next row and foll alt row.

Collar extension

Work without shaping on rem 47 sts until there is one row less than left front collar extension, so ending with a WS (p) row.

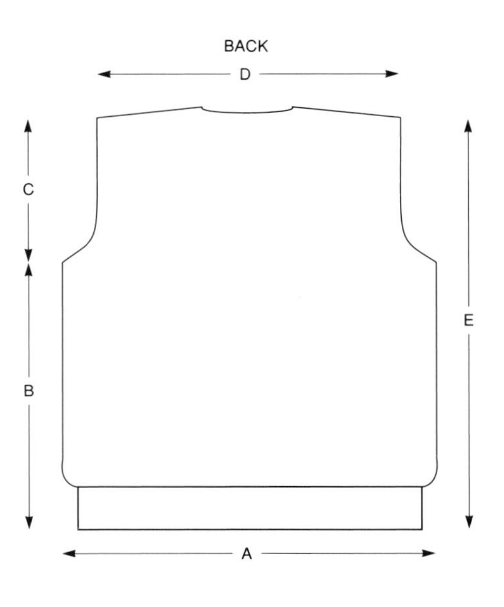

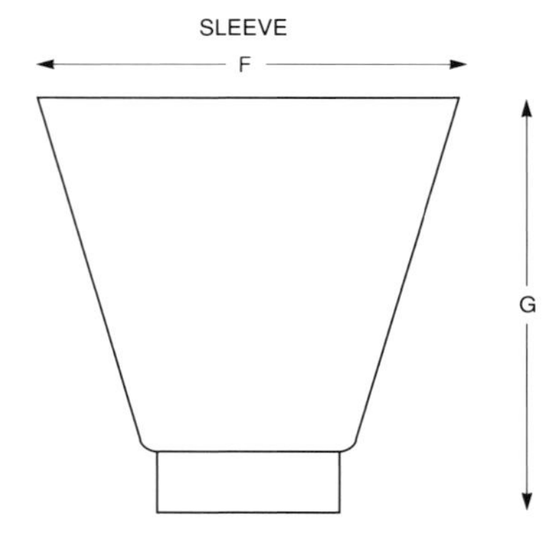

KEY
A = 65.5cm (26¼in)
B = 46cm (18in)
C = 26cm (10¼in)
D = 54.5cm (21¾in)
E = 72cm (28¼in)
F = 53.5cm (21¼in)
G = 58.5cm (23in)

Graft tog the left and right collar extensions.

SLEEVES

Using smaller needles and I, cast on 40 sts and work 2 rows in k2, p2 rib as for back.

Work 2 rib rows more in C.

Using A, cont in rib until ribbing measures 10cm/4in from cast-on edge, ending with a RS row.

Keeping rib correct, inc 8 sts evenly across next row as foll:

Next row (inc row) (WS) Rib 2, inc 1 into next st, *rib 4, inc 1 into next st*, rep from * to * 6 times more, rib 2. 48 sts.

Change to larger needles and beg patt chart from chart row 71 in st st as foll:

Chart row 71 (RS) Skip first 9 sts of chart, then work next 48 sts of chart, omitting last 9 sts.

Cont in st st foll chart for patt and rep 96-row repeat throughout *and at the same time* shape sleeve by inc one st at each end of 3rd row and then at each end of every foll 4th row 16 times in all, then every foll 5th row 8 times, working added sts into patt as set. 96 sts.

Work in patt without shaping until sleeve measures 58.5cm/23in from cast-on edge, ending with a WS row. Cast (bind) off all sts.

Make 2nd sleeve in same way.

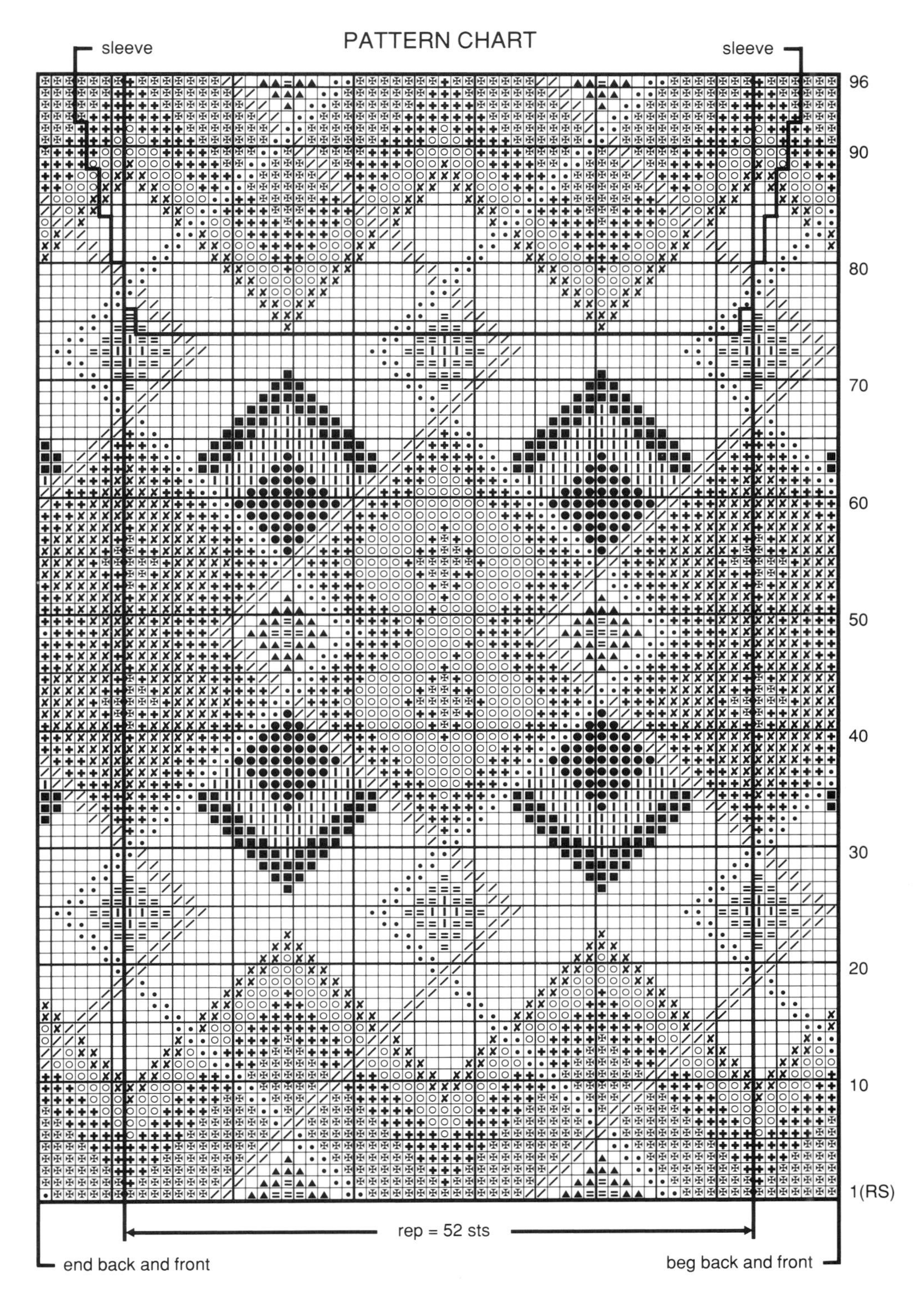

FINISHING

Press pieces lightly on WS with a warm iron over a damp cloth, omitting ribbing.

Join shoulder seams.

Placing centre of top of sleeve at shoulder seam, sew cast (bound) off edge of sleeves to armhole edge (including decreased edge).

Join side and sleeve seams.

Sew the edge of the collar extension to the back neck.

Turn 18-st collar facing on left side of front collar to WS at beg of neck divide, then place right side of collar inside the left side and fold 18 sts of the facing to the WS in the same way; at back neck, fold the collar in half, then stitch the collar neatly in place on the WS.

Press seams lightly on WS.

COLOUR KEY

□ = A
⊠ = B
◪ = C
⊟ = D
◫ = E
⊞ = F
✚ = G
◎ = H
⊡ = I
■ = J
● = L
▲ = M

May
June

ALMANAC

THIS IS A SWEATER THAT WILL TAKE YOU RIGHT THROUGH THE YEAR. KNIT IT IN WOOL FOR THE WINTER MONTHS AND THEN, TO HERALD THE SPRING, CREATE A PASTEL VERSION OF YOUR OWN. YOU MAY HAVE YOUR OWN PARTICULAR FAVOURITE MOTIFS TO DEPICT THE MONTHS OR YOU MIGHT EVEN LIKE TO CHANGE THE THEME: INSTEAD OF CALENDAR, WHAT ABOUT A BOTANIC, MUSICAL OR ASTROLOGICAL SWEATER?

SIZE

One size only to fit 86–102cm/ 34–40in bust

See diagram for finished knitted measurements.

MATERIALS

Rowan *Lightweight DK* 25g/1oz hanks as foll:

A (no.613: light taupe) 21 hanks
B (no.655: teal) 3 hanks
C (no.601: raspberry) 2 hanks
D (no.150: khaki) 2 hanks
E (no.86: caramel) 2 hanks
F (no.88: smokey blue) 2 hanks
G (no.663: sienna) 2 hanks
H (no.9: old gold) 2 hanks
J (no.430: olive) 1 hank
L (no.62: black) 1 hank
M (no.7: pale yellow) 1 hank
N (no.46: cherry) 1 hank
Q (no.412: dark rose) 1 hank
R (no.77: dark rust) 1 hank
S (no.80: dark brown) 1 hank
T (no.2: ecru) 1 hank
U (no.11: biscuit) 1 hank
V (no.151: dark blue) 1 hank

One pair each of 3mm (US size 3) and 3¾mm (US size 5) knitting needles

Set of four 3mm (US size 3) double-pointed needles for neckband

ALTERNATIVE COLOURWAY

This sweater can also be worked in the colourway shown below, where:
A = no.62: black
E = no.147: dusty apricot
S = no.28: brown
T = no.84: natural
V = no.57: dark blue
All remaining shades are same as for main colourway.

TENSION (GAUGE)

24 sts and 32 rows to 10cm/4in measured over st st worked on 3¾mm (US size 5) needles
26 sts and 33 rows to 10cm/4in measured over patt worked on 3¾mm (US size 5) needles

PLEASE CHECK YOUR TENSION (GAUGE) CAREFULLY AND CHANGE KNITTING NEEDLE SIZE IF NECESSARY

NOTES

When working the colourwork pattern, use the intarsia method, using a separate length of yarn for each isolated area of colour and twisting yarns together at back of work when changing colours to avoid making a hole.

Read charts from right to left for the RS (odd-numbered) rows and from left to right for the WS (even-numbered) rows.

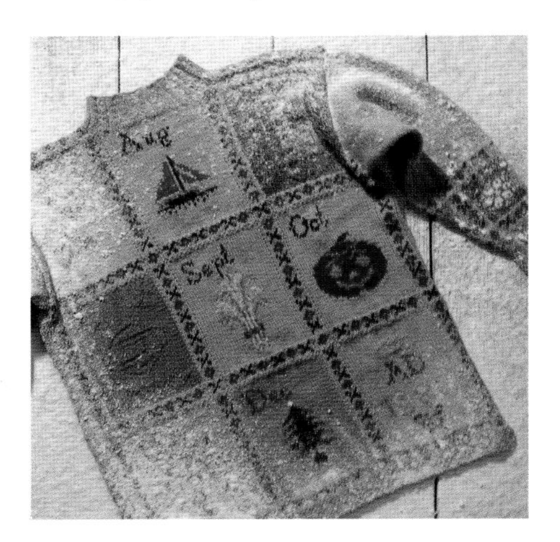

BACK

Using smaller needles and A, cast on 150 sts and beg double moss (seed) st as foll:

Row 1 (RS) *P1, k1, rep from * to end.
Row 2 As row 1.
Row 3 (RS) *K1, p1, rep from * to end.
Row 4 As row 3.

Rep last 4 rows until ribbing measures 3.5cm/1¼in from cast-on edge, ending with a WS row.

Change to larger needles and beg chart row 1, foll back patt chart (on page 31) until chart row 144 has been completed, so ending with a WS row.

Armhole shaping

Cont to foll chart throughout, dec one st at each end of next row, then at each end of every foll alt row 10 times in all. 130 sts.

Work without shaping until chart row 208 has been completed, so ending with a WS row.

Neck shaping

Chart row 209 (RS) Work first 50 sts in patt, turn leaving rem sts on a spare needle.

Working first side of neck only, dec one st at beg of next row (neck edge), then at neck edge on every foll row 8 times in all. 42 sts.

Work without shaping until chart row 220 has been completed.

Cast (bind) off.
Return to rem sts and with RS facing, slip centre 30 sts onto a st holder, rejoin yarn to rem sts and work in patt to end of row.
Complete 2nd side of neck to match first side, reversing shaping.

FRONT

Foll front chart (on page 33), work as for back until chart row 202 has been completed.

Neck shaping

Chart row 203 (RS) Work first 56 sts in patt, turn leaving rem sts on a spare needle.
Working first side of neck only, dec one st at beg of next row (neck edge), then at neck edge on every foll row 14 times in all. 42 sts.
Work without shaping until chart row 220 has been completed.
Cast (bind) off.
Return to rem sts and with RS facing, slip centre 18 sts onto a st holder, rejoin yarn to rem sts and work in patt to end of row.
Complete 2nd side of neck to match first side, reversing shaping.

SLEEVES

Using smaller needles and A, cast on 48 sts and beg rib patt on first row as foll:
Rib row 1 (RS) *P1, k1, p1, k2, p2, k2, rep from * to last 3 sts, p1, k1, p1.
Rib row 2 *K1, p1, k1, p2, k2, p2, rep from * to last 3 sts, k1, p1, k1.
Rib row 3 K1, *p1, k3, p2, k3, rep from * to last 2 sts, p1, k1.
Rib row 4 P1, *k1, p3, k2, p3, rep from * to last 2 sts, k1, p1.
Rep last 4 rows until ribbing measures 11.5cm/4½in from cast-on edge, ending with a RS row.
Keeping rib patt correct as set, increase 14 sts evenly across next row as foll:
Next row (inc row) (WS) Rib 4, work into front and back of next st – called *inc 1* –, * rib 2, inc 1 into next st*, rep from * to * 12 times more, rib 4. 62 sts.
Change to larger needles and beg with chart row 1, foll left sleeve chart (on opposite page) and inc one st at each end of 5th row, then every foll 4th row until chart row 44 has been completed. 82 sts.
Using A only and working in st st for remainder of sleeve, inc one st at each end of next row, then every foll 4th row until there are 118 sts in total.
Work without shaping until sleeve measures 51cm/20in or desired length from cast-on edge, ending with a WS row.
Cast (bind) off all sts.
Make left sleeve in same way, but foll right sleeve chart.

NECKBAND

Do not press.
Join shoulder seams using a small neat backstitch on very edge of work.
Using set of 4 double-pointed needles and A and with RS of front facing, beg at left shoulder and pick up k23 sts down left front neck, k18 sts from front neck st holder, pick up and k23 sts up right front neck, 16 sts down right back neck, k30 sts from back neck st holder, and pick up and k16 sts up left back neck. 126 sts.
Working in rounds (RS always facing), beg cable and rib patt on next row as foll:
Rib round 1 *K2, p2, k2, p1, k1, p1, rep from * to end.
Rib round 2 As round 1.
Rib round 3 *K2, p2, k2, k1, p1, k1, rep from * to end.

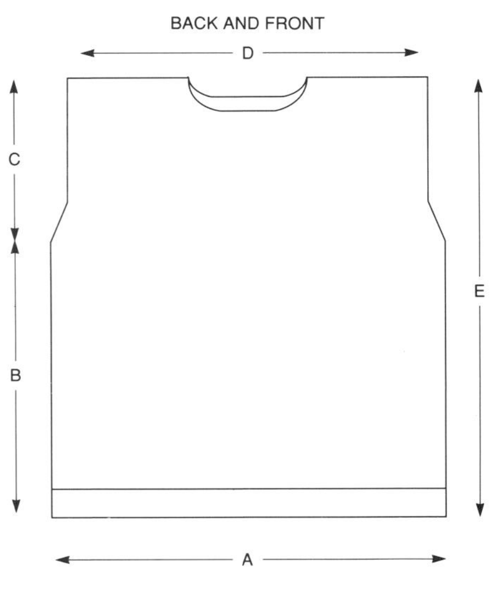

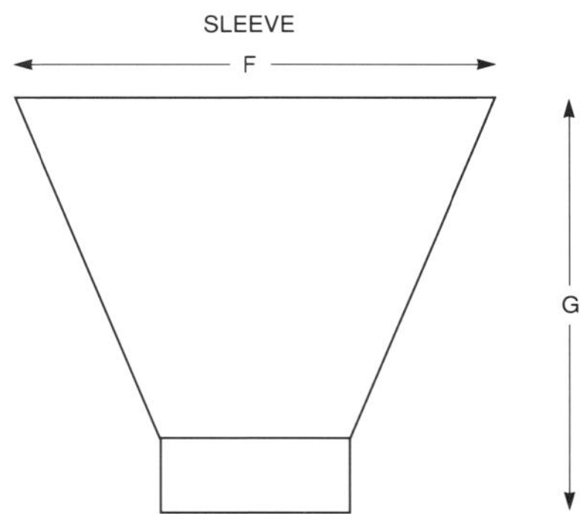

KEY
A = 58cm (23in)
B = 47cm (18¾in)
C = 23cm (9¼in)
D = 50cm (20in)
E = 70cm (28in)
F = 49cm (19¾in)
G = 51cm (20in)

Rib round 4 As round 3.
Rep last 4 rounds 4 times more to complete neckband.
Cast (bind) off in rib.

FINISHING

Join the seams using a small neat backstitch on the very edge of the work, except for the ribbing where an invisible slip stitch should be used instead.

Placing centre of top of sleeve at shoulder seam, sew cast (bound) off edge of sleeves to armhole edge (including decreased edge).

Join side and sleeve seams, leaving side seams at lower edge of back and lower edge of front unjoined for 5cm/2in to form slits.

Press seams lightly on WS.

LEFT SLEEVE CHART

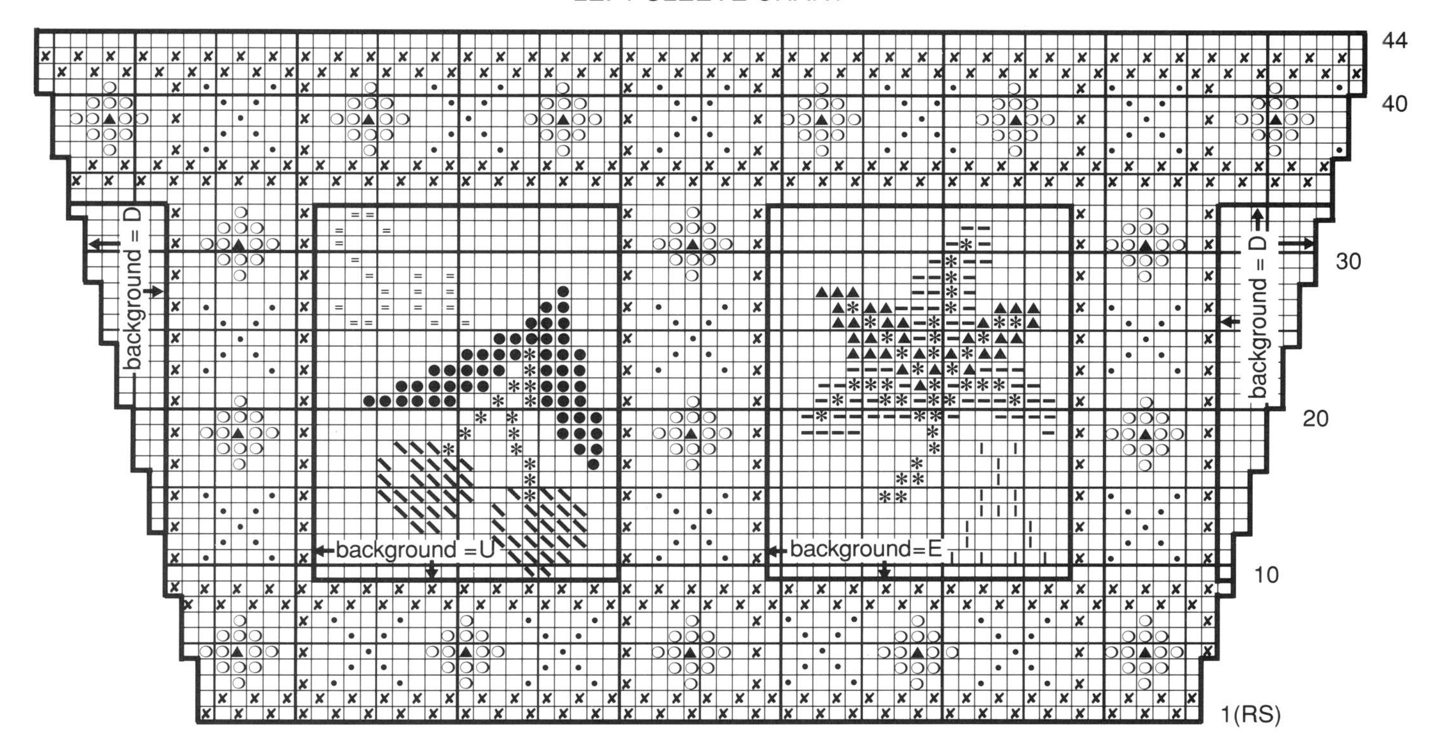

RIGHT SLEEVE CHART

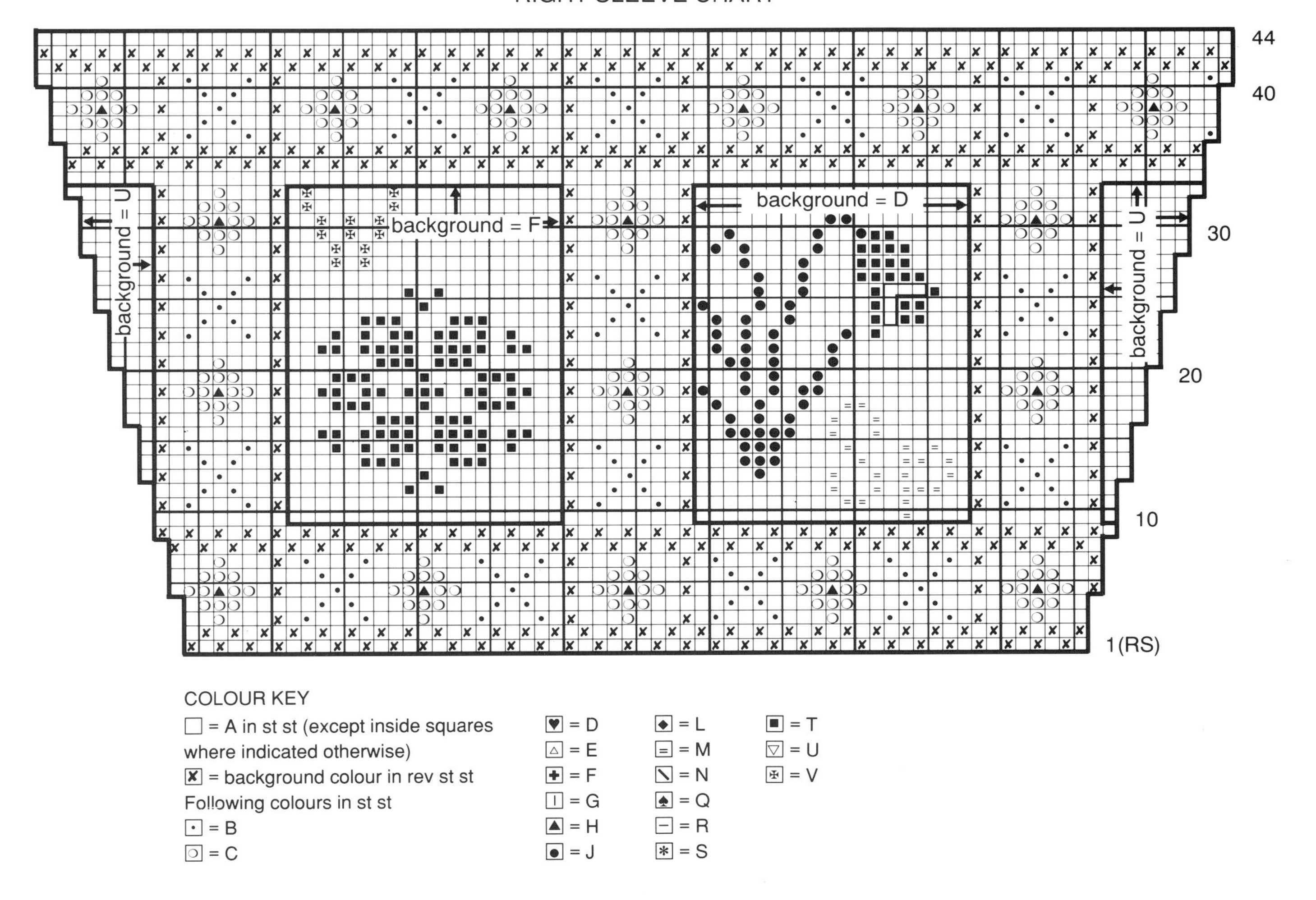

COLOUR KEY

☐ = A in st st (except inside squares where indicated otherwise)

☒ = background colour in rev st st

Following colours in st st

⊡ = B

◌ = C

♥ = D

△ = E

✚ = F

| = G

▲ = H

● = J

◆ = L

= = M

╲ = N

♠ = Q

− = R

✱ = S

■ = T

▽ = U

✠ = V

BACK CHART

COLOUR KEY
See right sleeve chart.

100
90
80
70
60
50
40
30
20
10
1(RS)
background = E
background = D

FRONT CHART

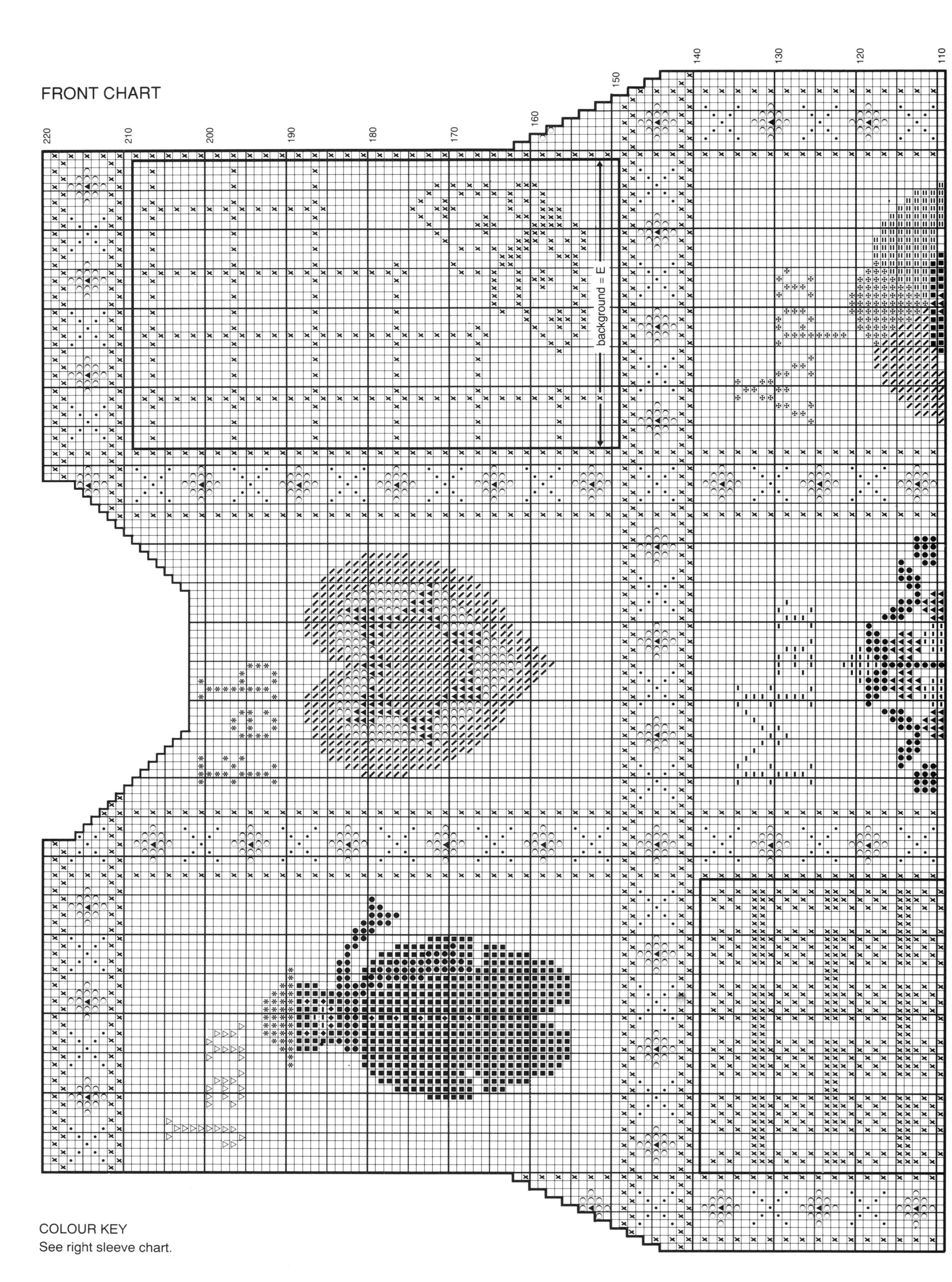

COLOUR KEY
See right sleeve chart.

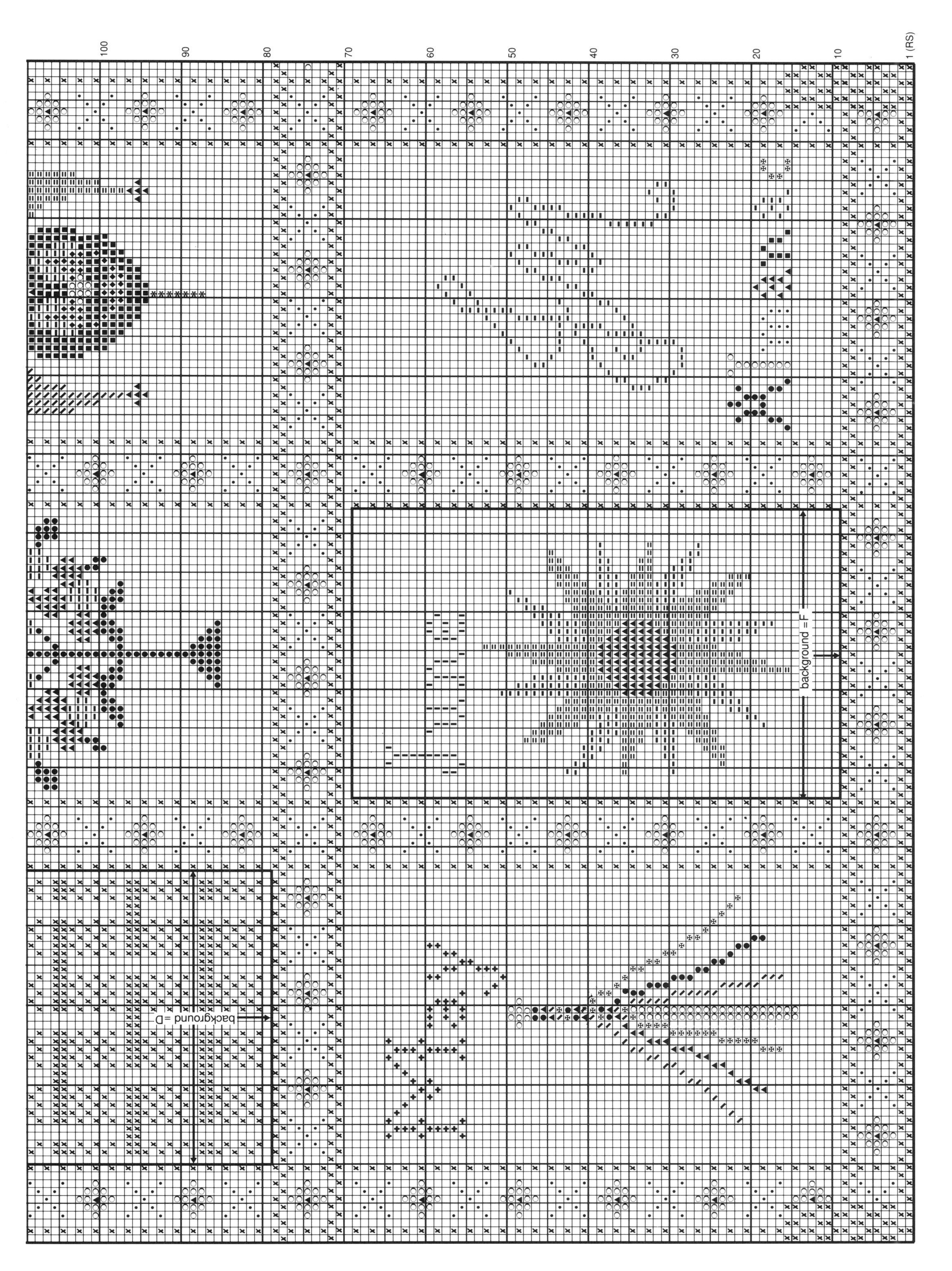
100
90
80
70
60
50
40
30
20
10
1 (RS)
background = F
background = D

SNOWDON

I'M VERY INTERESTED IN WORKING WITH POSITIVE AND NEGATIVE IMAGES, AND THIS JACKET IS INSPIRED BY A WONDERFUL MOROCCAN HAT WITH CHECKERBOARD PATTERNS THAT I BOUGHT IN THE SOUK IN MARRAKECH. I CHANGED THE ORIGINAL DIAMOND PATTERN TO A STAR-SHAPE. IF YOU'D ALSO LIKE TO MAKE IT A LITTLE DIFFERENT, WHY NOT TRY A SNOWFLAKE?

SIZES

To fit 6[8:10] yrs or 61[66:71]cm/ 24[26:28]in

Figures for larger sizes are given in brackets [ ]; where there is only one set of figures, it applies to all sizes.

See diagram for finished knitted measurements.

MATERIALS

Rowan *Designer DK* 50g/1¾oz balls as foll:

A (no.671: navy) 6[7:8] balls
B (no.649: natural) 4[4:5] balls
C (no.673: red) 1 ball
D (no.626: green) 1 ball
E (no.672: blue) 1 ball
F (no.675: yellow) 1 ball

One pair each of 3¼mm (US size 3) and 3¾mm (US size 5) needles

Five 18mm/¾in buttons

ALTERNATIVE COLOURWAY

This sweater can also be worked in the colourway shown right, where:

A = no.655: teal
B = no.661: turquoise
C, D, E and F = no.649: (1 ball only)

TENSION (GAUGE)

25 sts and 33 rows to 10cm/4in measured over patt worked on 3¾mm (US size 5) needles

PLEASE CHECK YOUR TENSION (GAUGE)

NOTES

When working the border pattern, strand colours A and B loosely across the back of work when not in use, but use separate lengths of C, D, E and F for centre of diamonds.

When working the colourwork pattern, use the intarsia method, using a separate length of A or B for each square stranding the background colour (A or B) only across that square and using a separate length for each of the other colours used in the square.

Read charts from right to left for the RS (odd-numbered) rows and from left to right for the WS (even-numbered) rows.

BACK

Using smaller needles and A, cast on 107[113:119] sts and work 10 rows in k1, p1 rib.

P 2 rows to form foldline for hem.

Beg with chart row 1, foll patt chart until chart row 10 has been completed, so ending with a WS row.

Change to larger needles and cont foll chart for patt, rep 48-row rep throughout, until back measures 29[30:31]cm/11½[11¾:12]in from hemline fold, ending with a WS row.

Armhole shaping

Keeping patt correct throughout, dec one st at each end of next row and then every foll alt row 8[9:10] times in all. 91[95:99] sts.

Work without shaping until back measures 46[48:50]cm/18¼[19:19¾]in from hemline, ending with a WS row.

Neck shaping

Next row (RS) Work first 32[34:36] sts in patt, turn leaving rem sts on a spare needle.

Working first side of neck only, dec one st at beg of next row (neck edge), then at neck edge on every foll row 4 times in all. 28[30:32] sts.

Slip rem onto a st holder.

Return to rem sts and with RS facing, slip centre 27 sts onto a st holder, rejoin yarn to rem sts and work in patt to end of row.

Complete 2nd side of neck to match first side, reversing shaping.

LEFT FRONT

Before beg front, work pocket lining.

Using larger needles and A, cast on 24 sts.

Beg with a k row, work 24 rows in st st, so ending with a WS row.

Break off yarn and slip sts onto a st holder.

Begin front

Using smaller needles and A, cast on 54[57:60] sts and work 10 rows in k1, p1 rib.

P 2 rows to form foldline for hem.

Beg with chart row 1, foll patt chart until chart row 10 has been

completed, so ending with a WS row. Change to larger needles and cont foll chart for patt until chart row 34 has been completed, so ending with a WS row.

Chart row 35 (RS) Work first 9[12:15] sts in patt foll chart, slip next 24 sts onto a st holder, then with RS of pocket lining facing work in patt across 24 sts of pocket lining, work rem 21 sts in patt.

Cont in patt and rep 48-row rep. Work without shaping until there are same number of rows as back to armhole, ending with a WS row.

Armhole shaping

Keeping patt correct throughout, dec one st at beg of next row (armhole edge) and then at armhole edge on every foll alt row 8[9:10] times in all. 46[48:50] sts.

Work without shaping until front measures 41[43:45]cm/16¼[17:17¾]in from hemline, ending with a RS row.

Neck shaping

Cast (bind) off 7 sts at beg of next row, then dec one st at neck edge on next row and every foll row 11 times in all. 28[30:32] sts.

Work without shaping until there are same number of rows as back to shoulder, ending with a RS row. Slip sts onto a st holder.

RIGHT FRONT

Work as for left front, foll chart for right front and reversing all shaping.

SLEEVES

Using smaller needles and A, cast on 41[41:45] sts and work 10 rows in k1, p1 rib for hem as for back, so ending with a WS row.

P 2 rows to form foldline for hem.

Beg with chart row 1, foll patt chart until chart row 10 has been completed, so ending with a WS row. Change to larger needles and cont foll chart for patt, rep 48-row rep throughout *and at the same time* inc one st at each end of 3rd row and then at each end of every foll 3rd row 16[19:21] times in all, then every foll 4th row 10[10:9] times. 93[99:105] sts.

Work in patt without shaping until sleeve measures 36[37:39.5]cm/ 14[14½:15½]in from hemline, ending with a WS row. Cast (bind) off.

BUTTON BAND

Press pieces lightly on WS with a warm iron, omitting ribbing.

Using larger needles and A, join left shoulder seam by placing WS of back and WS of left front tog, then with left front facing, knit through both layers along shoulder sts, taking one st from left front st holder tog with one st from back st holder with each st and casting (binding) off as the row is worked.

Join right shoulder seam in same way.

Placing centre of top of sleeve at shoulder seam, sew cast (bound) off edge of sleeves to armhole edge (including decreased edge).

Join side and sleeve seams.

Turn hem on back and fronts to WS along p row and slip stitch in place.

Turn hem on sleeves to WS and slip stitch in place.

Using smaller needles and A and with RS facing, pick up and k105[112:119] sts along right front for boy or left front for girl.

Using A, p one row.

Work from front band chart until chart row 7 has been completed, so ending with a RS row.

Using A only, p 2 rows, then work 9 rows in k1, p1 rib. Cast (bind) off.

Mark positions for 5 buttonholes, the first to beg 2cm/¾in from lower edge, the last to come 2cm/¾in above neck shaping (to be worked horizontally in neckband) and rem 3 evenly spaced between (each buttonhole to be worked over 3 sts).

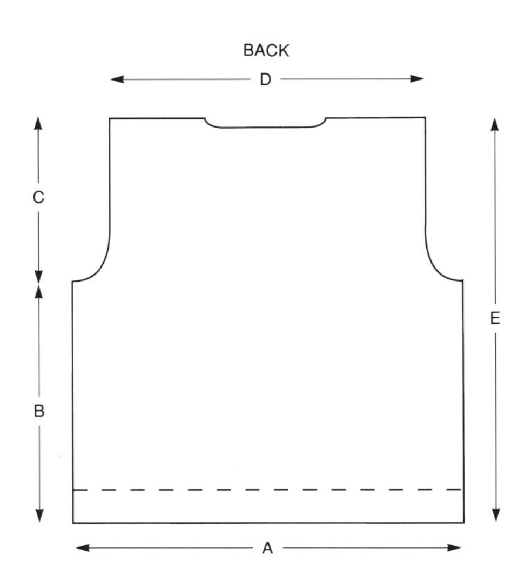

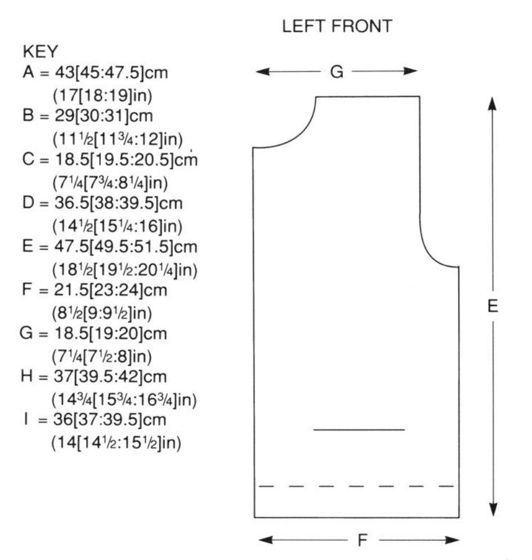

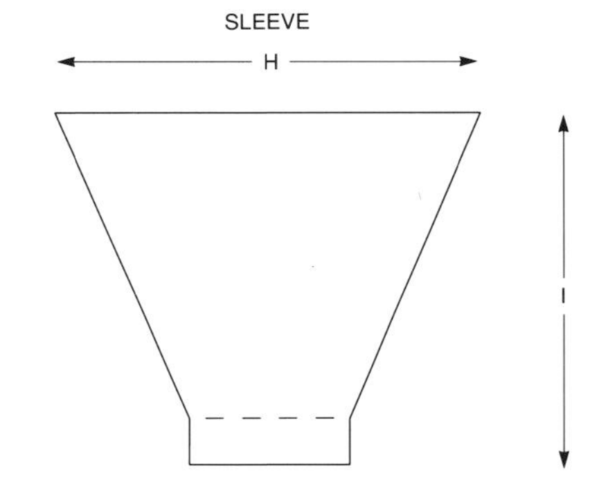

BUTTONHOLE BAND

Work as for button band along rem front *and at the same time* work buttonholes on chart row 3 by casting (binding) off 3 sts when position of each buttonhole is reached, then in foll row cast on

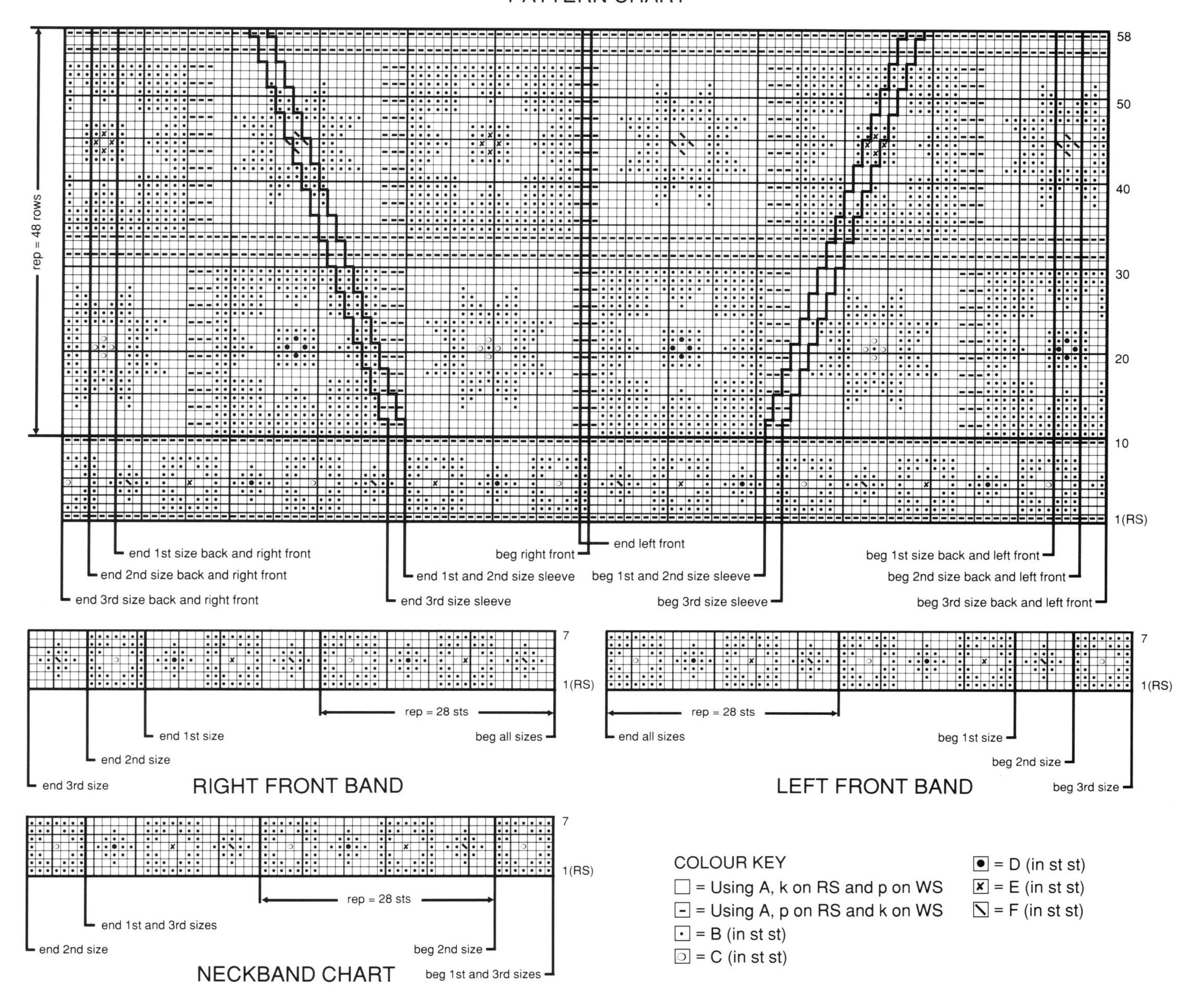

3 sts over those cast (bound) off, then work buttonholes over 4th and 5th rib rows in same places.

Turn front bands to WS along foldline and slip stitch in place.

NECKBAND

Using smaller needles and A and with RS facing, pick up and k31 sts evenly up right front neck, 4 sts down right back neck, k27 sts from back neck st holder, pick up and k4 sts up left back neck and 32 sts down left front neck. 98 sts.

Using A, p one row.

Work from neckband until chart row 7 has been completed *and at the same time* on chart row 3 cast (bind) off 3 sts (4 sts from edge) above buttonhole band, and in foll row cast on 3 sts over sts cast (bound) in last row.

Using A only, p 2 rows, then work 9 rows in k1, p1 rib *and at the same time* on 4th and 5th rib rows work a buttonhole in same place.

Cast (bind) off loosely in rib.

FINISHING

Turn neckband to WS along foldline and slip stitch in place.

Pocket hems

Using smaller needles and A and with RS facing, k across 24 sts of left front pocket. Work 4 rows in k1, p1 rib.

Cast (bind) off loosely in rib.

Work hem at top of right front pocket in same way.

Turn pocket hems to WS of fronts and slip stitch in place.

Slip stitch pocket linings to WS of fronts. Sew 2 layers of each buttonhole tog.

Press seams lightly on WS.

Sew buttons to button band and neckband opposite buttonholes.

HEARTSTRINGS

THIS VEST (WAISTCOAT) SHAPE IS ONE OF MY OLD FAVOURITES AS IT'S SO WEARABLE FOR BOTH MEN AND WOMEN. YOU CAN USE THE KNITTING PATTERN AGAIN AND AGAIN, CREATING A COMPLETELY DIFFERENT LOOK BY CHANGING THE COLOURS OF THE YARNS OR BY CHANGING THE HEARTS MOTIF. YOU COULD TRY USING DIAMONDS, TRIANGLES, OR ANY SMALL GEOMETRIC SHAPE FOR THE MOTIF, OR EVEN INVENT YOUR OWN DESIGN FOR THE SPECIAL PERSON IN YOUR LIFE.

SIZES

To fit 91–96[101–106:112–117]cm/ 36–38[40–42:44–46]in chest

Figures for larger sizes are given in brackets [ ]; where there is only one set of figures, it applies to all sizes.

See diagram for finished knitted measurements.

MATERIALS

Rowan *Wool and Cotton* 50g/1¾oz balls as foll:

A (no.924: black) 8[9:10] balls

B (no.911: dove) 3[3:4] balls

Rowan *Botany* 25g/1oz hanks as foll:

C (no.44: red) 2[2:3] hanks

One pair each of 2¼mm (US size 1) and 3¼ mm (US size 3) knitting needles

Five 2cm/¾in buttons

ALTERNATIVE COLOURWAY

This vest (waistcoat) can also be worked in the colourway shown on the right, where:

A = *Wool and Cotton* no.920: hazelnut

B = *Wool and Cotton* no.921: chocolate

C = *Botany* no.44: red

TENSION (GAUGE)

28 sts and 36 rows to 10cm/4in measured over st st worked on 3¼mm (US size 3) needles

28 sts and 33 rows to 10cm/4in measured over patt worked on 3¼mm (US size 3) needles

PLEASE CHECK YOUR TENSION (GAUGE) CAREFULLY AND CHANGE KNITTING NEEDLE SIZE IF NECESSARY

NOTES

When working the colourwork patterns, use the intarsia method, using a separate length of yarn for each isolated area of colour and twisting yarns together at WS when changing colours to avoid making a hole.

Read charts from right to left for the RS (odd-numbered) rows and the from left to right for the WS (even-numbered) rows.

BACK

Using smaller needles and A, cast on 127[139:151] sts and beg foll back ribbing chart as foll:

Chart rib row 1 (RS) Reading chart from right to left, work first 16[3:9] sts of chart before patt repeat begins as indicated on chart, rep 19-st patt repeat 5[7:7] times, work last 16[3:9] sts of chart as indicated.

Cont foll chart for rib patt until chart row 14 has been completed. Then work rows 1–13 again, so ending with a RS row.

Keeping rib correct as set, inc 23[25:27] sts evenly across next row as foll:

Next row (inc row) (WS) Rib 3, work into front and back of next st – called *inc 1* – , *rib 4, inc 1 into next st, rib 5, inc 1 into next st*, rep from * to * 10[11:12] times more, rib 2[3:4]. 150[164:178] sts.

Change to larger needles and beg with a k row, work 3 rows in st st, so ending with a RS row.

Then beg foll back heart patt chart from row 4 as foll:

Chart patt row 4 (WS) Reading chart from left to right, work 3[10:17] sts of chart before patt repeat begins as indicated on chart, rep 18-st repeat 8 times, work last 3[10:17] sts of chart.

Cont in this way foll chart for heart patt and rep 24-row repeat throughout, until back measures 40.5cm/16in from cast-on edge, ending with a WS row.

Armhole shaping

Keeping patt correct throughout, cast (bind) off 6[7:8] sts at beg of next 2 rows.

Dec one st at each end of next row and every foll row 20[22:24] times in all. 98[106:114] sts.

Work without shaping until back measures 68[69.5:70.5]cm/ 26¾[27¼:27¾]in) from cast-on edge, ending with a WS row.

Neck and shoulder shaping
Next row (RS) Work first 32[35:38] sts in patt, turn leaving rem sts on a spare needle.
Working on first side of neck only, dec one st at beg of next row (neck edge).
****Next row** (RS) Cast (bind) off 9[10:11] sts, work in patt to last 2 sts, k2tog.**
Dec one st at neck edge on next row.
Rep row from ** to ** once more.
Work one row without shaping.
Cast (bind) off rem 10[11:12] sts.
Return to rem sts and with RS facing, slip centre 34[36:38] sts onto a st holder, rejoin yarn to rem sts and work in heart patt as set to end of row.
Complete 2nd side of neck to match first side, reversing shaping.

LEFT FRONT

Before beg front, work pocket lining.

Pocket lining
Using larger needles and A, cast on 36 sts. Beg with a k row, work in st st until lining measures 11cm/4¼in from cast-on edge, ending with a WS row.
Break off yarn and slip sts onto a st holder.

Begin front
Using smaller needles and A, cast on 60[66:72] sts and beg foll left front ribbing chart as foll:
Chart rib row 1 (RS) Reading chart from right to left, work first 16[3:9] sts of chart before patt repeat begins as indicated on chart, rep 19-st patt repeat 2[3:3] times, work last 6 sts of chart as indicated.
Cont foll chart for rib patt until chart row 14 has been completed.
Then work rows 1–13 again, so ending with a RS row.
Keeping rib correct as set, inc 11[12:13] sts evenly across next row as foll:
Next row (inc row) (WS) Rib 2, inc 1 into next st, *rib 4, inc 1 into next st, rib 5, inc 1 into next st*, rep from * to * 4[4:5] times more, rib 2[5:3], inc 0[1:0] into next st, rib 0[2:0]. 71[78:85] sts.
Change to larger needles and beg with a k row, work 3 rows in st st, so ending with a RS row.
Then beg foll left front heart patt chart from row 4 as foll:
Chart patt row 4 (WS) Reading chart from left to right, work 14 sts of chart before patt repeat begins as indicated on chart, then rep 18-st repeat 3 times, work last 3[10:17] sts of chart.
Cont in this way foll chart for heart patt until chart row 24 has been completed.
Then work chart rows 1–14 again, so ending with a WS row.

Insert pocket lining
Cont to foll chart for heart patt, insert pocket lining on next row as foll:
Next row (chart row 15) (RS) Work first 12[19:26] sts in patt, slip next 36 sts onto a st holder, then with RS of pocket lining facing work in patt across 36 sts of pocket lining, work rem 23 sts in patt.
Cont in this way foll left front heart patt chart for heart patt and rep 24-row repeat throughout, until left front measures 35.5cm/14in from cast-on edge, ending with a WS row.

Neck and armhole shaping
Keeping patt correct throughout, dec one st at end of next row (neck edge) and at neck edge on every foll 6th row 10[13:16] times in all, then on every foll 7th row 7[5:3] times *and at the same time* when there are same number of rows as back to armhole, ending with a WS row,

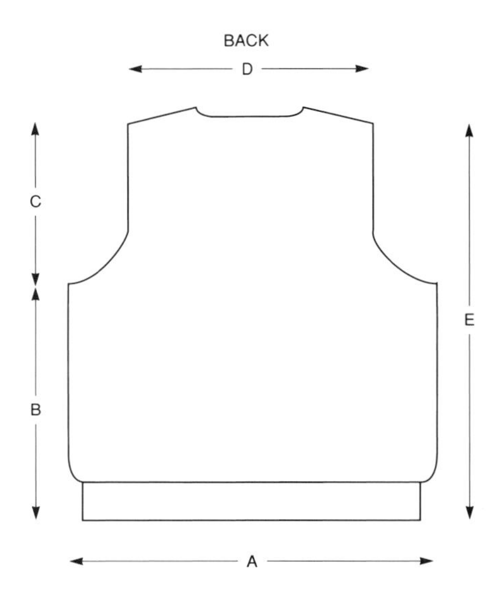

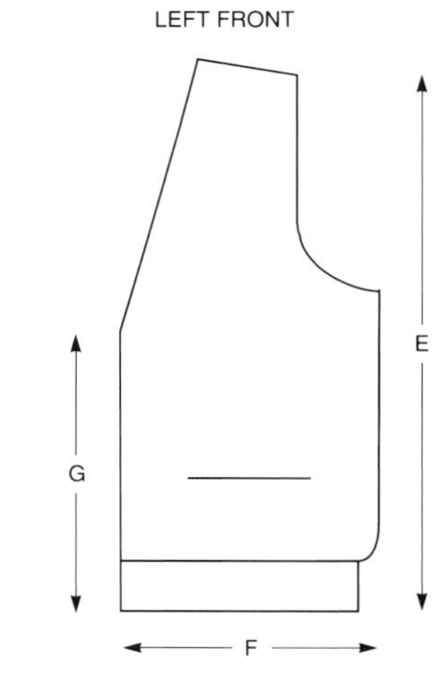

KEY
A = 54[59:64]cm (21½[23½:25½]in)
B = 40.5[16]cm
C = 28[29.5:30.5]cm (11[11½:12]in)
D = 35[38:41]cm (14[15¼:16¼]in)
E = 68.5[70:71]cm (27[27½:28]in)
F = 25.5[28:30.5]cm (10¼[11¼:12¼]in)
G = 30.5cm (14in)

work armhole shaping as foll:
Cast (bind) off 6[7:8] sts at beg of next row, work one row without shaping, then dec one st at armhole edge on next row and every foll row 20[22:24] times in all.
Keeping armhole edge straight, cont shaping V-neck until neck shaping has been completed. 28[31:34] sts.
Now work without shaping until there are same number of rows as back to beg of shoulder shaping, ending with a WS row.

Shoulder shaping
****Cast (bind) off 9[10:11] sts at beg of next row.

BACK RIBBING

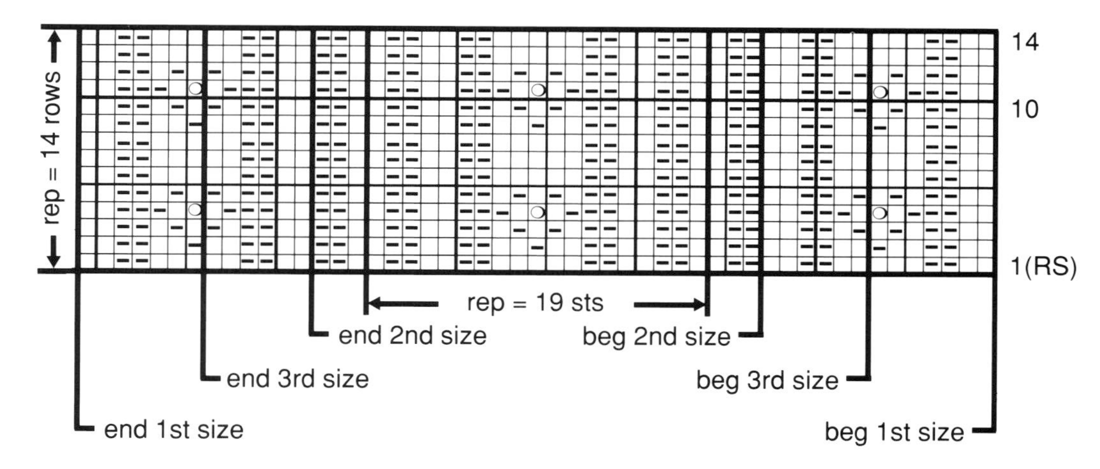

BACK HEART PATTERN

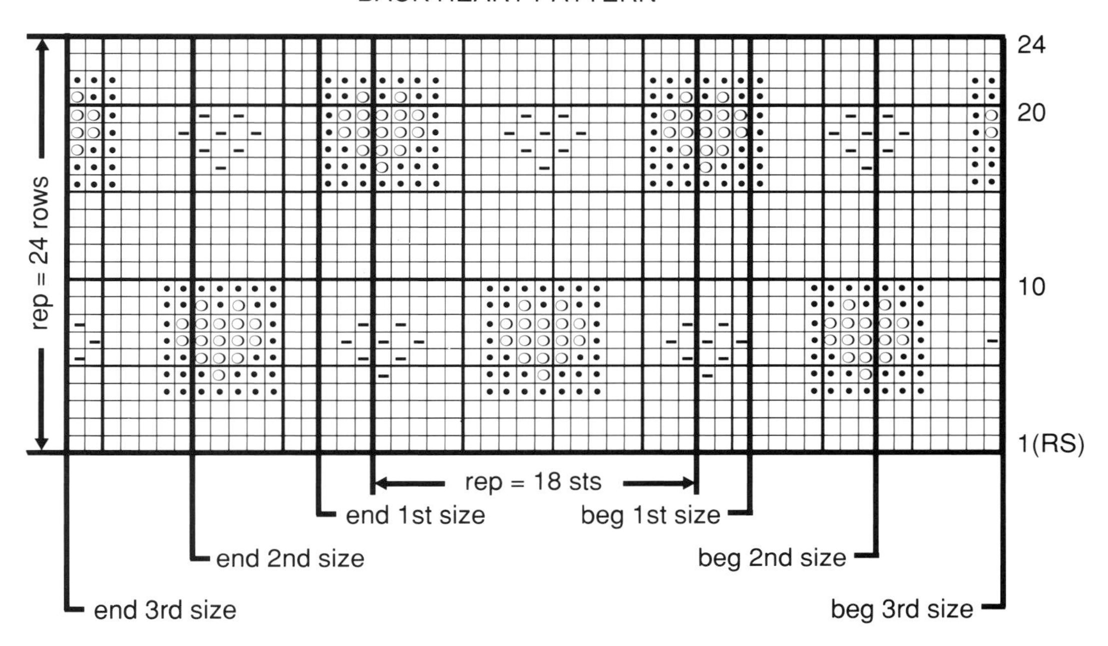

LEFT FRONT RIBBING

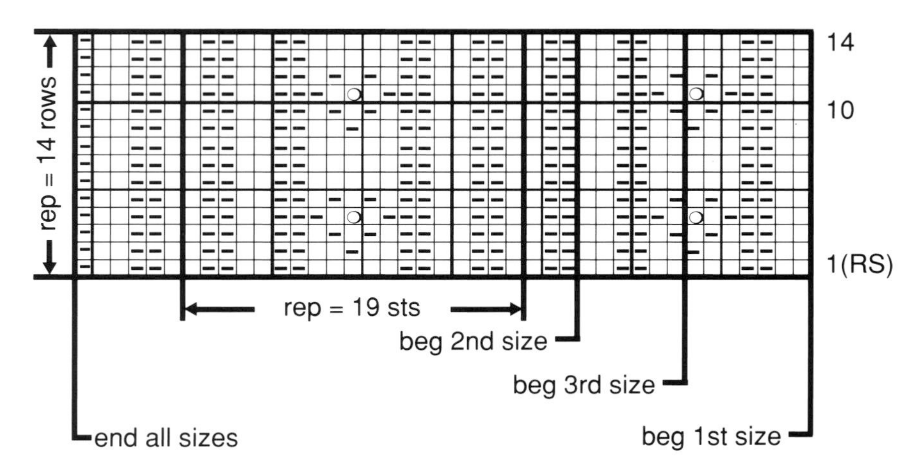

KEY

□ = Using A, k on RS and p on WS

⊟ = Using A, p on RS and k on WS

⊡ = Using B, k on RS and p on WS

◯ = Using C, k on RS and p on WS

LEFT FRONT HEART PATTERN

24
20
10
1(RS)
rep = 24 rows
rep = 18 sts
beg 1st size
beg 2nd size
beg 3rd size
end all sizes

ARMBAND RIBBING

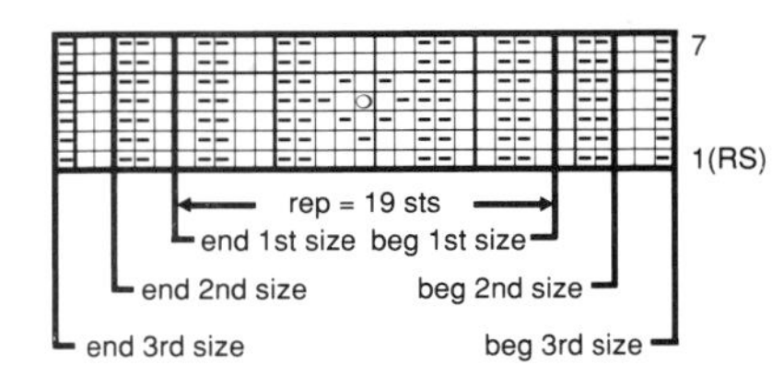

BUTTON BAND HEART PATT

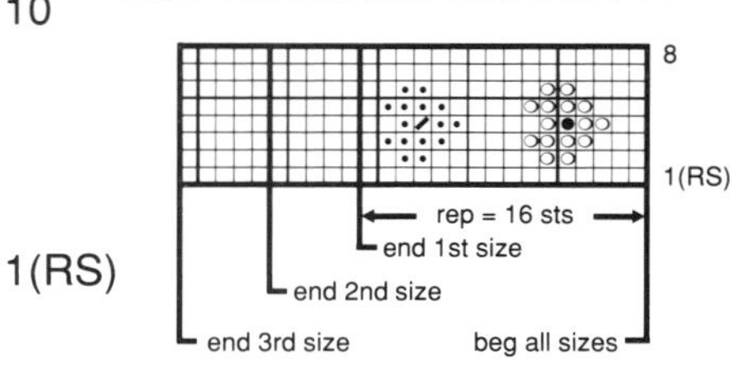

BUTTONHOLE BAND HEART PATT

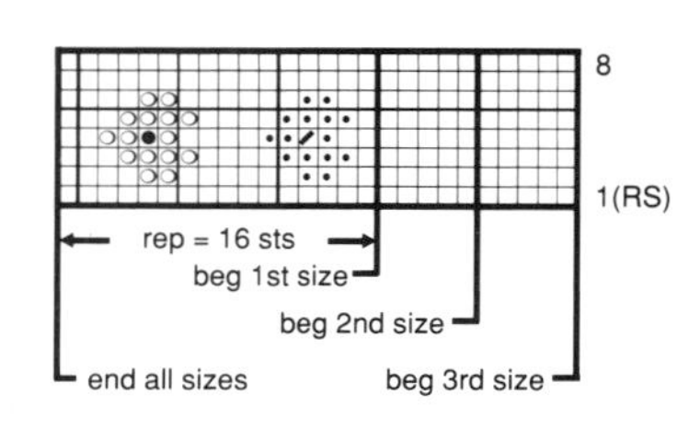

RIGHT FRONT RIBBING

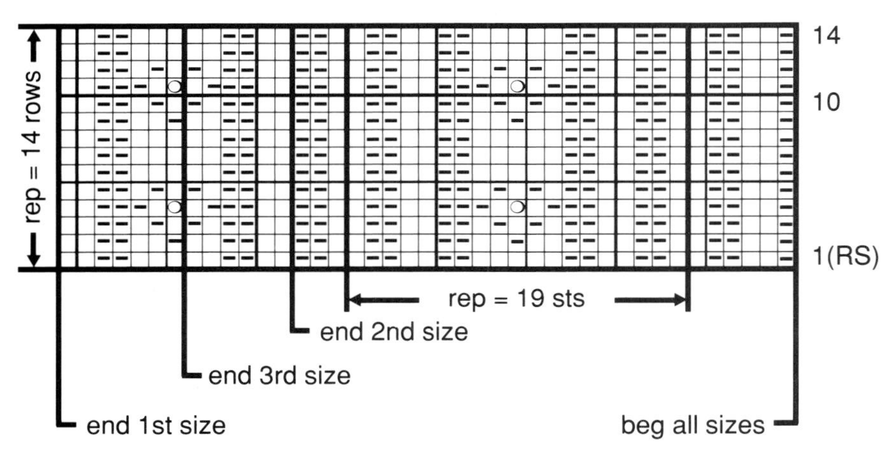

CENTRE BACK NECK HEART

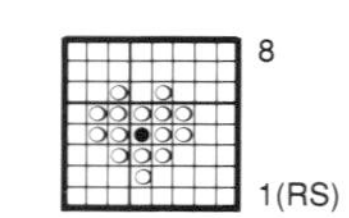

KEY
- ☐ = Using A, k on RS and p on WS
- ⊡ = Using B, k on RS and p on WS
- ⧄ = Using B, p on RS and k on WS
- ◌ = Using C, k on RS and p on WS
- ● = Using C, p on RS and k on WS

RIGHT FRONT HEART PATTERN

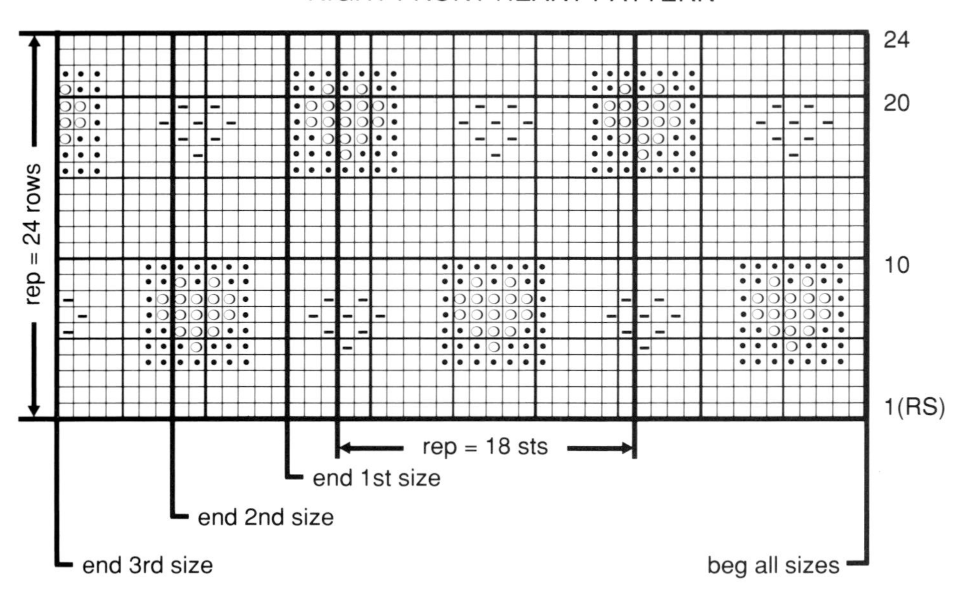

Work one row without shaping.****
Rep from **** to **** once.
Cast (bind) off rem 10[11:12] sts.

RIGHT FRONT

Work as for left front, but foll charts for right front and reversing all shaping and position of pocket.

ARMBANDS

Press pieces lightly on WS with a warm iron over a damp cloth, omitting ribbing.
Join shoulder seams, using a small

neat backstitch on very edge of work.
Using smaller needles and A and with RS facing, pick up and k171[177:183] sts evenly around left armhole edge.
P one row.
Beg foll armband ribbing chart on next row as foll:
Chart rib row 1 (RS) Reading chart from right to left, work first 0[3:6] sts of chart before patt repeat begins as indicated on chart, rep 19-st patt repeat 9 times, work last 0[3:6] sts of chart as indicated.
Cont foll chart for rib patt until chart row 7 has been completed, so ending with a RS row.
Cast (bind) off in rib.
Work right armband in same way.

BUTTON BAND

Using smaller needles and A and with RS facing, pick up and k211[215:219] sts evenly up right front from cast-on edge to back neck st holder, then k13[14:15] sts from back neck st holder. 224[229:234] sts.
P one row, k one row.
Beg foll button band heart patt chart from chart row 2 as foll:
Chart row 2 (WS) Reading chart from left to right, work 0[5:10] sts of chart before patt repeat begins as indicated on chart, rep 16-st patt repeat 14 times.
Cont foll chart for patt until chart row 8 has been completed, so ending with a WS row.
P the next row to form the foldline for the hem.
Work 9 rows in k1, p1 rib.
Cast (bind) off in rib.
Mark the positions for the 5 buttonholes, the first to beg 1.5cm/½in from the lower edge, the last to end at the beg of the neck shaping and the rem 3 evenly spaced between, with each buttonhole to be worked over 4 sts.

BUTTONHOLE BAND

Using smaller needles and A and with RS facing, slip first 8 sts on back neck st holder onto a safety pin, k rem 13[14:15] sts, then pick up and k211[215:219] sts evenly down left front from sts just worked to cast-on edge. 224[229:234] sts.
P one row, k one row.
Beg foll buttonhole band heart patt chart from chart row 2 as foll:
Chart row 2 (WS) Reading chart from left to right, rep 16-st repeat 14 times, work last 0[5:10] sts of chart.
Cont foll chart for patt until chart row 3 has been completed, so ending with a RS row.
Buttonhole row (chart row 4) (WS) Work in patt foll chart, casting (binding) off 4 sts when position of each buttonhole is reached.
Work chart row 5 casting on 4 sts over those cast (bound) off in previous row.
Cont foll chart until chart row 8 has been completed, so ending with a WS row.
P next row to form foldline for hem.
Work 4 rows in k1, p1 rib.
Work next row in rib, casting (binding) off 4 sts when each buttonhole is reached.
Work next row in rib, casting on 4 sts for those cast (bound) off in previous row.
Work 3 rows more in rib.
Cast (bind) off in rib.

Centre back neck heart

Using smaller needles and A and with RS facing, k8 sts from safety pin at centre back neck.
P one row, k one row.
Beg foll centre back neck heart chart from chart row 2 as foll:
Chart row 2 (WS) Reading chart from left to right, work 8 sts of chart.
Cont foll chart for patt until chart row 8 has been completed, so ending with a WS row.
P next row to form foldline for hem.
Work 9 rows in k1, p1 rib.
Cast (bind) off in rib.
Sew sides of centre back heart piece to side edges of front bands.
Turn button and buttonhole bands to WS along hemline fold and slip stitch in place.

FINISHING

Join side and armband seams, using a small neat backstitch on very edge of work, except for ribbing where an invisible overstitch (overcast st) should be used.

Pocket hems

Using larger needles and A and with RS facing, p across 36 sts of left front pocket to form foldline for hem.
Then work remainder of hem in k1, p1 rib as foll:

Change to smaller needles and work 5 rows in k1, p1 rib.

Cast (bind) off firmly in rib.

Work hem at top of right front pocket in same way as given for left front pocket hem.

Turn both pocket hems to WS of fronts and slip stitch in place.

Slip stitch both pocket linings to WS of fronts.

Sew two layers of each buttonhole tog all around the edge.

Press seams lightly on WS.

Sew the buttons to the button band in positions corresponding to the buttonholes.

CANDLEMAS

I LOVE TO WEAR THIS DRESS WHEN I'M FEELING LOW AS IT'S AN INSTANT PICK-ME-UP. WORN WITH LEGGINGS OR WARM, WOOLLY TIGHTS, IT'S GREAT FOR ADDING A SPLASH OF COLOUR, WARMTH AND CHEER TO DULL, WINTER DAYS. FOR A SPRINGTIME VERSION, KNIT IT IN LIGHTWEIGHT COTTON OR VISCOSE AND SPRINKLE A FEW FLOWERS AMONGST THE HEARTS.

SIZE

One size only to fit 81–96cm/ 32–38in bust

See diagram for finished knitted measurements.

MATERIALS

Rowan *Lightweight DK* 25g/1oz hanks as foll:

A (no.56: sapphire blue) 34 hanks
B (no.406: sage green) 2 hanks
C (no.53: teal blue) 2 hanks
D (no.125: turquoise) 2 hanks
E (no.405: lime green) 2 hanks
F (no.27: paprika) 2 hanks
G (no.67: bright red) 2 hanks
H (no.149: lilac) 2 hanks

One pair each of 3¼mm (US size 3) and 3¾mm (US size 5) knitting needles

One 3¼mm (US size 3) and one 3¾mm (US size 5) long circular needle

Set of four 3¼mm (US size 3) double-pointed needles for collar

Cable needle (cn)

30cm/12in of 1.5cm/½in wide firm tape for inside of shoulder seams

ALTERNATIVE COLOURWAY

This tunic dress can also be worked in the colourway shown on right, where colours are as foll:

A = no.88: smokey blue
B = no.77: dark rust
C = no.45: red
D = no.86: caramel
E = no.422: sky
F = no.78: tawny
G = no.412: dark rose
H = no.20: pale rose

TENSION (GAUGE)

30 sts and 36 rows to 10cm/4in measured over colourwork patt worked on 3¾mm (US size 5) needles

PLEASE CHECK YOUR TENSION (GAUGE) CAREFULLY AND CHANGE KNITTING NEEDLE SIZE IF NECESSARY

NOTES

When working the colourwork hearts from the charts, use the intarsia method, using a separate length of yarn for each isolated area of colour and twisting yarns together at WS when changing colours to avoid making a hole.

Note that all of the charts (except the collar chart) begin with a WS row, so that RS rows are even-numbered (instead of the usual odd-numbered). Read charts from right to left for the RS (even-numbered) rows and from left to right for the WS (odd-numbered) rows.

The collar chart is worked in the round and all rows are RS and are all read from right to left.

The number of sts in the hearts cable panel shifts between 36 sts and 28 sts – see chart row 35.

CABLE PATTERN SYMBOLS

The cable panels are charted using the following symbols:

C4R = *cable 4 right* – slip 2 sts onto a cn and hold at back of work, k2, then k2 from cn.

T2L = *twist 2 left* – skip one st and k the 2nd st tbl, then k2tog tbl (the skipped st and the k st), slip both sts from needle tog.

no sts = this represents the sts that disappear as the colourwork heart panels are decreased on each side or sts that disappear inside cable panel.

C4pR = *cable 4 right and p background* – slip 2 sts onto a cn and hold at back of work, k2, then p2 from cn.

C4pL = *cable 4 left and p background* – slip 2 sts onto cn and hold at front of work, p2, then k2 from cn.

C3R = *cable 3 right* – slip one st onto a cn and hold at back of work, k2, then p1 from cn.

C3L = *cable 3 left* – slip 2 sts onto a cn and hold at front of work, p1, then k2 from cn.

C4L = *cable 4 left* – slip 2 sts onto a cn and hold at front of work, k2, then k2 from cn.

C5L = *cable 5 left* – slip 2 sts onto a cn and hold at front of work, p3, then k2 from cn.

C5R = *cable 5 right* – slip 3 sts onto a cn and hold at back of work, k2, then p3 from cn.
work 5 tog = *work 5 sts tog* – slip 3 with yarn in front, drop yarn, then *pass 2nd st on RH needle over the first and off needle (centre st of dec), slip centre st back to LH needle and pass 2nd st on LH needle over it*, slip the centre st back to RH needle again and rep from * to * once more, now pick up yarn and k the centre st.
M1 = *make one* – lift running thread between the st just worked and the next st, and k into back of this thread.
inc2 = *double increase* – work (k1 tbl, k1) into same st, then insert tip of LH needle behind the vertical strand that runs downwards from between the 2 sts just made, and k1 tbl into this strand to make the 3rd st of the group.

BACK

Using smaller circular needle and A, cast on 286 sts.
Working back and forth in rows throughout, k 2 rows.
Beg charted cable ribbing as foll:
Chart rib row 1 (WS) K1, p4, *k2, p2, k2, p4, rep from * to last st, p1.
This sets positions of cables.
Work next row foll back patt chart as foll:
Chart rib row 2 (RS) Reading chart from right to left, work first 45 sts of chart, work next 80-st rep 3 times, p last st as indicated.
Beg with chart row 3, cont foll chart until chart row 8 has been completed, so ending with a RS row.
Change to larger circular needle and work chart row 9, so ending with a WS row.

Colourwork panel shaping

The colourwork panel shaping is begun on the next row as foll:
Chart row 10 (RS) P1 (edge st), sl 1-k1-psso, k40, k2tog, *work cable panel over next 36 sts as indicated, sl 1-k1-psso, k40, k2tog*, work from * to * twice more, p1 (edge st).
Note: The 80-st rep of the cable panel and colourwork panel is now a 78-st rep; this rep narrows as the colourwork panel is decreased.
Cont in this way foll chart for patt, working decs at either side of each colourwork panel (when reached) as in row 10 and working an edge st in rev st st at each side of back, until chart row 156 has been completed. 126 sts.
The colourwork panels have each narrowed into a single 4-st cable panel.
Cont foll chart on these 126 sts until chart row 179 has been completed, so ending with a WS row.

Armhole shaping

Chart row 180 (RS) Cast (bind) off first 5 sts (edge st and first 4-st cable panel), work in patt to end of row.
Chart row 181 (WS) Cast (bind) off first 5 sts, work cable panel over next 36 sts, *work 4-st cable at top of colourwork panel, work cable panel over next 36 sts*, rep from * to * once more. (*Note:* The broken line above chart row 181 indicates that the last 4-st cable on the side edge of the back has now been cast (bound) off, but the 4-st cable panel continues at the tops of the 2 rem colourwork panels.) 116 sts.
Chart row 182 Work cable panel over first 36 sts, *work 4-st cable panel, work cable panel over next 36 sts*, rep from * to *.
Cont in patt on these 116 sts until chart row 185 has been completed, so ending with a WS row.

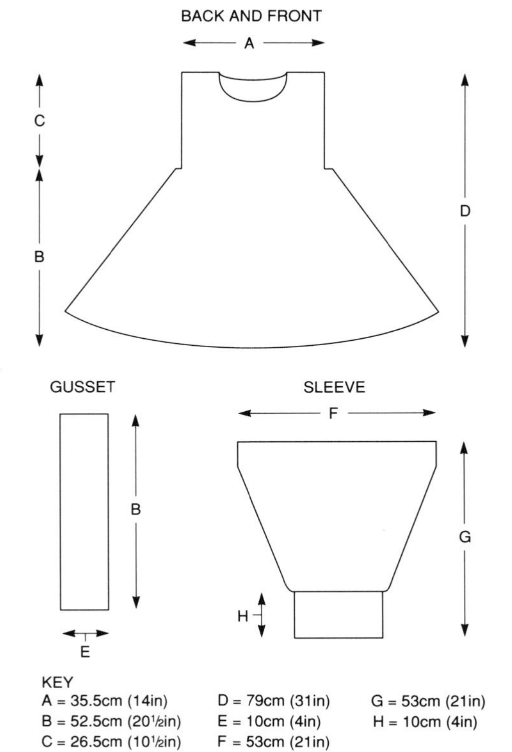

Keeping patt correct (as set between chart rows 158 and 185) throughout, cont without shaping until back measures 77.5cm/30½in from cast-on edge, ending with a WS row.

Neck shaping

Change to smaller needles and beg neck shaping as foll:
Next row (RS) Work first 37 sts in patt, turn leaving rem sts on a spare needle.
Working on first side of neck only, dec one st at beg of next row (neck edge), then dec one st at neck edge on every foll row 4 times in all.
Cast (bind) off rem 33 sts firmly in patt.
Return to rem sts and using smaller needles and with RS facing, slip centre 42 sts on a st holder, rejoin yarn to rem sts and work in patt to end of row.
Complete to match first side, reversing shaping.

FRONT

Work as for back until front measures 71.5cm/28¼in from cast-

BACK AND FRONT
PATTERN CHART
rep = 28 rows
185
179
170
160
158
150
140
130
120
110
100
90
80
70
60
50
40
30
20
10
2 (RS)
1 (WS)
gusset pattern
36 sts
rep these 2 panels twice more
(80-st rep)

NECKBAND PATTERN CHART

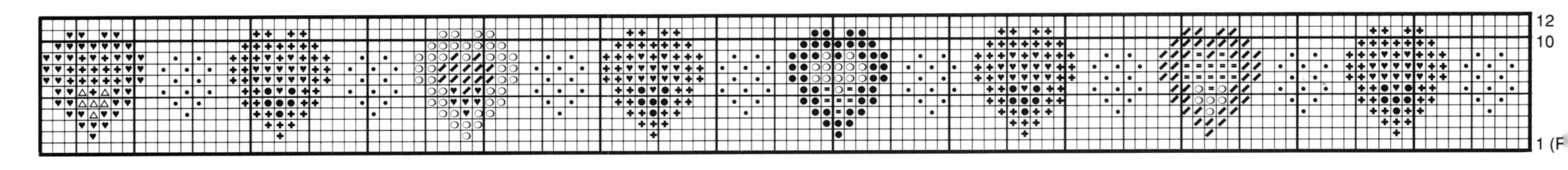

CUFF PATTERN CHART

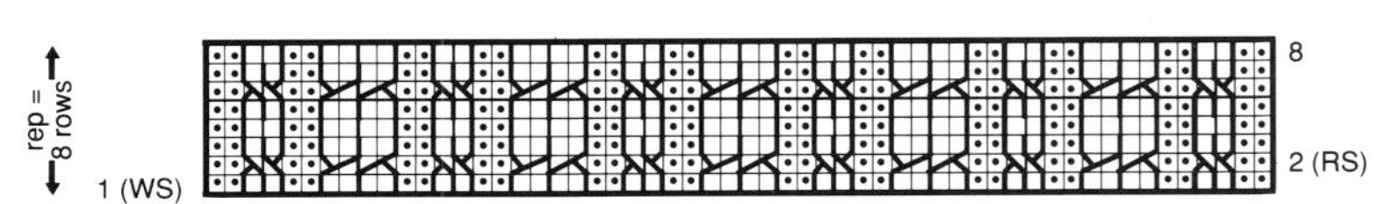

on edge, ending with a WS row.

Neck shaping

Still using larger needles, beg neck shaping as foll:

Next row (RS) work first 47 sts in patt, turn leaving rem sts on a spare needle.

Working on first side of neck only, dec one st at beg of next row (neck edge), then dec one st at neck edge on every foll row 14 times in all.

Work without shaping on rem 33 sts until front measures 77.5cm/30½in from cast-on edge (and there are same number of rows as back to beg of neck shaping), ending with a WS row.

Change to smaller needles and work 5 rows more.

Cast (bind) off firmly in patt.

Return to rem sts and using larger needles and with RS facing, slip centre 22 sts on a st holder, rejoin yarn to rem sts and work in patt to end of row.

Complete to match first side, reversing shaping.

GUSSETS

Using smaller needles and A, cast on 36 sts and k 2 rows.

Beg with chart row 1 of back patt chart, work 36-st cable panel only, foll chart until chart row 8 has been completed, so ending with a RS row.

Change to larger needles and cont foll chart using A only throughout, until chart row 179 has been completed, so ending with a WS row.

Cast (bind) off firmly in patt.

Make 2nd gusset in same way.

SLEEVES

Using smaller needles and A, cast on 56 sts and work in cable rib patt foll cuff chart from row 1 until chart row 8 has been completed.

Cont in rib patt rep rows 1–8 until 39 rows have been worked from cast-on, so ending with a 7th chart row (WS row).

Inc 18 sts evenly across next row as foll:

Next row (RS) P into front and back of first 2 sts, *k2, p into front and back of next st, p1, k1, k into front and back of next st, k2, p into front and back of next st, p1*, rep from * to * once more, k2, p into front and back of next st, p1, k4 (centre cable), p into front and back of next st, p1, rep from * to * twice, k2, p into front and back of last 2 sts. 74 sts.

Change to larger needles and beg with chart row 1, foll sleeve chart until chart row 148 has been completed *and at the same time* work shaping as indicated on chart by inc one st at each end of 4th row and then at each end of every foll 3rd row until there are 160 sts and then cont without shaping, changing to circular needle when there are too many sts to work comfortably.

Cast (bind) off in patt.

Make 2nd sleeve in same way.

NECKBAND

Press pieces very lightly and gently on WS with a warm iron, avoiding cables.

Join shoulder seams using a small neat backstitch on very edge of work. Then sew tape firmly along the WS of the shoulder seams, easing each seam in to measure 11cm/4¼in in length.

Using set of 4 double-pointed needles and A and with RS facing, beg at right shoulder seam pick up and k5 sts down right back neck edge, k42 sts from back neck st holder, pick up and k5 sts up left back neck, 9 sts down straight edge of left front neck, 18 sts down shaped edge, k22 sts from front neck st holder, pick up and k18 sts up shaped edge of right front neck and 9 sts up straight edge. 128 sts.

K one round.

Then beg with chart round 2, foll neckband patt chart, reading all rows from right to left, until chart round 12 has been completed.

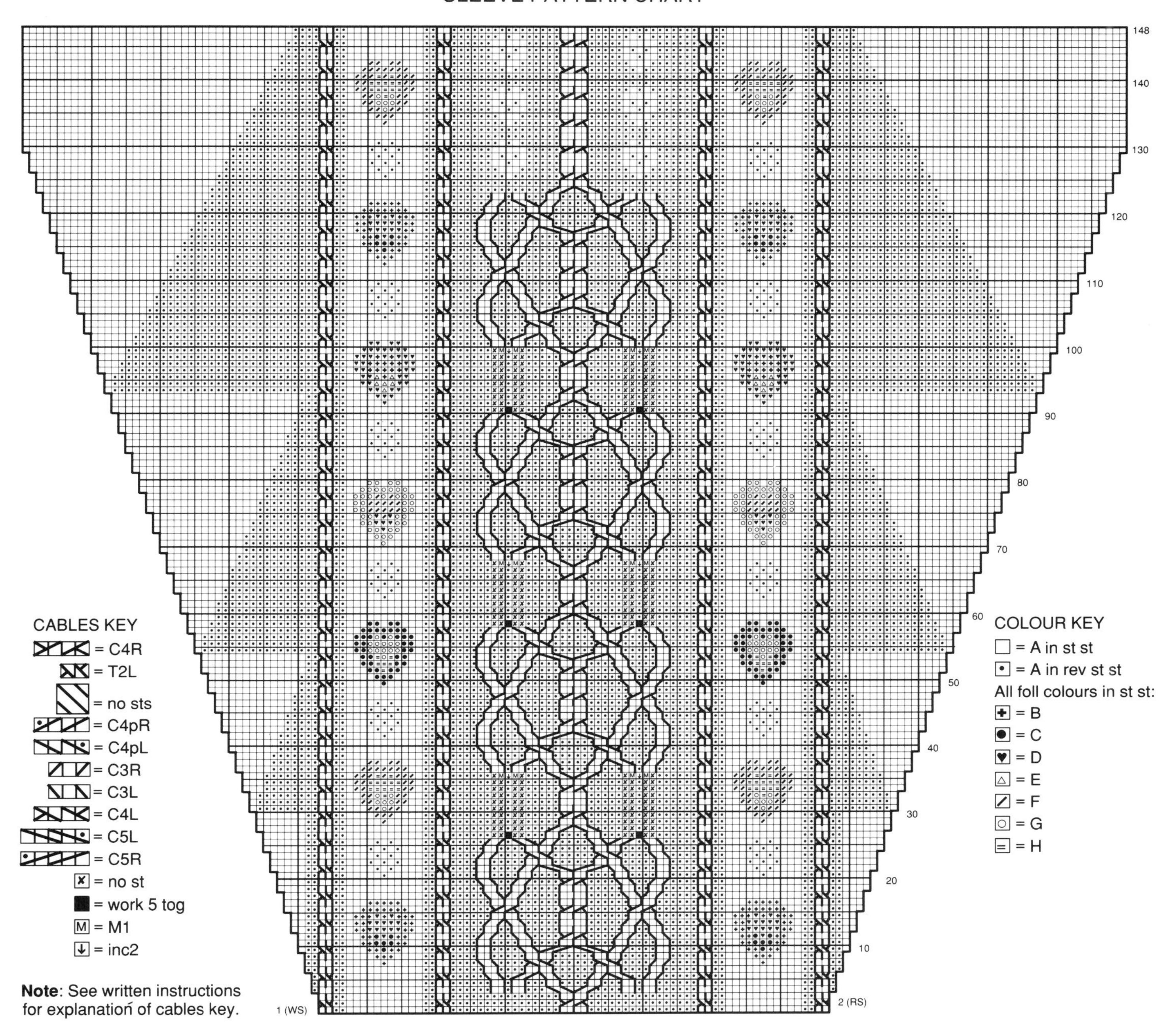

P one round to form fold for hemline.

Work 12 rounds in k1, p1 rib.

Cast (bind) off all sts in rib.

FINISHING

Turn neckband to WS along foldline and slip stitch neatly in place.

Using A, embroider a line of chain st along the first row of the neckband where sts were picked up.

Use a small neat backstitch on very edge of work for all seams except cuffs where a small overstitch (overcast st) should be used.

Join one gusset to each side of front, from cast-on edge to armhole. Then join back to rem sides of gussets.

Set in sleeves placing centre of top of each sleeve at shoulder seam and sewing cast (bound) off edge of sleeve to vertical edge of armhole and sewing sides of sleeve to armhole shaping and top of gusset, easing in top of gusset. Join the sleeve seams.

THE GARDENER'S WEEK-END BOOK
E. S. ROHDE & ERIC PARKER

SPRING

Spring

Even before the Winter is over I'm searching for clues that Spring is on the way. Snowdrops, crocuses and daffodils start to poke their noses through the warming soil. But it's only when I get an uncontrollable urge to dig the garden that I'm sure Spring is around the corner!

In the countryside it's the birth of a whole new year. Hares box in the fields, nests are full of fledglings, the trees sprout blossom and leaf buds unfurl overnight. What a wonderful surprise to see a whole new palette of colour emerging from the monochrome of the winter months: delicate and fragile pastel hues that will intensify and strengthen as the year moves on.

In our house we have always painted eggs and hidden them for the children to find at *Easter*. For me this is not a religious time, but more of a celebration of the wonder of rebirth – I'm constantly amazed by the profusion of creation that is Spring.

In Spring the skies are still clear and as the evenings get warmer, I love to get out into the garden and do a bit of *Stargazing*. Looking up into the great dome of the heavens makes me realise how small and precious our own planet is – and how vital is the need to look after it. I have always been intrigued by the myths and legends attached to the constellations – Orion, the hunter; Corona Borealis, the Northern crown given by Bacchus to Ariadne; and the splendid colour of Arcturus in Boötes, the herdsman.

Coming from the industrial North of England, I look forward every Spring to *Maytime* celebrations. As children in the 50s, my friends and I would dress up as May Queens using old clothes, curtains and sheets, and then parade around the streets. Each child would take it in turn throughout May to be the Queen and the rest of us would be her train-bearers. We would make maypoles out of broom handles and ribbons, and then joyously dance around them. This pleasure in celebrating the rites of Spring has remained with me and I still dance around the maypole each year in spirit if not in person.

EGGSHELL

THE SHAPE OF THIS SWEATER IS BORROWED FROM THE COTTON FISHERMEN'S SMOCKS WITH THEIR HUGE DOUBLE POCKETS, WHICH, I THINK, ARE PERFECT FOR ALL THE PRECIOUS PIECES OF JUNK THAT YOUNG CHILDREN LIKE TO CARRY AROUND. THE COLOURS ARE INSPIRED BY THE NEAPOLITAN ICE-CREAM PASTELS OF A BATTENBURG CAKE. BUT WHAT ABOUT A COTTON VERSION FOR SUMMER, USING A PAINTBOX OF BRIGHT PRIMARIES? OR LET YOUR CHILD CHOOSE THE PALETTE SHE LOVES FOR A SWEATER SHE'LL ALWAYS BE KEEN TO WEAR.

SIZES

To fit 4[6:8:10] yrs or 56[61:66:71]cm/22[24:26:28]in chest

Figures for larger sizes are given in brackets [ ]; where there is only one set of figures, it applies to all sizes.

See diagram for finished knitted measurements.

MATERIALS

Rowan *Lightweight DK* 25g/1oz hanks as foll:

A (no.2: ecru) 2 hanks
B (no.76: spring green) 2[3:4:4] hanks
C (no.112: pastel green) 2[3:4:4] hanks
D (no.4: buttermilk) 3[4:5:5] hanks
E (no.103: apricot) 3[4:5:5] hanks
F (no.6: yellow) 3[4:5:5] hanks

One pair each of 3mm (US size 3) and 3¾mm (US size 5) knitting needles

Set of four 3mm (US size 3) double-pointed needles for collar

Cable needle (cn)

ALTERNATIVE COLOURWAY

This sweater can also be worked in the colourway shown below, where:

A = no.83: shell
B = no.47: pale blue
C = no.416: green
D = no.4: buttermilk
E = no.79: dusty apricot
F = no.410: rose pink

TENSION (GAUGE)

24 sts and 32 rows to 10cm/4in measured over st st worked on 3¾mm (US size 5) needles

PLEASE CHECK YOUR TENSION (GAUGE) CAREFULLY AND CHANGE KNITTING NEEDLE SIZE IF NECESSARY

NOTES

When working the bicolour ribbing on this sweater, strand the colour not in use loosely across the WS.

When working with more than one colour in a row on the rest of the sweater, use the intarsia method, using a separate ball of yarn for each isolated area of colour and twisting yarns tog at WS when changing colour to avoid making a hole.

Note that the cable panels are worked in one colour only and the contrasting colour at the centre of the cable is embroidered with a simple running stitch after the sweater pieces have been completed.

MOSS (SEED) STITCH

The front pockets are worked in moss (seed) stitch.

To work moss (seed) st over an odd number of sts, work as foll:

Patt row 1 (WS) P1, *k1, p1, rep from * to end.

Rep last row to form patt.

To work moss (seed) st over an even number of sts, work as foll:

Patt row 2 (WS) *P1, k1, rep from * to end.

Patt row 2 (RS) *K1, p1, rep from * to end.

Rep last 2 rows to form patt.

BACK

**Using smaller needles and A, cast on 94[102:106:114] sts and beg k2, p2 bicolour rib (see *Notes* above) as foll:

Rib row 1 (RS) *K2 in A, p2 in F, rep from * to last 2 sts, k2 in A.

Rib row 2 *P2 in A, k2 in F, rep from * to last 2 sts, p2 in A.

Rep last 2 rows until ribbing measures 2.5cm/1in from cast-on edge, ending with a WS row and inc 1[0:1:0] st at each end of last row. 96[102:108:114] sts.**

Change to larger needles and working in st st with a central cable panel, beg colour patt and cable as foll:

Row 1 (RS) Using E k43[46:49:52]; then using F work p2, k6, p2 across 10 sts of cable panel; using D k43[46:49:52].

Row 2 Using D p43[46:49:52]; then

using F work k2, p6, k2 for cable panel; using E p43[46:49:52].
Rows 3 and 4 As rows 1 and 2.
Row 5 Using E k43[46:49:52]; then using F p2, sl next 3 sts onto a cable needle and hold at front of work, k3, then k3 sts from cable needle, p2; using D k43[46:49:52].
Row 6 As row 2.
Rep last 6 rows until back measures 15[16:17:18]cm/6[6¼:6½:7]in from cast-on edge, ending with a WS row.
Using F only and keeping st st and cable patt correct as set, work 6 rows, so ending with a WS row.
Cont to keep st st and cable patt correct as set throughout, change colours on next row as foll:
*****Next row** (RS) Using C k43[46:49:52]; then using F work 10 sts of cable panel; using B k43[46:49:52].***
Keeping to colours set in last row, work in patt until back measures 40[42.5:45:47.5]cm/ 15¾[16¾:17¾:18¾]in from cast-on edge, ending with a WS row.
Keeping colours correct, cast (bind) off first 28[31:32:34] sts and break off yarn, slip centre 40[40:44:46] sts onto a st holder for centre back neck, then rejoin yarn and cast (bind) off rem 28[31:32:34] sts.

FRONT

The front is worked in 2 separate pieces; the first piece is worked to the top of the pocket, then a second piece is worked to form the pocket lining and the remainder of the front. The 2 pieces are joined later when the sweater is sewn tog.

Begin pockets

Cast on sts and work ribbing as for back from ** to **.
Change to larger needles and working in st st with a central cable panel, beg colour patt and cable as foll:
Row 1 (RS) Using E work 43[46:49:52] sts in moss (seed) st; then using F work p2, k6, p2 across 10 sts of cable panel; using D work 43[46:49:52] sts in moss (seed) st.
Row 2 Using D work 43[46:49:52] in moss (seed) st; then using F work k2, p6, k2 for cable panel; using E work 43[46:49:52] in moss (seed) st.
Using these colours, cont as set working cable as for back, but working moss (seed) st on either side of cable panel (instead of st st), until pockets measure 15[16:17:18]cm/6[6¼:6½:7]in from cast-on edge, ending with a WS row. (Pockets should now measure same as back to horizontal stripe in F.)
Using smaller needles and F only, work k2, p2 rib across top of pockets while keeping cable panel correct as set as foll:
Next row (RS) K3[2:1:0], (p2, k2) 10[11:12:13] times; work cable panel over next 10 sts; then (k2, p2) 10[11:12:13] times, k3[2:1:0].
Next row P3[2:1:0], (k2, p2) 10[11:12:13] times; work cable panel over next 10 sts; then (p2, k2) 10[11:12:13] times, p3[2:1:0].
Still using F only, rep last 2 rows until ribbing measures 2cm/¾in), ending with a WS row (and making a note of last cable patt row.
Cast (bind) off all sts in rib.

Pocket lining and front

Using larger needles and A, cast on 96[102:108:114] sts and beg pocket lining and rest of front as foll:
Row 1 (RS) Using E k43[46:49:52]; then using F work p2, k6, p2 across 10 centre sts; using D k43[46:49:52].
Row 2 Using D p43[46:49:52]; then using F work k2, p6, k2 across 10 centre sts; using E p43[46:49:52].
Rep last 2 rows (thereby omitting working a cable up the centre

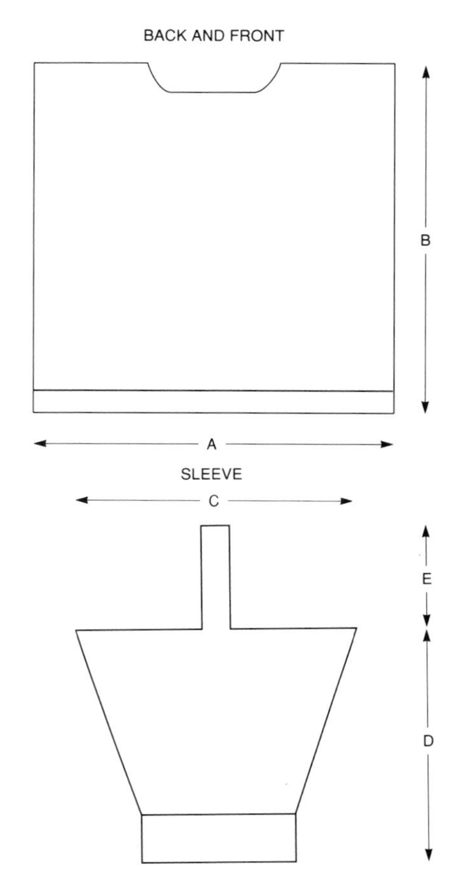

KEY
A = 39[42:44:47]cm (15½[16½:17½:18½]in)
B = 40[42.5:45:47.5]cm (15¾[16¾:17¾:18¾]in)
C = 35[38:40:43]cm (14[15:16:17]in)
D = 31[34.5:37:40.5]cm (12¼[13½:14½:16]in)
E = 12[13:13.5:14]cm (4¾[5:5¼:5¾]in)

10 sts) until front measures 12.5[13.5:14.5:15.5]cm/ 5[5¼:5½:6]in from cast-on edge, ending with a WS row. (Front should now measure same as back between lower ribbing and horizontal stripe in F.)
Using F only, work 6 rows in patt as set, so ending with a WS row.
Beg with row in cable patt which follows last row at top of pockets, work next row as for back from *** to ***.
Keeping to colours as set in last row and cont to work cable in central panel throughout, work in patt until front measures 34[36.5:38.5:41]cm/ 13½[14½:15¼:16¼]in from cast-on edge, ending with a WS row.

Neck shaping

Keeping to colours as set, beg neck

shaping on next row as foll:
Next row (RS) Work 36[39:41:43] sts in patt, then turn leaving rem sts on a spare needle.
Working on first side of neck only, dec one st at neck edge on next and every foll row 8[8:9:9] times in all. 28[31:32:34] sts.
Work without shaping until front measures same as back between top of ribbing and shoulder.
Cast (bind) off.
Return to rem sts and with RS facing, slip centre 24[24:26:28] sts onto a st holder, rejoin yarn to rem sts and work in patt to end of row.
Complete 2nd side of neck to match first side, reversing shaping.

RIGHT SLEEVE

Using smaller needles and C, cast on 42[42:46:50] sts and work in k2, p2 bicolour rib as for back, but using C and F (instead of A and F) until ribbing measures 6.5cm/2½in from cast-on edge, ending with a WS row.
Change to larger needles and working in st st with a central cable panel, beg colour patt and cable as foll:
Row 1 (RS) Using E k16[16:18:20]; then using F work p2, k6, p2 across 10 sts of cable panel; using D k16[16:18:20].
Row 2 Using D p16[16:18:20]; then using F work k2, p6, k2 for cable panel; using E p16[16:18:20].
Cont to work cable panel over 10 centre sts as for back and st st on either side of cable panel in colours as set in last 2 rows *and at the same time* shape sleeve by inc one st at each end of next row and every foll 3rd row 20[23:18:10] in all, then every foll 4th row 2[2:8:17] times. 86[92:98:104] sts.
Keeping patt correct, work without shaping until sleeve measures 31[34.5:37:40.5]cm/12¼[13½:14½:16]in from cast-on edge, ending with a WS row.
Keeping colours and cable patt correct, cast (bind) off 38[41:44:47] sts at beg of next 2 rows.
Using F only, cont in cable panel on rem 10 sts until cable strip measures 12[13:13.5:14]cm/4¾[5:5¼:5¾]in from cast (bound) off edge at top of sleeve, ending with a WS row.
Slip these 10 sts onto a st holder to be picked up later.

LEFT SLEEVE

Work as for right sleeve, but casting on with B and working bicolour rib in B and F.

COLLAR

Press pieces lightly on WS with a warm iron over a damp cloth, omitting cables and ribbing.
Using F and small, neat overstitch (overcast stitch) on very edge of work, sew cast (bound) off edges at top of back and front to side edges of cable strips at top of sleeves.
Using set of four double-pointed needles and A and with RS facing, k10 sts from st holder at top of cable strip on left sleeve, then pick up and k10[10:13:13] sts down left front neck, k24[24:26:28] sts from front st holder, pick up and k10[10:13:13] sts up right front neck, k10 sts from st holder at top of cable strip on right sleeve and k40[40:44:46] sts from back neck st holder.
104[104:116:120] sts.
Work in rounds of k2, p2 bicolour rib as foll:
Round 1 *K2 in A, p2 in F, rep from * to end of round.
Rep last round until ribbing measures 5cm/2in.
Using A, cast (bind) off loosely.

FINISHING

Using A and an invisible slip stitch, sew cast-on edge of pocket lining to WS of pockets just above ribbing.
Then using appropriate colours and a small neat overstitch (overcast st) on very edge of work throughout, sew cast (bound) off edge of sleeves to back and front.
Join side and sleeve seams, sewing through both thicknesses at pocket, but leaving lower ribbing open to form slits at side seams.

Embroidery

Using 4 strands of A, work a running stitch down the centre of the cables on the back and the sleeves, so that the strands of yarn A cover the rows between the cable crossings (see photo). Fasten the strands at the WS at the beg and the end of the running stitches.
Work a running stitch in the same way down the centre front cable, but working through both thicknesses on the pocket so that the pocket is secured to the pocket lining and is divided in two.
Press seams lightly on WS.

Equinox

This jacket was inspired by the ubiquitous waxed cotton jacket. I used a wool and silk yarn for its luxurious feel and added the Equinox design on the back with its sequined border for a bit of fun. If you prefer you can knit it without the motif, or you can add your own – a simple project where you can experiment and express your own creativity.

SIZE

One size only to fit 86–102cm/34–40in bust

See diagram for finished knitted measurements.

MATERIALS

Rowan *Silk and Wool* 20g/¾oz balls as foll:

A (no.851: camel) 57 balls
B (no.852: moss green) 1 ball
C (no.856: donkey) small amount
D (no.857: ecru) small amount

Rowan *Wool and Cotton* 50g/1¾oz balls as foll:

E (no.911: dove) 1 ball
F (no.921: chocolate) 1 ball
G (no.920: hazelnut) 1 ball

Rowan *Silkstones* as foll:

H (no.828: teal) small amount
I (no.826: chilli) small amount

One pair each of 3mm (US size 3), 3¾mm (US size 5) and 4mm (US size 6) knitting needles

Eight 2cm/¾in buttons

Four 14mm/½in buttons for pocket flaps

Four 1.5cm/⅝in buttons for hood (optional)

2.8m/3yd of matching cord for belt and hood

Small amount of yarn in contrasting colour for chain st embroidery around sun and moon

Approx seventy 1cm/⅜in flat sequins

ALTERNATIVE COLOURWAY

This jacket can also be worked in the colourway shown below, where:

A = *Silk and Wool* no.855: coral
B = *Silk and Wool* no.851: camel
C = *Silkstones* no.836: mulberry
D = *Silk and Wool* no.857: ecru
E = *Silkstones* no.825: dried rose
F = *Silk and Wool* no.848: royal blue
G = *Silkstones* no.832: blue mist
H = *Silkstones* no.835: eau de nil
I = *Wool and Cotton* no.913: musk

Plus small amount of pale yellow yarn for embroidery

TENSION (GAUGE)

21 sts and 29 rows to 10cm/4in measured over st st worked on 4mm (US size 6) needles and using yarn double

PLEASE CHECK YOUR TENSION (GAUGE) CAREFULLY AND CHANGE KNITTING NEEDLE SIZE IF NECESSARY

NOTES

Use all types of knitting yarn double throughout for all of the pieces of the knitting.

When working from the motif colourwork chart (for the back) use the intarsia method, using a separate length of yarn for each isolated area of colour and twisting yarns together at WS when changing colours to avoid making a hole.

Read chart from right to left for the RS (odd-numbered) rows and from left to right for the WS (even-numbered) rows.

BACK

Using 3mm (US size 3) needles and A (yarn used double throughout), cast on 132 sts and beg moss (seed) st as foll:

Row 1 (RS) *K1, p1, rep from * to end.

Row 2 *P1, k1, rep from * to end.

Rep last 2 rows 5 times more, so ending with a WS row.

Change to 4mm (US size 6) needles and beg with a k row, work in st st until back measures 33cm/13in from cast-on edge, ending with a WS (p) row.

Slip all sts onto a spare needle, but do not break off yarn.

Belt facing

Using 4mm (US size 6) needles and A doubled and with WS of sts on spare needle facing, pick up and k one st into back of each st in row 7 *rows below sts on spare needle*. 132 sts.

Mark each end of row along which sts have been picked up for belt facing.

Working on these picked up sts, work (k one row, p one row) 4 times. Break off yarn.

Now turn back so that RS is facing and with sts on spare needle in front of sts just worked and with both sets of sts lined up, then using yarn at end of spare needle k across working each st on spare needle tog with each st of belt facing, i.e. knit through both layers tog. 132 sts. This completes belt facing.

Beg with a p row, cont in st st until back measures 42cm/16½in from cast-on edge, ending with a WS (p) row.

Back motif

Beg charted motif on next row, using all colours double and positioning motif as foll:

Chart row 1 (RS) K34 using A, work the next 63 sts foll chart for colours, then using A only k rem 35 sts.

Chart row 2 P35 using A, work the next 63 sts foll chart for colours, then using A only k rem 34 sts.

Cont in this way foll chart for motif until all 81 chart rows have been completed and *at the same time* when back measures 52cm/20½in from cast-on edge, ending with a WS (p) row, beg armhole shaping.

Armhole shaping

****Next row** (RS) K3, sl 1-k1-psso, work in patt to last 5 sts, k2tog, k3. Work one row in patt without shaping.**

Rep from ** to ** 10 times more. 110 sts.

Cont in patt without shaping and after chart has been completed work in st st using A only until back measures 80cm/31½in from cast-on edge, ending with a WS (p) row.

Neck and shoulder shaping

Next row (RS) K first 12 sts and slip these 12 sts onto a st holder, k next 29 sts, turn leaving rem 69 sts on a spare needle.

Working on first side of neck only

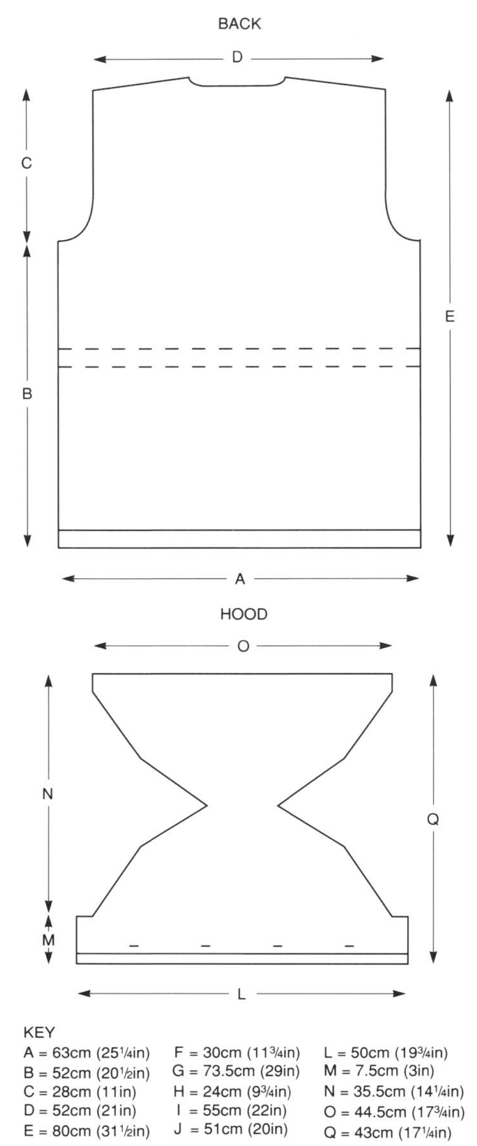

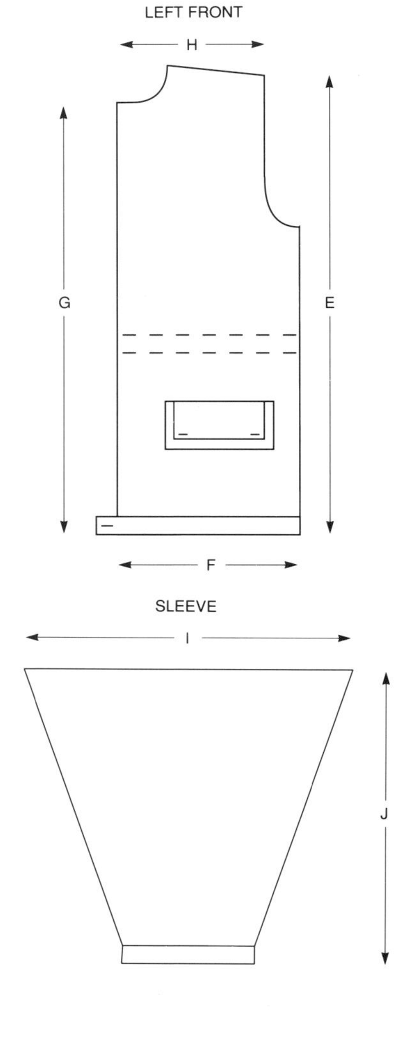

and cont in st st throughout, dec one st at beg (at neck edge) of next row.

Next row K first 13 sts and slip these 13 sts onto a st holder, k to last 2 sts, k2tog.

Dec one st at neck edge on next row.

Work one row without shaping.

Slip rem 13 sts onto a st holder.

Return to rem sts and with RS facing, slip centre 28 sts onto a st holder for centre back neck, rejoin yarn to rem sts and k to end of row.

Next row (WS) P first 12 sts and slip these 12 sts onto a st holder, p to last 2 sts, p2tog.

Dec one st at beg (neck edge) of next row and then work as foll:

Next row P first 13 sts and slip these 13 sts onto a st holder, p to last 2 sts, p2tog.

Work one row without shaping.

Slip rem 13 sts onto a st holder.

Note: Back and front shoulder sts are later cast (bound) off tog to form shoulder seams.

LEFT FRONT

***Before beg the front, work the pocket flap.

Pocket flap

Using 3¾mm (US size 5) needles and A doubled, cast on 36 sts and work 6 rows in moss (seed) st as for back, so ending with a WS row.

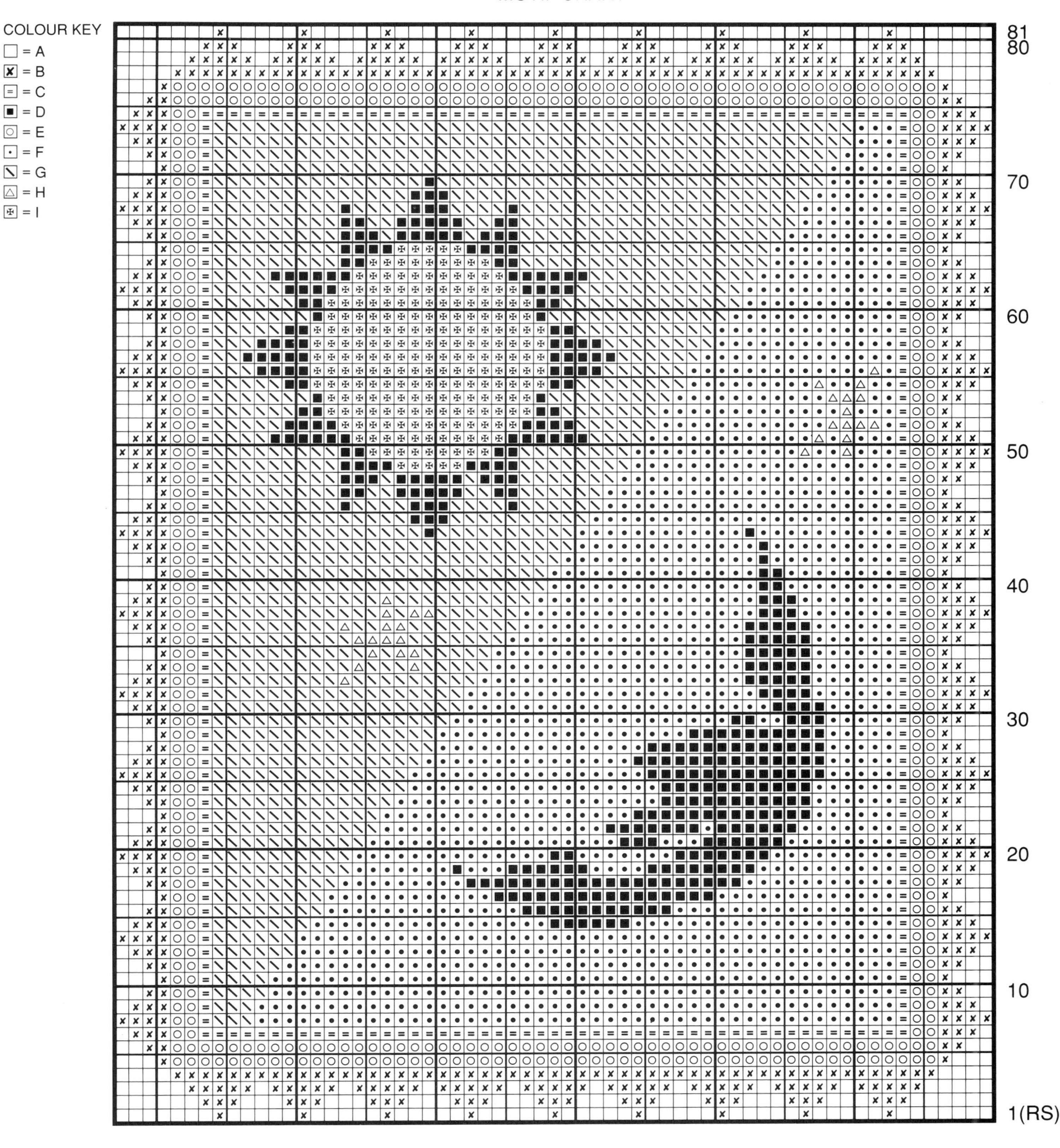

Next row (RS) Work first 4 sts in moss (seed) st as set, k28, work last 4 sts in moss (seed) st as set.

Next row Work first 4 sts in moss (seed) st as set, p28, work last 4 sts in moss (seed) st as set.

Keeping to patt as set with centre 28 sts in st st, work buttonholes over next 2 rows as foll:

Buttonhole row 1 (RS) Work 6 sts in patt, cast (bind) off 3 sts, work next 18 sts in patt (including st already on needle after cast (bind) off), cast (bind) off 3 sts, work in patt to end.

Buttonhole row 2 Work in patt, casting on 3 sts over those cast (bound) off in last row.
Cont in patt without shaping until flap measures 7.5cm/3in from cast-on edge, ending with a WS row.
Leave sts on a spare needle.***

Begin front

Using 3mm (US size 3) needles and A (used double throughout), cast on 69 sts and beg moss (seed) st as foll:
Row 1 (RS) K1, *p1, k1, rep from * to end.
Rep last row 11 times more, so ending with a WS row.
Change to 4mm (US size 6) needles and work next row as foll:
Next row (RS) K62 sts, turn leaving rem 7 sts on a st holder to be used later for front band.
Beg with a p row, cont in st st on these 62 sts until front measures 23.5cm/9¼in from cast-on edge, ending with a WS (p) row.

Insert flap

Insert flap on next row as foll:
Next row (RS) K11 sts, then place flap in front of rem sts on LH needle so that RS of flap is facing, k each of next 36 sts on LH needle tog with one st from pocket flap, k rem 15 sts.
Cont in st st throughout, work without shaping until there are same number of rows as back to beg of belt facing (row which has been marked on back), ending with a RS row. Front measures approx 31cm/12¼in from cast-on edge.
P one row, k one row.
Next row P14 sts, turn leaving rem sts on a spare needle.
Work 3 rows more on these 14 sts, so ending with a RS (k) row. Do not break off yarn. Slip these sts onto a spare needle.
Return to rem sts and using a separate ball of yarn and with WS facing, rejoin yarn and work 4 rows on these 48 sts, so ending with RS (k) row. Break off yarn.
With WS facing and beg with 14 sts on spare needle, p across entire row. 62 sts.
Slip all sts onto a spare needle, but do not break off yarn.

Belt facing

Using 4mm (US size 6) needles and A doubled and with WS of sts on spare needle facing, pick up and k one st into back of each st in row 7 *rows below sts on spare needle* in same way as for back but beg to pick up sts in 12th st from edge. 51 sts.
Working on these picked up sts, work (k one row, p one row) 4 times. Break off yarn.
Now turn front so that RS is facing and with sts on spare needle in front of sts just worked and with both sets of sts lined up, then using yarn at end of spare needle k across working each st on spare needle tog with each st of belt facing, i.e. knit through both layers tog across first 51 sts, then k rem 11 sts. 62 sts.
This completes belt facing.
Work without shaping until front measures 38cm/15in from beg, ending with a WS row.

Top pocket

Next row (RS) K24 sts, turn leaving rem sts on a spare needle.
Working on these 24 sts only, beg by casting on 48 sts and p to end of row. 72 sts.
Cont in st st on these sts until there are same number of rows as back to beg of armhole shaping, ending with a WS row.
Dec one st at armhole edge (work decs 3 sts from edge as on back) on next and every alt row 11 times in all *and at the same time* when front measures 53.5cm/21in from cast-on edge, ending with a RS (k) row, complete pocket as foll:
Next row (WS) Cast (bind) off 48 sts, p to end. Do not break off yarn.
Leave these sts on a spare needle.
Return to rem sts and with RS facing, rejoin yarn and k across these 38 sts.
Work on these sts until there are same number of rows as on other side of front, so ending with a WS (p) row. Break off yarn.
With RS facing and cont to work armhole shaping, work across all sts.
Cont to work armhole shaping until all 11 decs have been completed. 51 sts.
Work without shaping until front measures 73.5cm/29in from cast-on edge, ending with a RS (k) row.

Neck shaping

Next row (WS) P6 and slip these 6 sts onto a st holder, p to end. 45 sts.
Dec one st at end of next row (neck edge), then dec one st at neck edge on every foll alt row 7 times in all. 38 sts.
Work without shaping until there are same number of rows as back to shoulder shaping, ending with a WS row.
Next row (RS) K first 12 sts and slip these 12 sts onto a st holder, k to end.
Work one row without shaping.
Next row K first 13 sts and slip these 13 sts onto a st holder, k to end.
Work 2 rows without shaping.
Slip rem 13 sts onto a st holder.

RIGHT FRONT

Work a pocket flap as for left front from *** to ***.

Begin front

Using 3mm (US size 3) needles and A (used double throughout), cast on 69 sts and beg moss (seed) st as foll:

Row 1 (RS) K1, *p1, k1, rep from * to end.
Rep last row 3 times more, so ending with a WS row.
Keeping moss (seed) st correct as set, beg buttonhole on next row as foll:
Row 5 (RS) Work 3 sts in patt, turn leaving rem 66 sts on a spare needle.
Work 4 rows in patt on these 3 sts, so ending with a RS row. Break off yarn.
Return to rem sts and with RS facing, rejoin yarn and work in patt to end.
Work 4 rows more in patt on these 66 sts, so ending with a RS row. Do not break off yarn.
With WS facing and beg with group of 66 sts, work in patt across all sts in row. 69 sts.
Work 2 rows more in moss (seed) st, so ending with a WS row.
Change to 4mm (US size 6) needles and work next row as foll:
Next row (RS) Work first 7 sts in moss (seed st) and slip these 7 sts onto a st holder to be used later for front band, k rem 62 sts.
Beg with a p row, cont in st st on these 62 sts until there are same number of rows as left front to flap, ending with a WS (p) row.

Insert flap

Insert flap on next row as foll:
Next row (RS) K15 sts, then place flap in front of rem sts on LH needle so that RS of flap is facing, k each of next 36 sts on LH needle tog with one st from pocket flap, k rem 11 sts.
Cont in st st throughout, work without shaping until there are same number of rows as back to beg of belt facing (row which has been marked on back), ending with a RS row. Front measures approx 31cm/12¼in from cast-on edge.
P one row, k one row.
Next row P48 sts, turn leaving rem sts on a spare needle.
Work 3 rows more on these 48 sts, so ending with a RS (k) row. Do not break off yarn. Slip these sts onto a spare needle.
Return to rem sts and using a separate ball of yarn and with WS facing, rejoin yarn and work 4 rows on these 14 sts, so ending with RS (k) row. Break off yarn.
With WS facing and beg with 48 sts on spare needle, p across entire row. 62 sts.
Slip all sts onto a spare needle, but do not break off yarn.

Belt facing

Using 4mm (US size 6) needles and A doubled and with WS of sts on spare needle facing, pick up and k one st into back of each st in row 7 *rows below sts on spare needle* in same way as for back but do not pick up last 11 sts at end of row. 51 sts.
Working on these picked up sts, work (k one row, p one row) 4 times. Break off yarn.
Now turn front so that RS is facing and with sts on spare needle in front of sts just worked and with both sets of sts lined up, then using yarn at end of spare needle k first 11 sts, k across rem 51 sts working each st on spare needle tog with each st of belt facing, i.e. knit through both layers. 62 sts.
This completes belt facing.
Work without shaping until there are same number of rows as left front to beg of top pocket, ending with a WS (p) row.

Top pocket

Next row (RS) K38 sts, turn leaving rem sts on a spare needle.
Working on these 38 sts only, work without shaping until there is one row more than left front to top of pocket slit, so ending with a RS (k) row. Break off yarn.
Leave these sts on a spare needle.
Return to rem sts and with RS facing, rejoin yarn and cast on 48 sts at beg of row then k24 sts. 72 sts.
Work without shaping on these sts until there are same number of rows as back to beg of armhole shaping, ending with a WS row.
Dec one st at armhole edge (work decs 3 sts from edge as on back) on next and every alt row 11 times in all *and at the same time* when there is one row less than other side of right front, so ending with a WS (p) row, complete pocket as foll:
Next row (RS) Cast (bind) off 48 sts, k to end. Do not break off yarn.
With WS facing and cont to work armhole shaping, work across all sts.
Cont to work armhole shaping until all 11 decs have been completed.
51 sts.
Work without shaping until there is one more row than left front to neck shaping, so ending with a WS (p) row.

Neck shaping

Next row (RS) K6 and slip these 6 sts onto a st holder, k to end.
45 sts.
Dec one st at end of next row (neck edge), then dec one st at neck edge on every foll alt row 7 times in all.
38 sts.
Work without shaping until there are same number of rows as back to shoulder shaping, ending with a RS (k) row.
Next row (WS) P first 12 sts and slip these 12 sts onto a st holder, p to end.
Work one row without shaping.
Next row P first 13 sts and slip these 13 sts onto a st holder, p to end.

Work one row without shaping.
Slip rem 13 sts onto a st holder.

SLEEVES

Using 3mm (US size 3) needles and A (used double throughout), cast on 40 sts and work 12 rows in moss (seed) st as for back, ending with a WS row.
Change to 4mm (US size 6) needles and beg with a k row work in st st, inc one st at each end of 3rd row and then every foll 3rd row 24 times in all (88 sts), then every foll 4th row 14 times. 116 sts.
Work in st st without shaping until sleeve measures 51cm/20in from cast-on edge, or desired length, ending with a WS (p) row.
Cast (bind) off all sts.
Make 2nd sleeve in same way.

POCKET TRIM

Work the trim along the top pocket on the left front as foll:
With the RS of the left front facing, place the vertical side edge of the pocket lining along the left edge of the pocket slit (with the p sides of the pocket lining and the left front facing). Then using 3mm (US size 3) needles and A doubled, beg at lower end of slit and pick up and k31 sts evenly along the slit, picking up each st through both layers (the front and the pocket lining).
Work 3.5cm/1¼in in moss (seed) st as given for left front.
Cast (bind) off in patt.
Fold the pocket lining in half and slipstitch the top and bottom seams tog. Do not stitch the pocket lining to the WS of the front, but leave it loose.
Slipstitch the side edge of the pocket trim to the RS of the front.
Work the pocket trim on the right front and finish in the same way as given for the left front.

BUTTON BAND

Using 3mm (US size 3) needles and A doubled and with RS facing, work in moss (seed) st as set across 7 sts on st holder at lower edge of left front, inc one st at beg of row (inside edge of band). 8 sts.
Cont in moss (seed) st throughout, work without shaping until band when slightly stretched fits to beg of neck shaping, ending with a RS row (at outside edge).
Cast (bind) off first 3 sts in patt and slip rem 5 sts onto a safety pin.
Break off yarn.
Sew inside edge of band to left front.
Mark positions for buttonholes on band, the first 1.5cm/½in above cast-on edge, the last 2.5cm/1in below cast (bound) off edge and the rem 6 evenly spaced between. The buttonholes are vertical and are 1.5cm/½in long, so the positions marked are the positions for the beginnings of the buttonholes.

BUTTONHOLE BAND

Using 3mm (US size 3) needles and A doubled and with WS facing, work in moss (seed) st as set across 7 sts on st holder at lower edge of right front, inc one st at beg of row (inside edge of band). 8 sts.
Cont in moss (seed) st throughout, work without shaping as for button band, but when positions for buttonholes are reached work them, beg on a RS row as foll:
Buttonhole row 1 (RS) Work first 3 sts in patt, turn leaving rem sts on a spare needle.
Work 4 rows more on these 3 sts, so ending with a RS row.
Break off yarn.
Return to rem sts and with RS facing, rejoin yarn and work 5 rows in patt on these 5 sts, so ending with a RS row.
On next row work across all 8 sts and cont until next buttonhole position is reached.
When last buttonhole has been worked and buttonhole band is same length as button band, ending with a WS row, cast (bind) off first 3 sts of next (RS) row. Slip rem 5 sts onto a safety pin. Do not break off yarn.
Sew band to right front.

COLLAR

Using 4mm (US size 6) needles and A doubled, join left shoulder seam by placing WS of left front and WS of back tog, then with left front facing, knit through both layers along all 38 sts of shoulder, taking one st from front tog with one st from back with each st and casting (binding) off as the row is worked. This forms a decorative seam on the RS of the garment.
Join the right shoulder seam in the same way, working the cast (bind) off with the right front facing.
Using 3mm (US size 3) needles and A doubled and with RS facing, beg at right front neck edge k first 3 sts from safety pin at top of band, k next 2 sts on pin tog, k6 sts from st holder, pick up and k21 sts up right front neck, 4 sts down right back neck, k28 sts from back neck st holder, pick up and k4 sts up left back neck, 21 sts down left front neck, k6 sts from st holder, k first 2 sts on safety pin tog, and k rem 3 sts. 98 sts.
Beg k1, p1 rib on next row as foll:
Rib row 1 *K1, p1, rep from * to end.
Rep last row until ribbing measures 1.5cm/½in, ending at right front neck edge.
Change to 3¾mm (US size 5)

needles and beg next row as foll:
Row 1 (K1, p1) twice, (p1, k1) to last 4 sts, (k1, p1) twice.
Row 2 K1, p1, k1, p into front and back of next st to inc one st, k1, (p1, k1) to last 5 sts, p into front and back of next st, (k1, p1) twice.
Cont in this way working 4 sts in k1, p1 rib at each edge of collar, working moss (seed) st between these edge sts and inc one st at each end of every alt row (between rib and moss st) until collar measures 7.5cm/3in.
Work 2 rows more in patt as set without shaping.
Cast (bind) off in patt.

POCKETS

Using 4mm (US size 6) needles and A (used double throughout), cast on 22 sts.
Beg with a k row, work 7 rows in st st, inc one st at each end of every row. 36 sts.
Cont in st st throughout, work without shaping until pocket measures 18cm/7in from cast-on edge. Cast (bind) off all sts.
Work an identical 2nd pocket.

HOOD

The hood is optional and the jacket can be worn with or without the hood buttoned to the neckline under the collar.
Using 3mm (US size 3) needles and A doubled, cast on 105 sts and beg k1, p1 rib as foll:
Rib row 1 (RS) K1, *p1, k1, rep from * to end.
Rib row 2 P1, *k1, p1, rep from * to end.
Rep last 2 rows until ribbing measures 2cm/¾in from cast-on edge, ending with a WS row.
Change to 4mm (US size 6) needles and work buttonholes as foll:
Buttonhole row 1 (RS) K18, cast (bind) off next 3 sts, k21 including st already on needle after cast (bind) off, cast (bind) off next 3 sts, k15 including st already on needle, cast (bind) off next 3 sts, k21 including st already on needle, cast (bind) off next 3 sts, k to end.
Buttonhole row 2 (WS) P to end, casting on 3 sts over those cast (bound) off in last row.
Cont in st st throughout and beg with a k row, work without shaping until hood measures 7.5cm/3in from cast-on edge, ending with a WS (p) row.
Cast (bind) off 6 sts at beg of next 2 rows. 93 sts.
Dec one st at each end of next row and every foll alt row 14 times in all, then at each end of every foll row 20 times. 25 sts.
Work 2 rows without shaping.
Inc one st at each end of next row and every foll row 20 times in all, then at each end of every foll alt row 14 times. 93 sts.
Work 7 rows without shaping.
Cast (bind) off all sts.
Fold hood in half right sides tog, so that foldline is formed between 2 rows of 25 sts worked without shaping as centre of hood.
Join seams using a small, neat backstitch on very edge of work, beg at foldline and joining last 7 rows before final cast (bind) off to 6 sts cast (bound off) 7.5cm/3in from cast-on edge.
Then fold 2.5cm/1in of hood to WS all along edge without ribbing.
Slipstitch in place on WS, leaving cast-on edge of ribbing open for inserting cord.

FINISHING

Join seams using a small neat backstitch on very edge of work, except for moss (seed) st where an invisible overstitch (overcast st) should be used.

Placing centre of top of sleeve at shoulder seam, sew cast (bound) off edge of sleeves to armhole edge (including decreased edge).

Join side and sleeve seams, leaving belt facings open.

Sew patch pockets to RS of fronts, positioning the cast (bound) off edge directly under flaps.

Embroidery
Using a blunt-pointed needle and a small amount of contrasting yarn, work chain st as evenly as possible around the circumference of the sun and around the edge of moon on the back of the jacket.

Sequins
Sew a sequin to the centre of each point on the zigzag edge around the border of the motif, to the centre of each point on the sun, to the centre of each star, to each end of the moon and to the 'eye' on the moon.

Sew eight buttons to the button band and then two buttons to each patch pocket, in positions corresponding to the buttonholes worked in the knitting.

Sew buttons underneath the collar on the k1, p1 ribbing to correspond to the buttonholes on the lower edge of the hood.

Cut a piece of matching cord to the required length for the belt and knot one end of it. Slide the unknotted end of the cord through the belt facing, beg at the opening on the left front and coming out at the opening on the right front.
Check that the cord is the correct length, then knot the other end of it. Trim each end of the cord close to the knot.

Insert matching cord through the hood facing in the same way as given for the belt.

SKYLARK

INSPIRED BY THE PASTA SHAPES THAT MY SON, FELIX, IS HOOKED ON, THIS SWEATER IS A FANTASY OF SCIENCE FICTION. I LOVE THE IDEA OF THE MOTIF BECOMING AN INTEGRATED PART OF THE WELTS, AS IN THE ROCKET EXHAUST AT THE HEM AND THE MARTIAN'S LEGS ON THE SLEEVES. THE STARS, PLANETS AND SATELLITES ARE SPREAD RANDOMLY OVER THE SWEATER, SO IF YOUR CHILD HAS A FAVOURITE SPACE OBJECT, YOU CAN ADD OR SUBSTITUTE IT.

SIZES

To fit 7–8[10–12] yrs or 64–66[71–76]cm/25–26[28–30]in chest

Figures for larger size are given in brackets [ ]; where there is only one set of figures, it applies to both sizes.

See diagram for finished knitted measurements.

MATERIALS

Rowan *Cotton Glacé* 50g/1¾oz balls as foll:

A (no.729: navy) 8[9] balls
B (no.731: thistledown) 1 ball
C (no.726: bleached) 1 ball
D (no.735: butterscotch) 1 ball
E (no.732: harebell) 1 ball

Rowan *Nice Cotton* 50g/1¾oz balls as foll:

F (no.433: parakeet) 1 ball
G (no.437: fiesta) 1 ball

One pair each of 2¾mm (US size 2) and 3¼mm (US size 3) knitting needles

Set of four 2¾mm (US size 2) double-pointed knitting needles for neckband

ALTERNATIVE COLOURWAY

This sweater can also be worked in the colourway shown below, where:

A = *Cotton Glacé* no.725: ecru
B = *Nice Cotton* no.431: rio
C = *Cotton Glacé* no.744: provence
D = *Cotton Glacé* no.738: clay
E = *Nice Cotton* no.436: mardi gras
F = *Nice Cotton* no.433: parakeet
G = *Nice Cotton* no.432: carnival

TENSION (GAUGE)

24 sts and 32 rows to 10cm/4in measured over st st worked on 3¼mm (US size 3) needles

PLEASE CHECK YOUR TENSION (GAUGE) CAREFULLY AND CHANGE KNITTING NEEDLE SIZE IF NECESSARY

NOTES

When working the colourwork pattern, use the intarsia method, using a separate length of yarn for each isolated area of colour and twisting yarns together when changing colours to avoid making a hole.

Read back, front and sleeve charts from right to left for the RS (odd-numbered) rows and from left to right for the WS (even-numbered) rows. The neckband chart is worked in the round and all rows are RS and are read from right to left.

BACK

Using smaller needles and A, cast on 108[120] sts and beg multicoloured k1, p1 rib as foll:

Rib row 1 (RS) Using A k1, (p1, k1) 1[4] times, *using B p1, (using G k1, using B p1) twice, using A k1, (p1, k1) 4 times, rep from * to last 7[13] sts, using B p1, (using G k1, using B p1) twice, using A (k1, p1) 1[4] times.

Rib row 2 Using A k1, (p1, k1) 1[4] times, *using G p1, using A k1, using G p1, using A (k1, p1) 5 times, k1, rep from * to last 7[13] sts, using G p1, using A k1, using G p1, using A (k1, p1) 2[5] times.

Rep last 2 rows 6 times more, so ending with a WS row.

Change to larger needles and beg with a k row, work in st st foll back patt chart (see pages 70 and 71 for chart) until chart row 84[88] has been completed, so ending with a WS row.

Armhole shaping

Cont in st st foll chart throughout, beg armhole shaping on next row as foll:

Chart row 85[89] (dec row) (RS) k2, sl 1-k1-psso, work in patt to last 4 sts, k2tog, k2.

Work one row without shaping. Rep dec row once more.

Rep from ** to ** 5[7] times more. 94[102] sts.

Work without shaping until chart row 148[156] has been completed, so ending with a WS row.

Neck shaping

Chart row 149[157] (RS) Work first 31[35] sts in patt, turn leaving rem sts on a spare needle.

Working first side of neck only, dec one st at beg of next row (neck edge), then at neck edge on every foll row 3 times in all, so ending with a WS row.

Slip rem 28[32] sts onto a st holder.

Return to rem sts and with RS facing, slip centre 32 sts onto a st holder, rejoin yarn to rem sts and work in patt to end of row.

Complete 2nd side of neck to match first side, reversing shaping.

FRONT

Work as for back until chart row 132[140] has been completed, so ending with a WS row.

Neck shaping

Chart row 133 [141] (RS) Work first 41[45] sts in patt, turn leaving rem sts on a spare needle.

Working first side of neck only, cast (bind) off 3 sts at beg of next row.

Work one row without shaping.

Cast (bind) off 3 sts at beg of next row.

Dec one st at end of next row (neck edge), then at neck edge on every foll row 7 times in all.

Work without shaping until chart row 152[160] has been completed.

Slip rem 28[32] sts onto a st holder.

Return to rem sts and with RS facing, slip centre 12 sts onto a st holder, rejoin yarn to rem sts and work in patt to end of row.

Complete 2nd side of neck to match first side, reversing shaping.

SLEEVES

Using smaller needles and A, cast on 42 sts and beg k1, p1 rib as foll:

Rib row 1 (RS) Using A k1, p1, k1, *using B k3, using A k1, using B k3, using A (k1, p1) 3 times, k1*, rep from * to * once more, using B k3, using A k1, using B k3, using A (k1, p1) twice.

Rib row 2 Using A (k1, p1) twice, *using B p3, using A p1, using B p3, using A (p1, k1) 3 times, p1*, rep from * to * once more, using B p3, using A p1, using B p3, using A p1, k1, p1.

Rib row 3 Using A (k1, p1) twice, using *G k1, using A p1, k1, p1, using G k1, using A (p1, k1) 4 times, p1*, rep from * to * once more, using G k1, using A p1, k1, p1, using G k1, using A (p1, k1) twice, p1.

Rib row 4 Using A (k1, p1) twice, k1, *using G p1, using A k1, p1, k1, using G p1, using A (k1, p1) 4 times, k1*, rep from * to * once more, using G p1, using A k1, p1, k1, using G p1, using A (k1, p1) twice.

Rib rows 5–10 Rep 3rd and 4th rows 3 times more.

Rib row 11 As row 3.

Rib row 12 Using A k into front and back of first st, (p1, k1) twice, using G p1, using A k1, p1, k1, *using G p1, using A k1, p into front and back of next st, k1, p1, k into front and back of next st, p1, k1, p into front and back of next st, k1*, rep from * to * once more, using G p1, using A k1, p1, k1, using G p1, using A k1, p1, k1, p into front and back of last st. 50 sts.

Change to larger needles and beg with a k row, work in st st foll sleeve patt chart and inc one st at each end of 4th row, then every foll 3rd row until there are 102[108] sts.

Work without shaping until chart row 100[104] has been completed, so ending with a WS row.

Cast (bind) off all sts.

Make 2nd sleeve in same way.

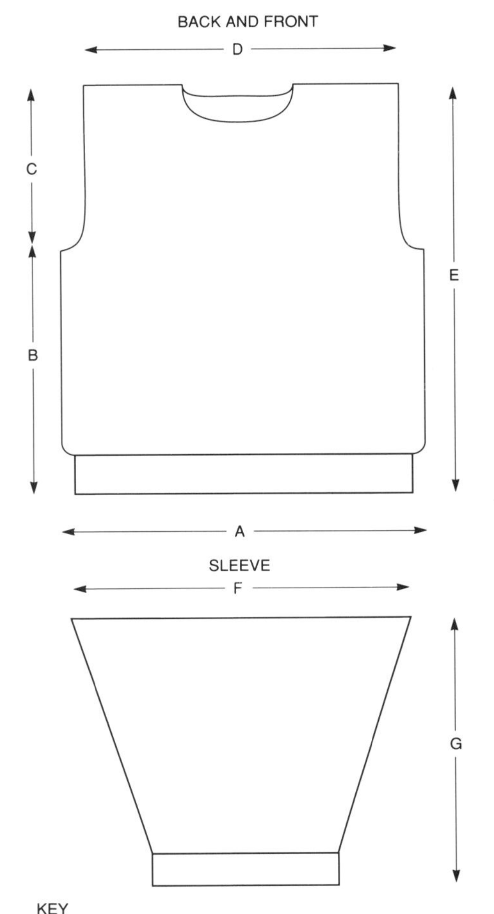

NECKBAND

Press pieces lightly on WS with a warm iron over a damp cloth, omitting ribbing.

Using larger needles and A, join left shoulder seam by placing WS of back and WS of front tog, then with back facing, knit through both layers along the 28[32] shoulder sts, taking one st from back st holder tog with one st from front st holder with each st and casting (binding) off as the row is worked. This forms a decorative seam on the RS.

Join the right shoulder seam in the same way, working the cast (bind) off with the back facing.

Using set of 4 double-pointed needles and A and with RS facing, beg at left shoulder seam and pick

SLEEVE PATTERN CHART

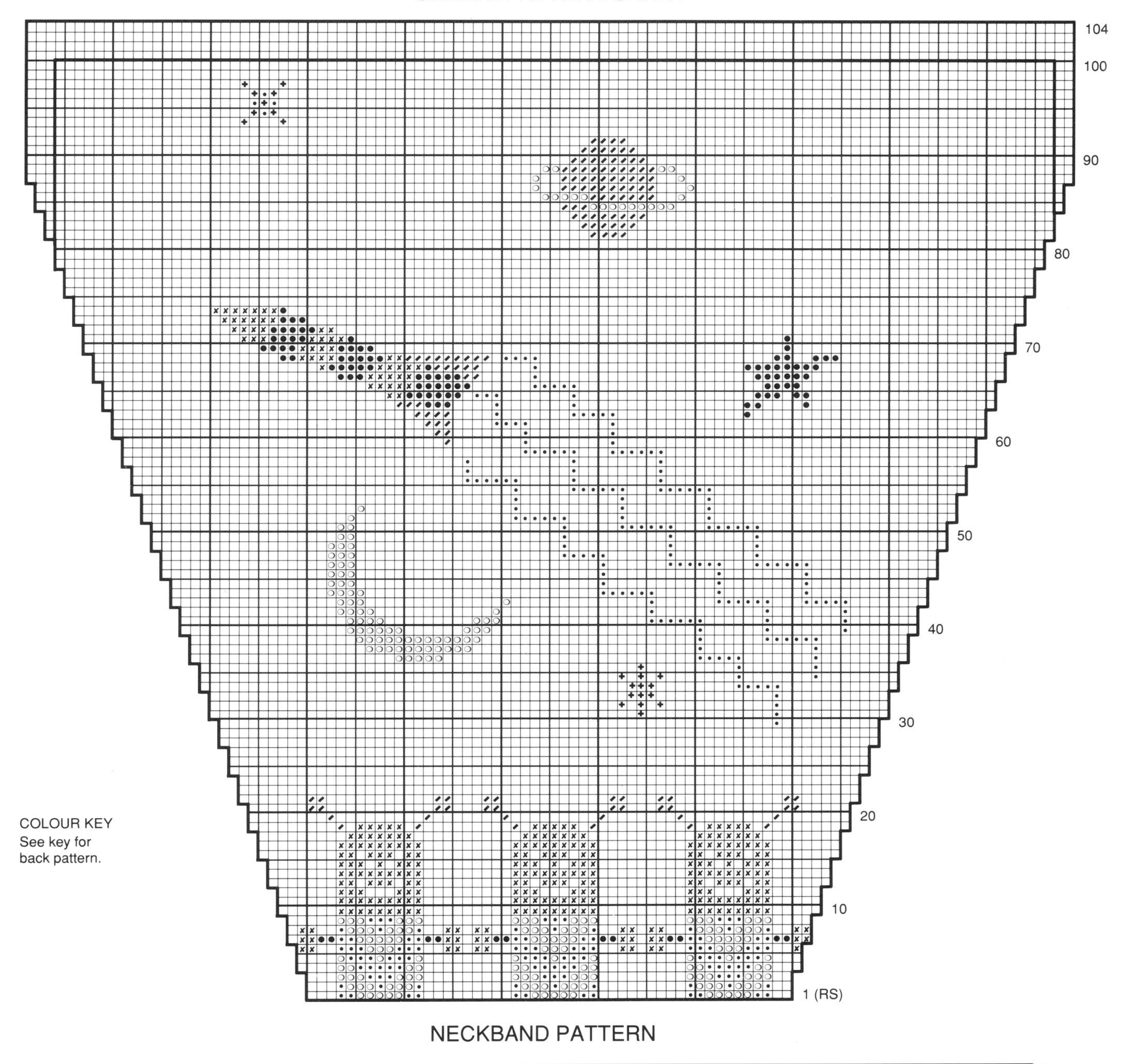

NECKBAND PATTERN

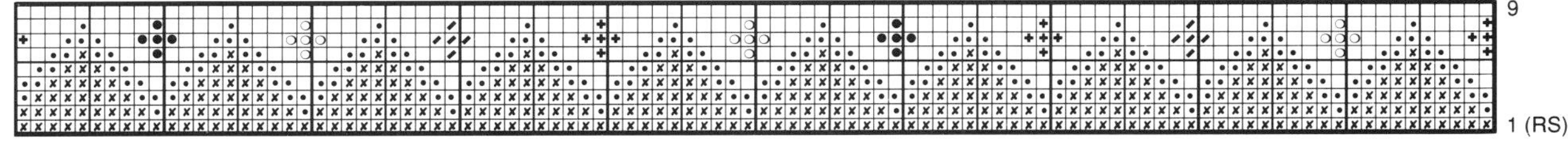

up and k9 sts down straight edge of left front neck, 15 sts along shaped edge, k12 sts from front neck st holder, pick up and k15 sts up shaped edge of right front neck, 9 sts up straight edge, 4 sts down right back neck, k32 sts from back neck st holder, pick up and k4 sts up left back neck. 100 sts.

Then beg with chart row 1, work in rounds in st st foll neckband patt chart, reading all rows from right to left, until chart round 9 has been completed.

Using A only, p one round, then k 9 rounds.

Cast (bind) off all sts loosely.

FINISHING

Join seams using a small neat backstitch on very edge of work, except for ribbing where an invisible overstitch (overcast stitch) should be used.

Placing centre of top of sleeve at shoulder seam, sew cast (bound) off edge of sleeves to armhole edge (including decreased edge).

Join side and sleeve seams.

Press seams lightly on WS.

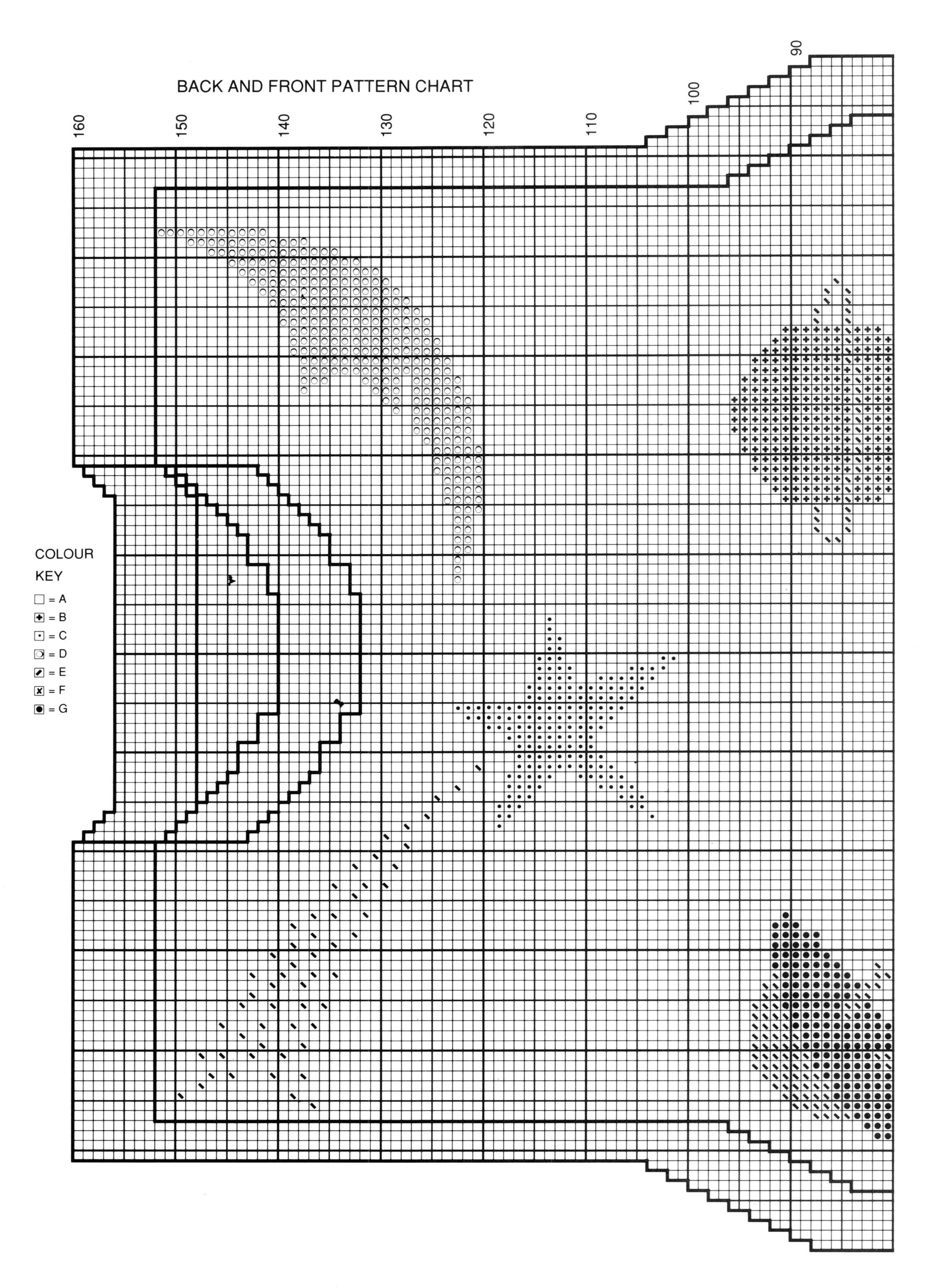
BACK AND FRONT PATTERN CHART
160
150
140
130
120
110
100
90
COLOUR
KEY
= A
= B
= C
= D
= E
= F
= G

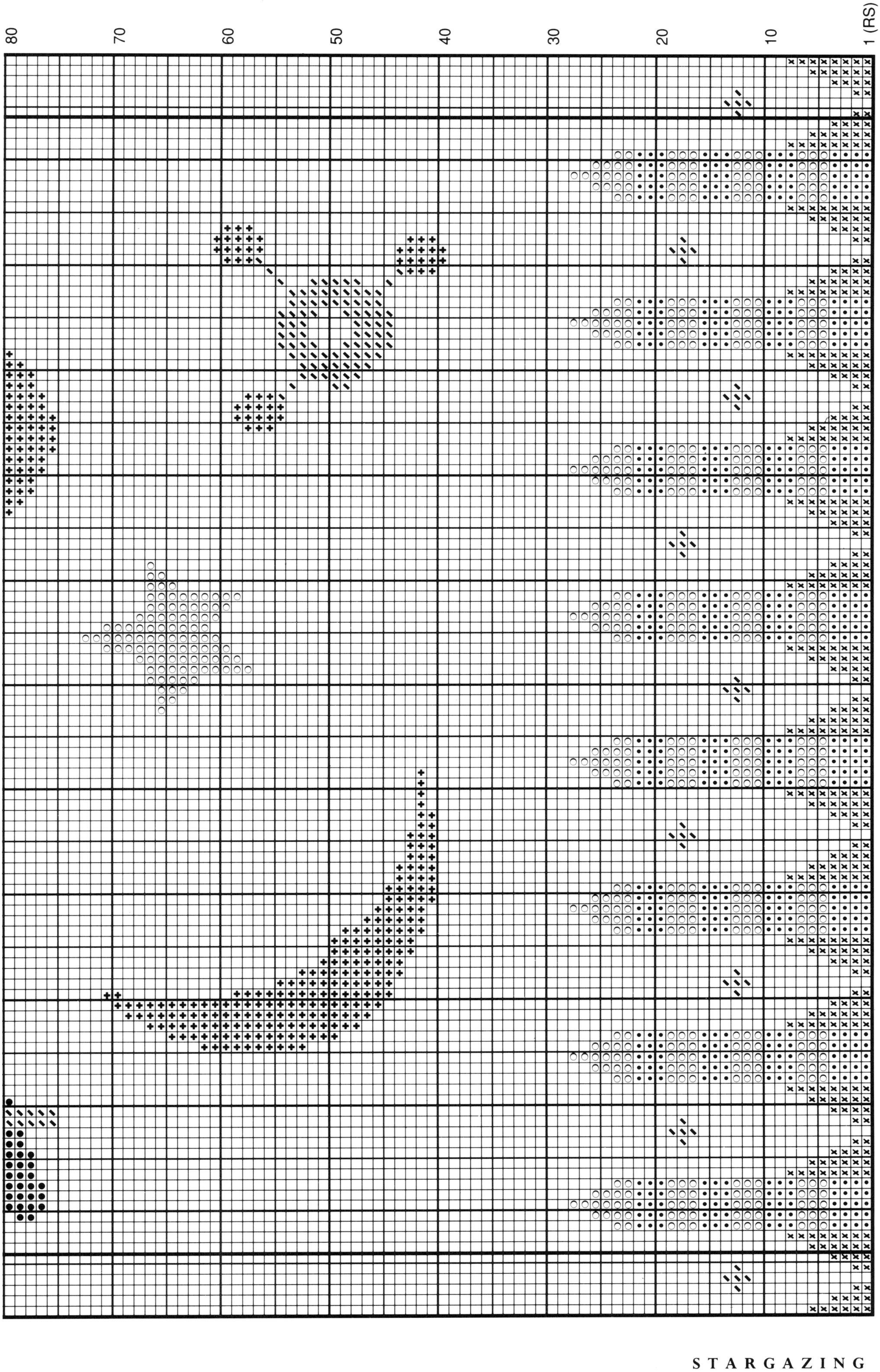

80 70 60 50 40 30 20 10 1 (RS)

MAYQUEEN

THIS DRESS MAKES ME WISH I HAD A DAUGHTER SO THAT I COULD KNIT IT FOR HER. FOR ME IT'S A FAIRYTALE, INSPIRED BY HANS CHRISTIAN ANDERSEN STORIES, CARL LARSSON PAINTINGS, AND EASTERN EUROPEAN EMBROIDERIES. A MAGICAL MIXTURE THAT'S BOTH ENCHANTING TO LOOK AT AND DELIGHTFUL TO KNIT.

SIZE

One size only to fit 4–5 yrs or 56–58cm/22–23in chest

See diagram for finished knitted measurements.

MATERIALS

Rowan *Cabled Mercerised Cotton*

50g/1¾oz balls as foll:

A (no.328: pale pink) 4 balls
B (no.314: furnace) 4 balls
C (no.334: speedwell) 1 ball
D (no.315: claret) 1 ball
E (no.337: firethorn) 1 ball
F (no.336: saffron) 1 ball
G (no.329: khaki) 1 ball
H (no.325: mushroom) 1 ball
I (no.335: aspen) 1 ball

One pair each of 2¾mm (US size 2) and 3¼mm (US size 3) knitting needles

Cable needle (cn)

Five 12mm/½in buttons

ALTERNATIVE COLOURWAY

This dress can also be worked in the colourway shown right, where:

A = no.313: pastel peach
B = no.328: pale pink
C = no.311: pale mauve
D = no.302: bleached
E = no.306: blue scan
F = no.312: wild rose
G = no.327: lichen
H = no.325: mushroom
I = no.329: khaki

TENSION (GAUGE)

29 sts and 41 rows to 10cm/4in measured over st st worked on 3¼mm (US size 3) needles

36 sts and 42 rows to 10cm/4in measured over smock st patt worked on 3¼mm (US size 3) needles

PLEASE CHECK YOUR TENSION (GAUGE) CAREFULLY AND CHANGE KNITTING NEEDLE SIZE IF NECESSARY

NOTES

When working the colourwork patterns, use the intarsia method, using a separate length of yarn for each isolated area of colour and twisting yarns together when changing colours to avoid making a hole.

Read charts from right to left for the RS (odd-numbered) rows and from left to right for the WS (even-numbered) rows.

FRONT

Using smaller needles and B, cast on 200 sts.

Beg with a k row, work 16 rows in st st, so ending with a WS row.

Change to larger needles and work picot edge on next row as foll:

Picot row (RS) K1, *k2tog, yarn to front of work between 2 needles, then over top of RH needle to back of work to make a new st – called *yarn over* or *yo* –, rep from * to last st, k1.

P one row.

Beg with chart row 1, foll skirt border chart (pages 76 and 77) until chart row 14 has been completed, so ending with a WS row.

Beg skirt chart (page 75) as foll:

Chart row 1 (RS) Using B only, k to end.

Chart row 2 Reading chart from left to right, work first 12 sts of chart, (work next 50 sts of chart) 3 times in all, work last 38 sts of chart.

Beg with chart row 3, cont foll chart until chart row 12 has been completed, working 50-st repeat 3 times on each row and so ending with a WS row.

Colourwork panel shaping

The colourwork panel shaping is begun on the next row as foll:

Chart row 13 (RS) Work first 11 sts of chart, with B k2tog, work next 25 sts in A foll chart, *with B sl 1-k1-psso, work next 21 sts of chart, with B k2tog, work next 25 sts in A foll chart*, rep from * to * twice more rep same 50-st repeat on chart, with B sl 1-k1, psso, work last 10 sts of chart.

Note: The 50-st rep of the 2 panels is now a 48-st rep; this rep narrows as the colourwork panel is decreased at each side on every foll 12th row as indicated on the chart.

Cont in this way foll chart for patt, working decs on every foll 12th row on either side of each of 3 centre colourwork panels and at only one side of half panels at sides as in row 13, until chart row 148 has been completed, so ending with a WS row. 104 sts.**

Yoke

Using B only throughout for remainder of front, beg smock st patt as foll:

Row 1 (RS) P2, *k1, p3, rep from *, ending last rep p1 instead of p3.

Row 2 K1, *p1, k3, rep from *, ending last rep k2 instead of k3.

Row 3 P2, *slip next 5 sts onto cn and hold at front of work, wind yarn 3 times around 5 sts on cn in anti-clockwise (counterclockwise) direction, then k1, p3, k1 from cn – called *cluster 5* or *cl 5* –, p3, rep from *, ending last rep p1 instead of p3.

Row 4 As row 2.

Rows 5–8 Rep rows 1 and 2 twice.

Row 9 Slip first 3 sts onto cn and hold at front of work, wind yarn 3 times around 3 sts on cn in anti-clockwise (counterclockwise) direction, then p2, k1 from cn – called *cluster 3* or *cl 3* –, *p3, cl 5, rep from * to last 5 sts, p3, slip last 2 sts onto cn and hold at front of work, wind yarn 3 times around 2 sts on cn in anti-clockwise (counterclockwise) direction, then k1, p1 from cn – called – *cluster 2* or *cl 2*.

Row 10 As row 2.

Rows 11 and 12 As rows 1 and 2.

Rows 1–12 are repeated to form the smock st patt.

Rep rows 1–4 once more, so ending with a WS row.

Armhole shaping

Keeping smock st patt correct as set throughout (working cluster over 2, 3 or 4 sts at edge where necessary), cast (bind) off 11 sts at beg of next 2 rows. 82 sts.

Work 34 rows more in patt, so ending with a WS row. Yoke measures approx 12.5cm/5in.

Neck shaping

Beg neck shaping on next row as foll:

Next row (RS) Work 21 sts in patt, then turn leaving rem sts on a spare needle.

Working on first side of neck only, work 24 rows in patt without shaping, so ending with a RS row.

Cast (bind) off.

Return to rem sts and with RS facing, slip centre 40 sts onto a st holder, rejoin yarn to rem sts and work in patt to end of row.

Work 25 rows in patt without shaping on these 31 sts, so ending with a WS row.

Cast (bind) off.

BACK

Work as for front to **.

Right back yoke

Using B only throughout for remainder of back, divide for back opening and beg smock st patt as foll:

Row 1 (RS) *P2, (k1, p3) 12 times*, (50 sts now on RH needle), turn leaving rem sts on a spare needle.

Working on first side of back only, cont in patt as foll:

Row 2 K3, *p1, k3, rep from *, ending last rep k2 instead of k3.

Row 3 P2, *cl 5, p3, rep from *.

Row 4 As row 2.

Rows 5–8 Rep rows 1 (working from * to * on row 1) and 2 twice.

Row 9 Cl 3, *p3, cl 5, rep from * to last 7 sts, p3, slip last 4 sts onto cn and hold at front of work, wind yarn 3 times around 4 sts on cn in anti-clockwise (counterclockwise) direction, then k1, p3 from cn – called *cluster 4* or *cl 4*.

Row 10 As row 2.

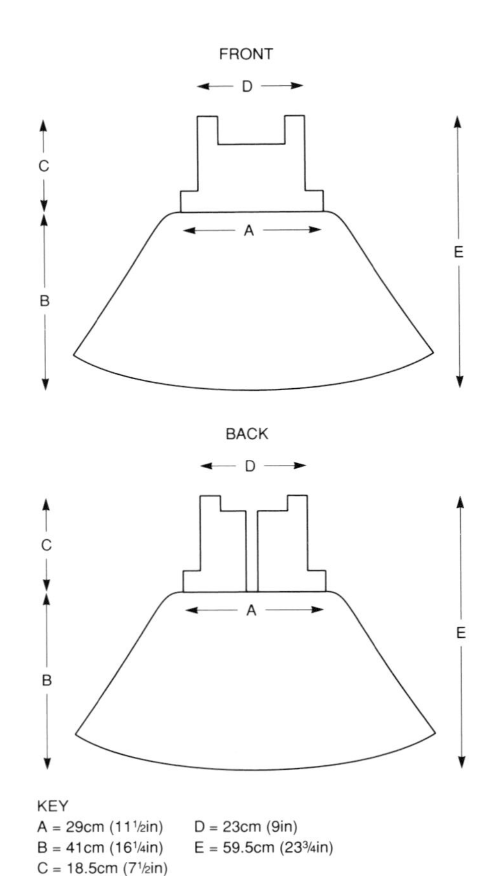

Rows 11 and 12 As rows 1 and 2.

Rows 1–12 are repeated to form the smock st patt.

Rep rows 1–4 once more, so ending with a WS row.

Armhole shaping

Keeping smock st patt correct as set throughout (working cluster over 2, 3 or 4 sts at edge where necessary), cast (bind) off 11 sts at beg of next row. 39 sts.

Work 49 rows more in patt, so ending with a WS row. Right back yoke measures approx 16cm/6¼in.

Neck shaping

Beg neck shaping on next row as foll:

Next row (RS) Work 21 sts in patt, then turn leaving rem 18 sts on a st holder.

Working on first side of neck only, work 10 rows in patt without shaping, so ending with a RS row.

Cast (bind) off.

Left back yoke

Return to rem sts from skirt and

SKIRT CHART

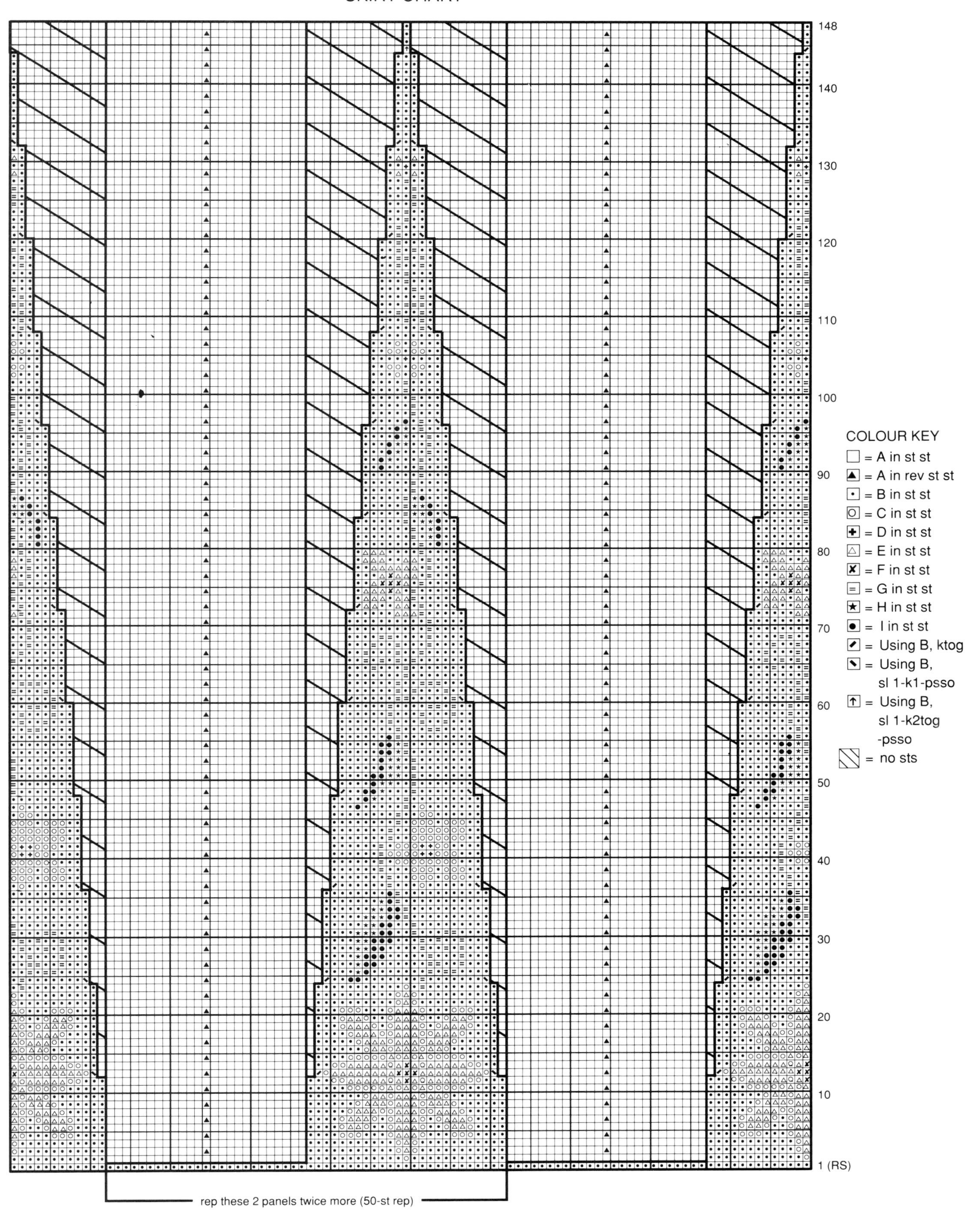
148
140
130
120
110
100
90
80
70
60
50
40
30
20
10
1 (RS)
rep these 2 panels twice more (50-st rep)
COLOUR KEY
= A in st st
= A in rev st st
= B in st st
= C in st st
= D in st st
= E in st st
= F in st st
= G in st st
= H in st st
= I in st st
= Using B, ktog
= Using B, sl 1-k1-psso
= Using B, sl 1-k2tog -psso
= no sts

SKIRT BORDER CHART

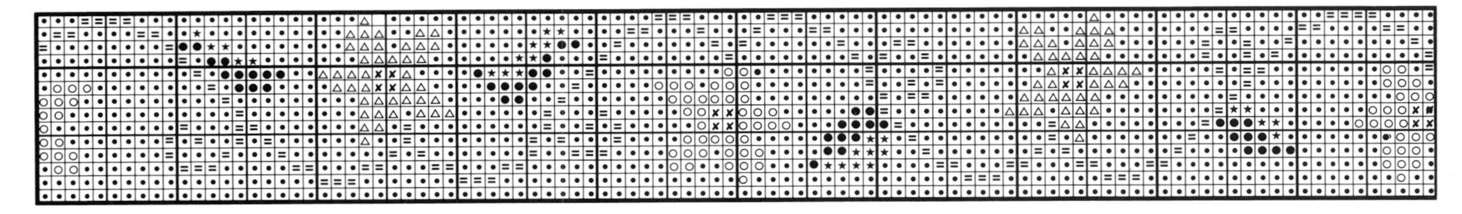

with RS facing and using A, cast (bind) off centre 3 sts, (one st now on RH needle), slip next st onto RH needle and pass first st on RH needle over 2nd and off needle, slip rem st on RH needle back onto LH needle. 50 sts.

Using B only throughout for remainder of back and with RS still facing, beg smock st patt as foll:

Row 1 (RS) *K1, p3, rep from *, ending last rep p1 instead of p3.

Row 2 K1, *p1, k3, rep from * to last st, p1.

Row 3 K1, *p3, cl 5, rep from * to last st, p1.

Row 4 As row 2.

Rows 5–8 Rep rows 1 and 2 twice.

Row 9 *Cl 5, p3, rep from * to last 2 sts, cl 2.

Row 10 As row 2.

Rows 11 and 12 As rows 1 and 2.

Rows 1–12 are repeated to form the smock st patt.

Rep rows 1–5 once more, so ending with a RS row.

Armhole shaping

Keeping smock st patt correct as set throughout (working cluster over 2, 3 or 4 sts at edge where necessary), cast (bind) off 11 sts at beg of next row. 39 sts.

Work 49 rows more in patt, so ending with a RS row. Left back yoke measures approx same as right back yoke to neck shaping.

Neck shaping

Beg neck shaping on next row as foll:

Next row (WS) Work 21 sts in patt, then turn leaving rem 18 sts on a st holder.

Work 10 rows in patt without shaping, so ending with a WS row.

Cast (bind) off.

ARMBANDS

Press pieces lightly on WS with warm iron over damp cloth, but do not stretch and avoid pressing smocking st patt.

Join shoulder seams, using a small neat backstitch on very edge of work.

Using larger needles and A and with RS facing, pick up and k94 sts evenly along right armhole edge, including cast (bound) off edges.

P one row.

Beg with chart row 1, foll armband chart, until chart row 20 has been completed, so ending with a WS row.

Work picot row as for front.

P one row.

Change to smaller needles and beg k1, p1 rib as foll:

Rib row 1 *K1, p1, rep from * to end.

Rep 17 times more.

Cast (bind) off in rib.

Work armband along left armhole in same way.

CENTRE FRONT NECKBAND

Using smaller needles and A and with RS facing, k40 sts from centre front st holder.

Beg with chart row 2, foll centre front neckband chart, dec one st at each end of 3rd, 5th and 7th rows as indicated, until chart row 8 has been completed, so ending with a WS row. 34 sts.

Work picot row as for front.

P one row.

Working in k1, p1 rib and keeping rib correct, inc one st at each end of next row and foll 2 alt rows. 40 sts.

Work one row in rib without shaping.

Cast (bind) off in rib.

CENTRE BACK NECKBANDS

Using smaller needles and A and with RS facing, k18 sts from left back st holder.

Beg with chart row 2, foll centre left back neckband chart, dec one st at end of 3rd, 5th and 7th rows as indicated, until chart row 8 has been completed, so ending with a WS row. 15 sts.

Picot row (RS) *K2tog, yo, rep from * to last st, k1.

P one row.

Working in k1, p1 rib and keeping rib correct, inc one st at end of next row and foll 2 alt rows. 18 sts.

Work one row in rib without shaping.

Cast (bind) off in rib.

Work centre right back neckband in same way, foll centre right back neckband chart and reversing shaping.

SIDE NECKBANDS

Using smaller needles and A and with RS facing, pick up and k28 sts evenly along vertical edge of right

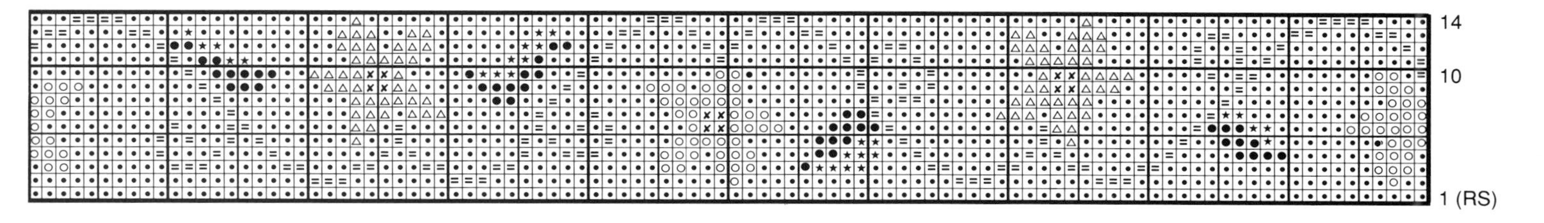

CENTRE FRONT AND BACK NECKBAND CHART

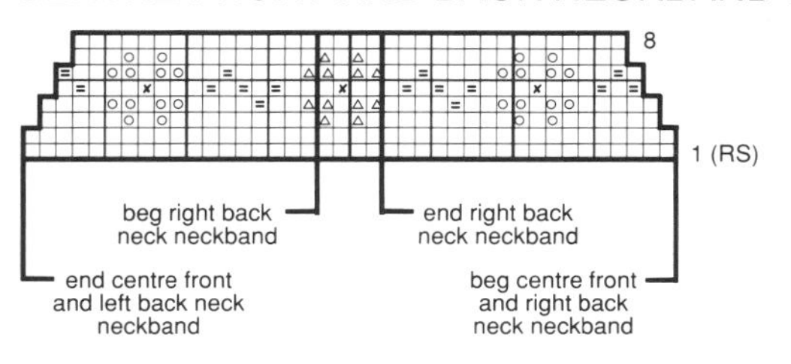

SIDE OF NECK NECKBAND CHART

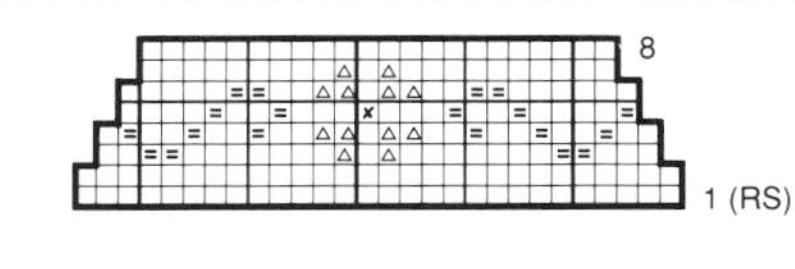

ARMBAND CHART

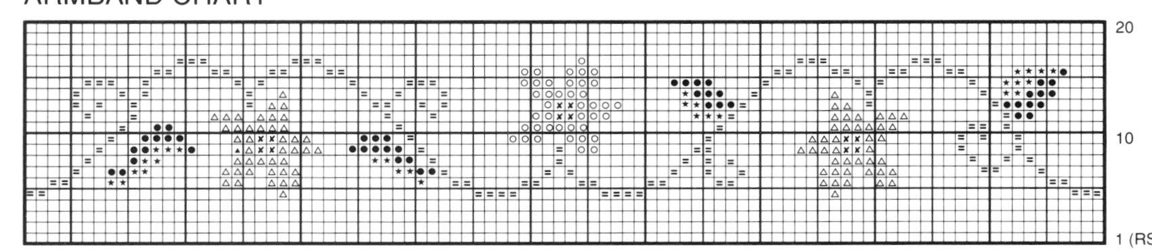

COLOUR KEY

- = A in st st
- = A in rev st st
- = B in st st
- = C in st st
- = D in st st
- = E in st st
- = F in st st
- = G in st st
- = H in st st
- = I in st st
- = Using B, ktog
- = Using B, sl 1-k1-psso
- = Using B, sl 1-k2tog -psso
- = no sts

neck edge from front to back.

Beg with chart row 2, foll side of neck neckband chart, dec one st at each end of 3rd, 5th and 7th rows as indicated, until chart row 8 has been completed, so ending with a WS row. 22 sts.

Work picot row as for front.

P one row.

Working in k1, p1 rib and keeping rib correct throughout, inc one st at each end of next row and foll 2 alt rows. 28 sts.

Work one row in rib without shaping.

Cast (bind) off in rib.

Work neckband on left side of neck in same way.

BUTTON BAND

Join mitred edges of neckband, using an invisible st on inside. Fold neckband ribbing to WS along picot row and slip stitch in place.

Using smaller needles and A and with RS facing, pick up and k58 sts along left back opening, beg at skirt edge and ending at top edge of neckband.

Work 5 rows in k1, p1 rib.

Cast (bind) off in rib.

BUTTONHOLE BAND

Using smaller needles and A and with RS facing, pick up and k58 sts along right back opening, beg at top edge of neckband and ending at skirt edge.

Work 1 row in k1, p1 rib.

Keeping rib correct throughout, work buttonholes on next 2 rows as foll:

Buttonhole row 1 (RS) Rib 4, cast (bind) off 2 sts, *rib 10 (including st already on needle after cast (bind) off), cast off 2 sts*, rep from * to * 3 times more, rib to end.

Buttonhole row 2 Rib to end, casting on 2 sts over each of 2 cast (bound) off in last row.

Work 2 rows more in rib.

Cast (bind) off in rib.

FINISHING

Join all seams using a small neat backstitch on the very edge of the work.

Then join the side and the armband seams.

Fold the hem to the WS along the picot row at the lower edge of the skirt and slip stitch in place.

Fold the armband ribbing to the WS along the picot row and slip stitch neatly in place.

Sew the bottom of button and buttonhole band to cast (bound) off edge at the top of the skirt.

Sew the buttons to the button band in positions corresponding to the buttonholes.

Rosebay

I've always been fascinated by textural stitches and loved this one instantly for its circular, lacey pattern which is so uncommon in knitting. To complement the look of the sweater, I chose a lacey knitted border for the hem and sleeve edges. This is an easy sweater to lengthen if you feel the cropped look is not for you. Just add the required number of centimetres before shaping the neckline.

SIZE

One size only to fit 81–96cm/ 32–38in bust

See diagram for finished knitted measurements.

MATERIALS

Rowan *Handknit DK Cotton* (no.240: raspberry) 12 x 50g/1¾ oz balls

One pair each of 3¼mm (US size 3) and 4mm (US size 6) knitting needles

Set of four 3¼mm (US size 3) double-pointed needles for neckband

ALTERNATIVE COLOURWAY

This sweater can also be worked in the colour shown on the right, which is no.259: peacock.

TENSION (GAUGE)

21 sts and 26 rows to 10cm/4in measured over circle lace patt worked on 4mm (US size 6) needles

Lace edging measures 5cm/2in wide worked on 3¼mm (US size 3) needles

Please check your tension (gauge) carefully and change knitting needle size if necessary

NOTE

To check your tension (gauge) cast on 27 sts and work circle lace patt from patt row 1.

BACK

Using smaller needles, cast on 8 sts.

Beg working lace edging (lengthwise) as foll:

Row 1 (WS) Sl 1, k1, *yarn to front of work between 2 needles, then over top of RH needle to back of work and to front again between 2 needles to make a new st – called *yarn over* or *yo* –, p2tog, (k1, p1, k1) all into next st*, rep from * to * once more. (12 sts)

Row 2 (K3, yo, p2tog) twice, k2.

Row 3 Sl 1, k1, (yo, p2tog, k3) twice.

Row 4 Cast (bind) off first 2 sts knitwise (one st on RH needle), yo, p2tog, cast (bind) off next 2 sts knitwise (4 sts on RH needle), yo, p2tog, k2. (8 sts)

Rep last 4 rows until 152 edging patt rows have been worked from beg and edging measures approx

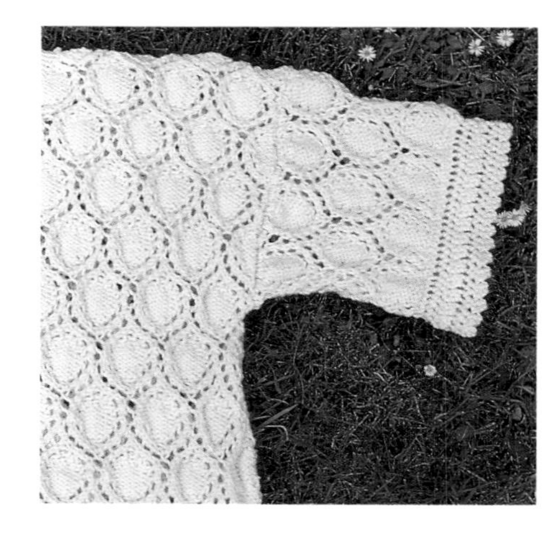

58.5cm (23½in) from cast-on edge, ending with a 4th row.

Cast (bind) off knitwise.

Mark positions on edging dividing it into 8 equal sections along heading (straight side of edging).

Using larger needles and with WS facing, pick up and k15 sts along first section of heading, *16 sts along next section, k15 sts along next section*, rep from * to * twice more, then pick up and k15 sts along last section of heading. 123 sts.

Beg circle lace patt as foll:

Patt row 1 (RS) K1, k2tog, *yarn to front of work between 2 needles, then over top of RH needle to back of work to make a new st – called *yarn over* or *yo* –, k2tog, yo (see row 1 of edging for working yo before a p st), p5, yo (taking yarn over top of RH needle before next st is worked), slip the next 2 sts knitwise one at a time, then insert tip of LH needle into fronts of 2 slipped sts and k2tog – called *slip, slip, knit* or *ssk* –, yo, sl 1-k2tog-psso, rep from *, ending last rep ssk, k1, instead of sl 1-k2tog-psso.

Patt row 2 P5, *k5, p7, rep from *, ending last rep p5, instead of p7.

Row 3 K1, *yo, k3tog, yo, p7, yo, ssk, rep from * to last 2 sts, yo, k2tog.

Row 4 P4, *k7, p5, rep from *, ending last rep p4, instead of p5.

Row 5 Ssk, yo, *ssk, yo, p7, yo, sl 2-k1-p2sso, yo, rep from * to last st, k1.

Row 6 As row 4.

Row 7 K1, *yo, sl 2-k1-p2sso, yo, p7, yo, k2tog, rep from * to last 2 sts, yo, k2tog.

Row 8 As row 4.
Row 9 K1, insert RH needle downwards into back of st in row below next st on LH needle and k, then k st on needle – called *inc 1* –, *yo, ssk, yo, p2tog, p3tog, p2tog, yo, k2tog, yo, (k1 tbl, k1) both into next st, then insert tip of LH needle behind the vertical strand that runs downwards from between the 2 sts just made and k1 tbl into this strand to make a 3rd st on needle – called *double inc* –, rep from *, ending last rep inc 1, k1 instead of double inc.
Row 10 P6, *k3tog, p9, rep from *, ending last rep p6, instead of p9.
Row 11 K1, inc 1, *(yo, ssk) twice, p1, (k2tog, yo) twice, double inc, rep from *, ending last rep inc 1, k1, instead of double inc.
Row 12 P7, *k1, p11, rep from *, ending last rep p7, instead of p11.
Row 13 K1, p3, *yo, ssk, yo, sl 1-k2tog-psso, yo, k2tog, yo, p5, rep from *, ending last rep p3, k1, instead of p5.
Row 14 P1, k3, *p7, k5, rep from *, ending last rep k3, p1, instead of k5.
Row 15 K1, p4, *yo, ssk, yo, k3tog, yo, p7, rep from *, ending last rep p4, k1, instead of p7.
Row 16 P1, k4, *p5, k7, rep from *, ending last rep k4, p1, instead of k7.
Row 17 K1, p4, *yo, sl 2-k1-p2sso, yo, ssk, yo, p7, rep from *, ending last rep p4, k1, instead of p7.
Row 18 As row 16.
Row 19 K1, p4, *yo, k2tog, yo, sl 2-k1-p2sso, yo, p7, rep from *, ending last rep p4, k1, instead of p7.
Row 20 As row 16.
Row 21 K1, p2tog, *p2tog, yo, k2tog, yo, double inc, yo, ssk, yo, p2tog, p3tog, rep from *, ending last rep p2tog, k1, instead of p3tog.
Row 22 P1, k2tog, *p9, k3tog, rep from *, ending last rep k2tog, p1, instead of k3tog.
Row 23 K1, p1, *(k2tog, yo) twice, double inc, (yo, ssk) twice, p1, rep from * to last st, k1.
Row 24 P1, k1, *p11, k1, rep from * to last st, p1.
Rep rows 1–24 throughout, cont in circle lace patt until back measures 47cm/18½in from lower edge (including edging), ending with a WS row.

Neck shaping

Keeping patt correct throughout, beg neck shaping as foll:
Next row (RS) Work first 46 sts in patt, turn leaving rem sts on a spare needle.
Working first side of neck only, dec one st at beg of next row (neck edge), then at neck edge on every foll row 4 times in all.
Cast (bind) off rem 42 sts.
Return to rem sts and with RS facing, slip centre 31 sts onto a st holder, rejoin yarn to rem sts and work in patt to end of row.
Complete 2nd side of neck to match first side, reversing shaping.

FRONT

Work as for back until front measures 42cm/16½in from lower edge (including edging), ending with a WS row.

Neck shaping

Keeping patt correct throughout, beg neck shaping as foll:
Next row (RS) Work first 51 sts in patt, turn leaving rem sts on a spare needle.
Working first side of neck only, dec one st at beg of next row (neck edge), then at neck edge on every foll row 9 times in all. 42 sts.
Work without shaping until there are same number of rows as back to shoulder.

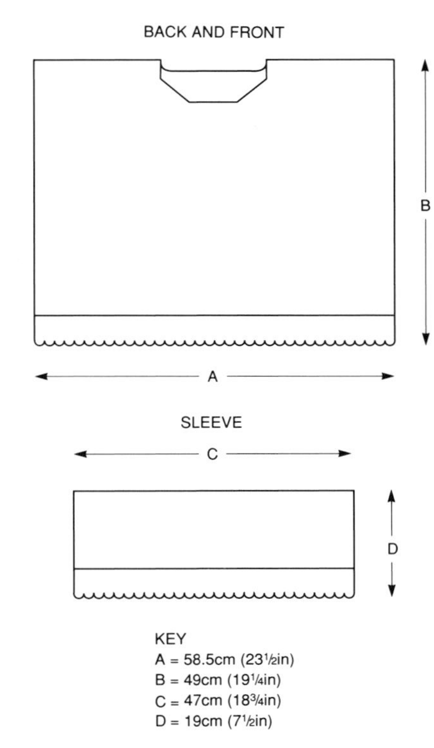

Cast (bind) off.
Return to rem sts and with RS facing, slip centre 21 sts onto a st holder, rejoin yarn to rem sts and work in patt to end of row.
Complete 2nd side of neck to match first side, reversing shaping.

SLEEVES

Using smaller needles, cast on 8 sts.
Rep 4 lace edging patt rows as for back until 120 edging patt rows have been worked from beg and edging measures approx 47cm/18¾in from cast-on edge, ending with a 4th row.
Cast (bind) off knitwise.
Mark positions on edging dividing it into 8 equal sections along heading.
Using larger needles and with RS facing, pick up and k12 sts along first section of heading, *13 sts along next section, k12 sts along next section*, rep from * to * twice more, then pick up and k12 sts along last section of heading. 99 sts.
Rep patt rows 1–24 of circle lace throughout, work in circle lace patt until sleeve measures 19cm/7½in from lower edge (including edging),

ending with a WS row.
Cast (bind) off all sts.
Make 2nd sleeve in same way.

NECKBAND

Do not press.
Join shoulder seams using a small neat backstitch on very edge of work.
Using set of 4 double-pointed needles and with RS of front facing, beg at left shoulder and pick up k17 sts down left front neck, k21 sts from front neck st holder, pick up and k17 sts up right front neck, 4 sts down right back neck, k31 sts from back neck st holder, and pick up and k4 sts up left back neck. 94 sts.
Working in rounds (RS always facing), beg k1, p1 rib as foll:
Rib round 1 *K1, p1, rep from * to end.
Rep last round 3 times more.
Cast (bind) off in rib.

FINISHING

Join seams using a flat invisible stitch.

Measure 23.5cm/9½in down from shoulder seams on back and front and mark positions of armholes.

Placing centre of top of sleeve at shoulder seam, sew cast (bound) off edge of sleeves to armhole edge between markers.

Join side and sleeve seams.

SUMMER

Summer

For me Summer is a time to live outdoors as much as possible, to open the windows, let in the fresh air, and enjoy being able to spill out into the garden after so many months being cooped up inside. Everything seems overblown, a season of excesses, when the days are long and you can sit around a barbecue into the early hours. The world seems less urgent and people are much happier and more relaxed. Maybe it's because this is traditionally the holiday season.

One of the first signs that Summer is well and truly here is when the farmers start *Haymaking*. The heady scent of the meadow hay as it is turned and dried before being brought in is one of my favourite smells. Having horses, there's nothing I like better than to know that their hay is in for the Winter. I will even put up with the hayfever that it sometimes brings on!

Another thing I love about Summer is being able to hold *Parties* in the garden. Whatever the occasion – someone's birthday, an anniversary, or just any old excuse – there's something so delicious about being with friends and family out of doors on a warm, sunny day, sharing good food and a bottle of wine.

I can't think of Summer without thinking of the seaside and *Boating*. Although I'm no sailor, I love to watch those who do sail. There is something fascinating about being around boats, with their ropes, nets, sails, masts, flaking paint and tar and all the other paraphernalia that goes with them. Boats are such beautiful pieces of design. Colourful narrowboats on canals, sleek sailing yachts in marinas, humble dinghies decaying on beaches – they are all wonderful sources of inspiration for the designer. Weather-beaten and salt-sprayed hulks open up a world of new ideas for colour combin ɔns, which seem to become more exciting and vivid in the strong sunlight.

I take photographs whenever I get the chance, as I love to capture those scorching summer colours on film so that I can reflect on them months later from the depths of a cold, grey Winter.

OBERON

THE FOLKLORIC SIGNIFICANCE OF CELTIC KNOTS INTRIGUES ME. KNOTS FOR ME ARE A FRIENDLY SYMBOL OF TRADITION, CONTINUITY AND HOPE FOR THE FUTURE, AND I LOVE THE IDEA OF EXPRESSING THIS ON A SWEATER. I HAVE LIMITED THIS DESIGN TO THREE COLOURS, AS I SOMETIMES ENJOY THE DISCIPLINE OF ECONOMY AND THE CHALLENGE OF FINDING SHADES WHICH CAN HAPPILY LIVE TOGETHER.

SIZE

One size only to fit 96–112cm/38–44in chest

See diagram for finished knitted measurements.

MATERIALS

Rowan *Cotton Glacé* 50g/1¾oz balls as foll:

A (no.744: provence) 15 balls

B (no.729: navy) 2 balls

Rowan *Sea Breeze* 50g/1¾oz balls as foll:

C (no.560: bronze) 1 ball

One pair each of 2¼mm (US size 1) and 3¼mm (US size 3) knitting needles

Set of four 2¼mm (US size 1) double-pointed needles for neckband

ALTERNATIVE COLOURWAY

This sweater can also be worked in the colourway shown on the right, where:

A = *Wool and Cotton* no.909: alabaster (13 balls)

B = *Wool and Cotton* no.911: dove (3 balls)

C = *Wool and Cotton* no.916: coral (2 balls)

TENSION (GAUGE)

25 sts and 31 rows to 10cm/4in measured over celtic knot patt worked on 3¼mm (US size 3) needles

PLEASE CHECK YOUR TENSION (GAUGE) CAREFULLY AND CHANGE KNITTING NEEDLE SIZE IF NECESSARY

NOTES

When working the bicolour ribbing in A and B, strand the colour not in use loosely across the WS, but use a separate strand of C for each isolated area of colour, twisting yarns together at the back of the work when changing colours to avoid making a hole.

When working celtic knot patt, use the intarsia method, using a separate length of B or C for each isolated area of colour and twisting yarns together when changing colours.

For celtic knot chart and ribbing chart, read from right to left for the RS (odd-numbered) rows and from left to right for the WS (even-numbered) rows.

For neckband chart read all rows from right to left.

BACK

Using smaller needles and A, cast on 126 sts and beg foll ribbing chart as foll:

Chart rib row 1 (RS) Work first 3 sts of chart before patt repeat begins as indicated on chart, rep 24-st repeat 5 times, work last 3 sts of chart as indicated.

Cont foll patt for ribbing patt until 27 rows of chart have been completed, so ending with a RS row. Keeping rib correct, inc 42 sts evenly across row as foll:

Chart rib row 28 (inc row) (WS) Rib 1, work into front and back of next st – called *inc 1* –, *rib 2, inc 1 into next st*, rep from * to * 40 times more, rib 1. 168 sts.

Change to larger needles and beg foll celtic knot patt chart as foll:

Chart row 1 (RS) Work first 11 sts of chart before patt repeat begins as indicated on chart, rep 49-st repeat 3 times, work last 10 sts of chart as indicated.

Cont foll chart for celtic knot patt and rep 98-row repeat throughout, until back measures 42cm/16½in from cast-on edge, ending with a WS row.

Armhole shaping

Keeping celtic knot patt correct throughout, beg armhole shaping as foll:

Next row (dec row) (RS) K2, sl 1-k1-psso, work in patt to last 4 sts, k2tog, k2.

Work one row without shaping. Rep dec row once.

Rep from ** to ** 9 times more. 146 sts.***

Work without shaping until back

measures 65.5cm/25¾in from cast-on edge, ending with a WS row.

Neck shaping

Next row (RS) Work first 53 sts in patt, then turn leaving rem sts on a spare needle.

Working on first side of neck only, dec one st at beg of next row (neck edge), then at neck edge on every foll row 5 times in all.

Slip rem 48 sts onto a st holder.

Return to rem sts and with RS facing, slip centre 40 sts onto a st holder, rejoin yarn to rem sts and work in patt to end of row.

Complete 2nd side of neck to match first side, reversing shaping.

FRONT

Work as for back to ***.

Work without shaping until back measures 60cm/23½in from cast-on edge, ending with a WS row.

Neck shaping

Next row (RS) Work first 60 sts in patt, then turn leaving rem sts on a spare needle.

Working on first side of neck only, dec one st at beg of next row (neck edge), then at neck edge on every foll row 7 times in all, then dec one st at neck edge on every foll alt row 5 times in all. 48 sts.

Work without shaping until there are same number of rows as back to shoulder.

Slip these sts onto a st holder.

Return to rem sts and with RS facing, slip centre 26 sts onto a st holder, rejoin yarn to rem sts and work in patt to end of row.

Complete 2nd side of neck to match first side, reversing shaping.

SLEEVES

Using smaller needles and A, cast on 52 sts and beg foll ribbing chart on the right as foll:

Chart rib row 1 (RS) Work first 2 sts of chart before patt repeat begins as indicated on chart, rep 24-st repeat twice, work last 2 sts of chart as indicated.

Cont foll patt for ribbing patt until 27 rows of chart have been completed, so ending with a RS row.

Keeping rib correct, inc 18 sts evenly across row as foll:

Chart rib row 28 (inc row) (WS) Inc 1 into first st, *rib 2, inc 1 into next st*, rep from * to * 16 times more. 70 sts.

Change to larger needles and beg foll celtic knot patt chart as foll:

Chart row 1 (RS) Work first 11 sts of chart before patt repeat begins as indicated on chart, work 49-st repeat once, work last 10 sts of chart as indicated.

Cont foll chart for celtic knot patt and rep 98-row repeat throughout *and at the same time* shape sleeve by inc one st at each end of 3rd row and then at each end of every foll 4th row until there are 134 sts, working all added sts into patt as set.

Work without shaping until sleeve measures 55.5cm/22in from cast-on edge or desired length, ending with a WS row.

Cast (bind) off all sts.

Make 2nd sleeve in same way.

COLLAR

Do not press.

Using smaller needles and A, join left shoulder seam by placing WS of back and front tog, then with back facing, knit through both layers along the 48 shoulder sts, taking one st from back st holder tog with one st from front st holder with each st and casting (binding) off as the row is worked, thereby forming a decorative seam on the right side of the garment.

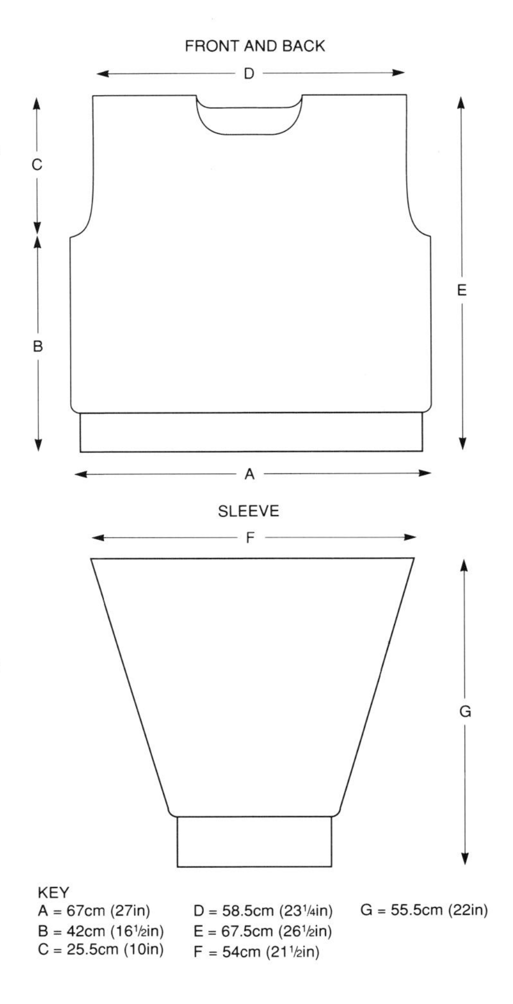

RIBBING CHART

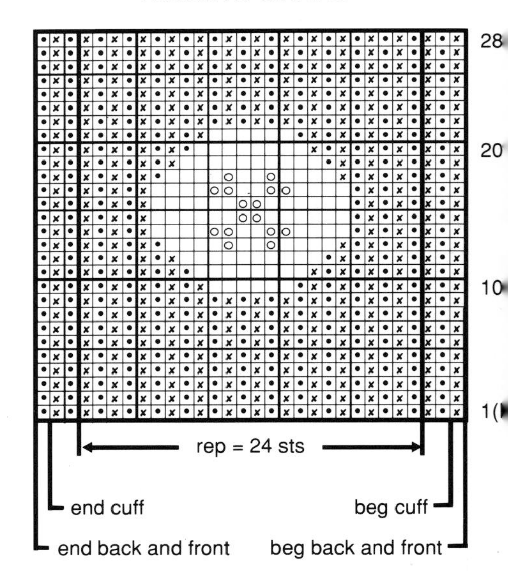

NECKBAND CHART

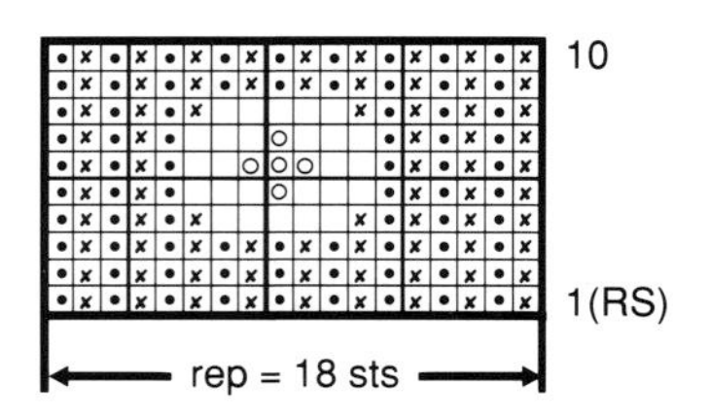

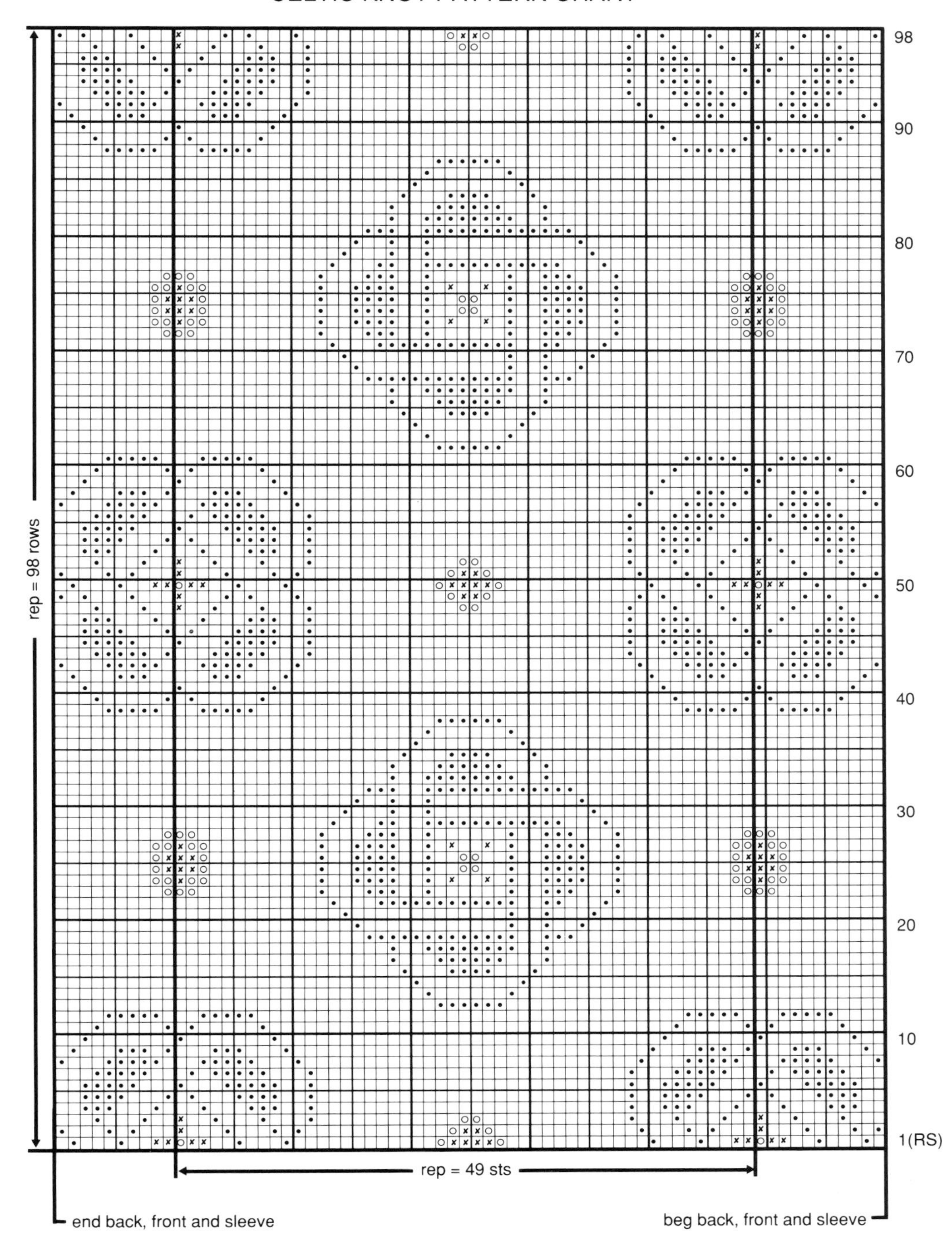

Join the right shoulder seam in the same way as the left shoulder seam, working the cast (bind) off with the back facing.

Using set of 2¼ mm (US size 1) double-pointed needles and A and with with RS facing, beg at left shoulder and pick up and k25 sts down left front neck, k26 sts from centre front neck st holder, pick up and k25 sts up right front neck, 5 sts down right back neck, k40 sts from back neck st holder and pick up and k5 sts up left back neck. 126 sts.

Working in rounds (RS always facing), beg neckband chart as foll:

Chart rib round 1 (RS) Work 18-st repeat 7 times.

Cont foll chart until chart row 10 has been completed.

Using A, cast (bind) off in rib.

FINISHING

Join seams using a small neat backstitch on very edge of work, except for ribbing where an invisible slip stitch should be used.

Placing centre of top of sleeve at shoulder seam, sew cast (bound) off edge of sleeves to armhole edge (including decreased edge).

Join side and sleeve seams.

Press seams lightly on WS.

SOLSTICE

THIS SWEATER TAKES ITS INSPIRATION FROM THE HOT, SPICY COLOURS AND GEOMETRIC SHAPES OF GUATEMALAN WEAVINGS. I REALLY ENJOY THE IDEA OF HAVING THE INDIAN BELLS AS BUTTONS, BUT I THINK IT WOULD ALSO LOOK GREAT WITH A CREW NECK – JUST OMIT THE PLACKET SHAPING.

SIZE

One size only to fit 86–101cm/34–40in bust

See diagram for finished knitted measurements.

MATERIALS

Rowan *Cotton Glacé* 50g/1¾oz balls as foll:

A (no.745: quince) 7 balls

B (no.743: gentian) 7 balls

C (no.744: provence) 2 balls

D (no.737: spice) 1 ball

Rowan *Wool and Cotton* 40g/1½oz balls as foll:

E (no.928: rajastan) 2 balls

Rowan *Nice Cotton* 50g/1¾oz balls as foll:

F (no.433: parakeet) 1 ball

G (no.431: rio) 1 ball

H (no.432: carnival) 1 ball

J (no.435: samba) 1 ball

One pair each of 2¼mm (US size 1) and 3¼mm (US size 3) knitting needles

2¼mm (US size 1) circular needle for neckband

Three 1.5cm/⅝in buttons

ALTERNATIVE COLOURWAY

This sweater can also be worked in the colourway shown right, where:

A = *Cotton Glacé* no.737: spice

B = *Nice Cotton* no.435: samba

C = *Nice Cotton* no.432: carnival

D = *Nice Cotton* no.431: rio

E = *Wool and Cotton* no.928: rajastan

F = *Cotton Glacé* no.745: quince

G = *Soft Cotton* no.560: bronze

H = *Cotton Glacé* no.744: provence

J = *Nice Cotton* no.436: mardi gras

TENSION (GAUGE)

25 sts and 34 rows to 10cm/4in measured over st st worked on 3¼mm (US size 3) needles

PLEASE CHECK YOUR TENSION (GAUGE) CAREFULLY AND CHANGE KNITTING NEEDLE SIZE IF NECESSARY

NOTES

When working from the chart, use the intarsia method, using a separate length (or ball) of yarn for each isolated area of colour and twisting yarns together when changing colours to avoid making a hole.

Read charts from right to left for the RS (odd-numbered) rows and from left to right for the WS (even-numbered) rows.

BACK

Using smaller needles and B, cast on 158 sts and beg bicolour rib as foll:

Row 1 (RS) *Using B k2, using A p2, rep from * to last 2 sts, using B k2.

Row 2 *Using B p2, using A k2, rep from * to last 2 sts, using B p2.

Rep last 2 rows until ribbing measures 3.5cm/1¼in from cast-on edge, ending with a WS row.

Change to larger needles and beg with a k row, work in st st foll back chart until chart row 132 has been completed, so ending with a WS row.

Armhole shaping

Cont to foll chart throughout, cast (bind) off 14 sts at beg of next 2 rows. 130 sts.

Work without shaping until chart row 208 has been completed, so ending with a WS row.

Neck shaping

Chart row 209 (RS) Work first 49 sts in patt, turn leaving rem sts on a spare needle.

Working first side of neck only, dec one st at beg of next row (neck edge), then at neck edge on every foll row 3 times in all, so ending with chart row 212. 46 sts.

Cast (bind) off.

Return to rem sts and with RS facing, slip centre 32 sts onto a st holder, rejoin yarn to rem sts and work in patt to end of row.

Complete 2nd side of neck to match first side, reversing shaping.

FRONT

Work as for back until chart row 142 has been completed.

Divide for neck

Chart row 143 (RS) Work first 62 sts in patt, turn leaving rem sts on a spare needle.

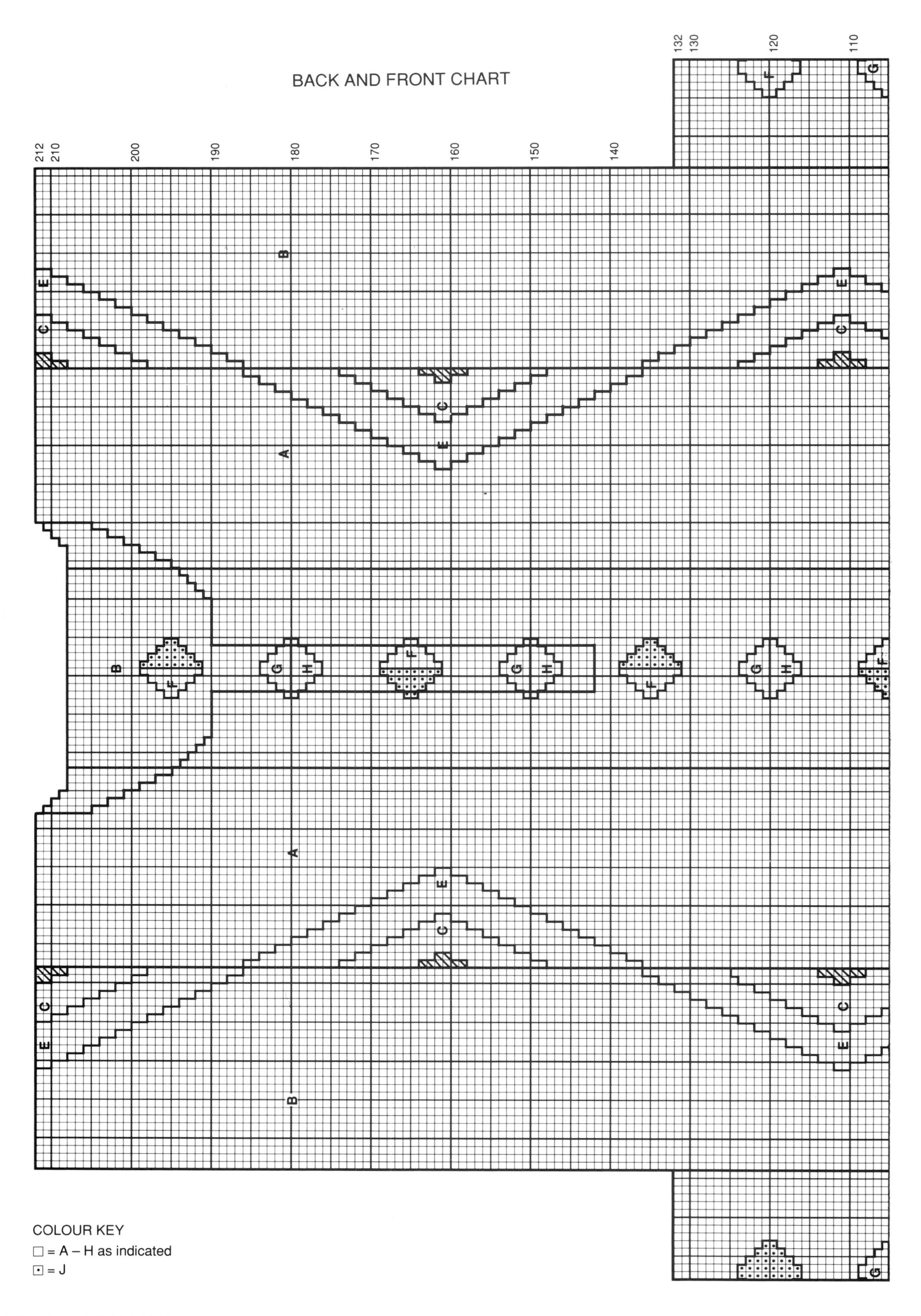
BACK AND FRONT CHART
212
210
200
190
180
170
160
150
140
132
130
120
110
A
B
C
E
F
G
H
COLOUR KEY
□ = A – H as indicated
⊡ = J

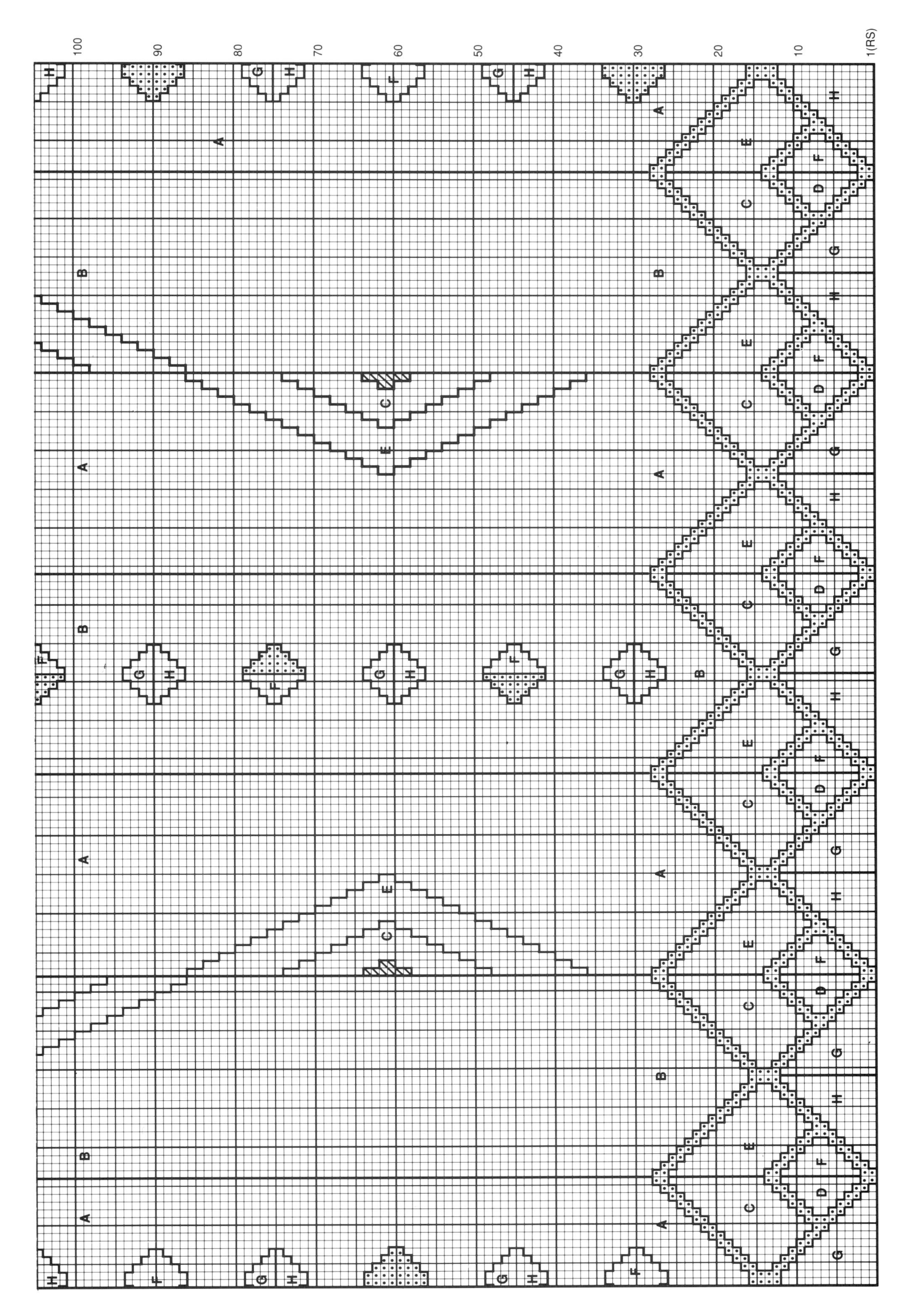

Working first side of neck only, work without shaping (omitting centre diamond motifs) until chart row 190 has been completed.

Neck shaping

Chart row 191 Work in patt to last 6 sts, slip last 6 sts onto a st holder.

Dec one st at beg of next row (neck edge) and at neck edge on every foll row 5 times in all, then on every foll alt row 5 times. 46 sts.

Work without shaping until chart row 212 has been completed.

Cast (bind) off.

Return to rem sts and with RS facing, slip centre 6 sts onto a st holder, rejoin yarn to rem sts and work in patt to end of row.

Complete 2nd side of neck to match first side, reversing shaping.

SLEEVES

Using smaller needles and B, cast on 56 sts and beg bicolour rib as foll:

Row 1 (RS) *Using B k2, using A p2, rep from * to end.

Row 2 *Using A k2, using B p2, rep from * to end.

Rep last 2 rows until ribbing measures 3.5cm/1¼in from cast-on edge, ending with a WS row.

Change to larger needles and beg with a k row, work in st st foll sleeve chart from chart row 1 *and at the same time* shape sleeve by inc one st at each end of 4th row, then every foll 3rd row 10 times in all (76 sts), then every foll 4th row 23 times. 122 sts.

Cont to foll chart, work without shaping until chart row 140 has been completed. Cast (bind) off all sts.

Make 2nd sleeve in same way.

BUTTON BAND

Press pieces lightly on WS with warm iron over damp cloth, omitting ribbing.

Using smaller needles and J, cast on 6 sts.

Work in moss (seed) st as foll:

Row 1 (RS) *K1, p1, rep from * to end.

Row 2 *P1, k1, rep from * to end.

Rep last 2 rows until band fits from neck divide to beg of neck shaping, ending with a WS row.

Do not break off yarn, but slip sts onto a st holder.

Mark the positions of two 4-row vertical buttonholes on button band, the first buttonhole (horizontal) to be 5mm/¼in above top of band in the neckband, the last vertical buttonhole to be 4cm/1½in from cast-on edge of band and the other vertical buttonhole to be evenly spaced between.

BUTTONHOLE BAND

Using smaller needles and J and with RS facing, work in moss (seed) st, as for button band, across 6 sts on st holder at neck divide.

Keeping moss (seed) st correct throughout, work as for button band, but working buttonholes over 4 rows when position for buttonhole is reached as foll:

Next row Work 3 sts in patt, turn leaving rem 3 sts unworked.

Work 3 rows more on these 3 sts, do not break off yarn.

Using separate length of J, work 4 rows on 3 sts left unworked and break off yarn.

Return to first set of sts and work in patt across all 6 sts.

When band has been completed, break off yarn and slip sts onto a st holder.

NECKBAND

Join shoulder seams using a small neat backstitch on very edge of work so that cast (bound) off edge does not show.

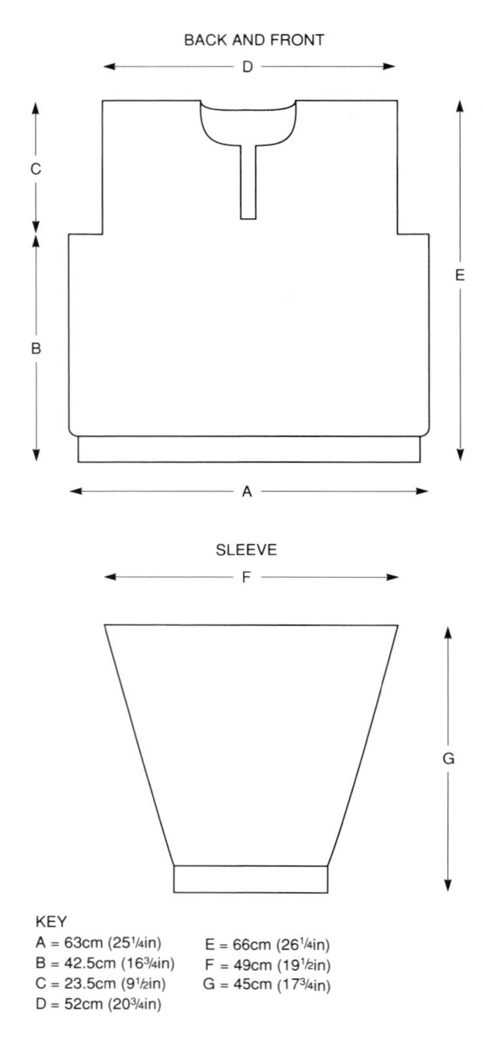

Keeping top of buttonhole band on st holder and using a small overstitch (overcast st), join band to right side of neck opening so that top of band is even with beg of neck shaping. Then join cast-on edge of button band to WS at beg of neck opening *behind* buttonhole band and stitch side of band to rem right side of neck opening, keeping top of band on st holder.

Using circular needle and J and with RS facing, work across 6 sts from buttonhole band st holder in moss (seed) st, k6 sts from right front neck st holder, then pick up and k22 up right front neck, 5 sts down right back neck, k32 sts from back neck st holder, pick up and k5 sts up left

SLEEVE CHART

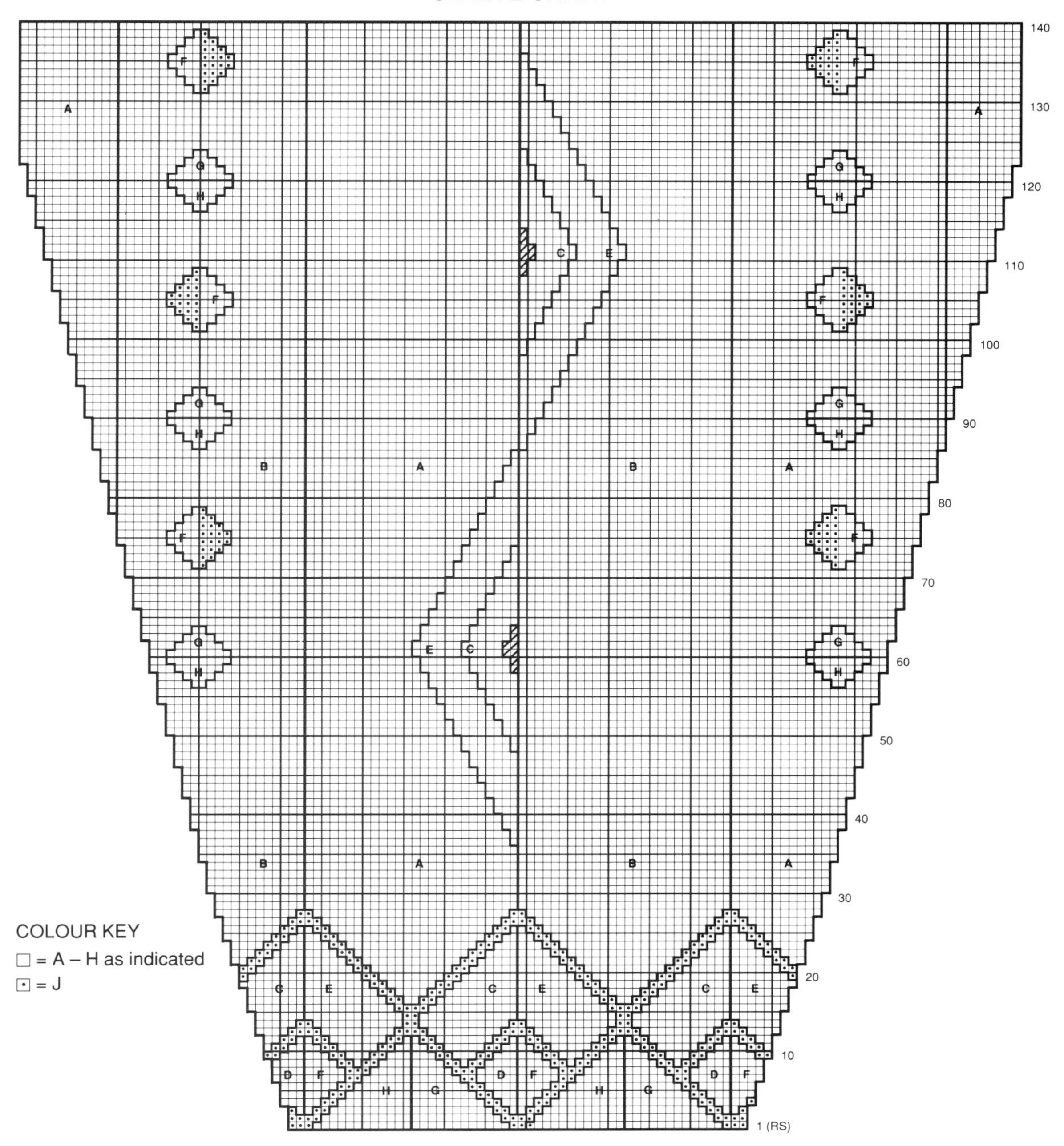

back neck, 22 sts down left front neck, k6 sts from left front neck st holder and work across 6 sts from button band st holder in moss (seed) st. 112 sts.

Working back and forth on neckband sts in rows, work 3 rows in moss (seed) st, so ending with a WS row.

Beg buttonhole on next row as foll:

Buttonhole row 1 (RS) Keeping moss (seed) st correct across row, work 2 sts in patt, cast (bind) off next 3 sts, work in patt to end.

Buttonhole row 2 Purl, casting on 3 sts over those cast (bound) off in last row.

Using A, work one row in k1, p1 rib.

Using B, work one row more in k1, p1 rib.

Still using B, cast (bind) off in rib.

FINISHING

Join seams using a small neat backstitch on very edge of work, except for ribbing where an invisible slip stitch should be used.

Placing centre of top of sleeve at shoulder seam, sew cast (bound) off edge of sleeves to horizontal armhole edge and join cast (bound) off edge of armhole to side of sleeve.

Join side and sleeve seams, making sure that patterns match. Press seams lightly on WS.

Sew the buttons to the button band in positions corresponding to the buttonholes.

HAYCOCK

THIS EASY-TO-KNIT LITTLE VEST FELL INTO SHAPE ONE AFTERNOON WHEN I WAS PLAYING AROUND WITH SOME ART DECO DESIGNS. ONE OF MY GREAT PASSIONS IS TO MIX TEXTURE AND COLOUR AND I ENJOY THE TWO-TONE EFFECT OF THE SIMPLE WRONG-SIDE STRIPE. IF YOU HAVEN'T KNITTED INTARSIA BEFORE, THIS IS A PERFECT SWEATER WITH WHICH TO BEGIN.

SIZES

To fit 4[6:8] yrs or 56[61:66]cm/ 22[24:26]in chest

Figures for larger sizes are given in brackets [ ]; where there is only one set of figures, it applies to all sizes. *See diagram for finished knitted measurements.*

MATERIALS

Rowan *Handknit DK Cotton* 50g/1¾oz balls as foll:

A (no.267: china) 3[4:4] balls
B (no.294: royal) 2 balls
C (no.259: peacock) 1 ball
D (no.274: spring green) 1 ball
E (no.248: azure) 1 ball

One pair each of 3¼mm (US size 3) and 4½mm (US size 7) knitting needles

Set of four 3¼mm (US size 3) double-pointed needles

ALTERNATIVE COLOURWAY

This sweater can also be worked in the colourway shown on the right, where:

A = no.254: flame
B = no.297: nut
C = no.249: pimpernel
D = no.261: sunflower
E = no.262: mango

TENSION (GAUGE)

19 sts and 27 rows to 10cm/4in measured over patt worked on 4½mm (US size 7) needles

PLEASE CHECK YOUR TENSION (GAUGE) CAREFULLY AND CHANGE KNITTING NEEDLE SIZE IF NECESSARY

NOTES

When working the colourwork pattern, use the intarsia method, using a separate length of yarn for each isolated area of colour and twisting yarns together when changing colours to avoid making a hole.

Read charts from right to left for the RS (odd-numbered) rows and from left to right for the WS (even-numbered) rows.

BACK

Using smaller needles and A, cast on 60[64:70] sts and beg bicolour k1, p1 rib as foll:

Rib row 1 (RS) *Using B k1, using A p1, rep from * to end.

Rib row 2 *Using A k1, using B p1, rep from * to end.

Rep last 2 rib rows until ribbing measures 5cm/2in from cast-on edge, ending with a RS row.

Keeping rib correct, inc 9[11:11] sts evenly across next row as foll:

Next row (inc row) (WS) Rib 5[6:4], work into front and back of next st – called *inc 1* –, * rib 5[4:5], inc 1 into next st*, rep from * to * 7[9:9] times more, rib 6[7:5]. 69[75:81] sts.

Break off B.

Change to larger needles and using A, k one row.

Then beg foll patt chart as foll:

Chart row 2 (WS) Foll chart from left to right, work 2[5:8] sts before patt rep as indicated, rep 13-st patt rep 5 times, work last 2[5:8] sts after patt repeat as indicated.

Cont foll chart for patt and rep 34-row repeat throughout, until back measures 22[23:24]cm/8½[9:9½]in from cast-on edge, ending with a WS row.

Armhole shaping

Keeping patt correct throughout, cast (bind) off 3[4:5] sts at beg of next 2 rows.

Then dec one st at each end of next and every foll row 7 times in all. 49[53:57] sts.**

Work without shaping until back measures 39.5[42:44.5]cm/ 15½[16½:17½]in from cast-on edge, ending with a WS row.

Neck shaping

Next row (RS) Work first 15[16:17] sts in patt, turn leaving rem sts on a spare needle.

Working first side of neck only, dec one st at beg of next row (neck edge), then at neck edge on every foll row 3 times in all, so ending with a WS row.

Cast (bind) off rem 12[13:14] sts.
Return to rem sts and with RS facing, slip centre 19[21:23] sts onto a st holder, rejoin yarn to rem sts and work in patt to end of row.
Dec one st at end of next row (neck edge), then at neck edge on every foll row 3 times in all, so ending with a WS row.
Cast (bind) off rem 12[13:14] sts.

FRONT

Work as for back to **.
Work without shaping until front measures 25.5[27:28]cm/10[10½:11]in from cast-on edge, ending with a WS row.

V-neck shaping

Next row (RS) Work first 24[26:28] sts in patt, turn leaving rem sts on a spare needle.
Working first side of neck only, dec one st at beg of next row (neck edge), then at neck edge on every foll 3rd row 12[13:14] times in all.
Work without shaping until there are same number of rows as back to shoulder and front measures 41[43.5:46]cm/16[17:18]in from cast-on edge, ending with a WS row.
Cast (bind) off rem 12[13:14] sts.
Return to rem sts and with RS facing, slip centre st onto a st holder, rejoin yarn to rem sts and work in patt to end of row.
Dec one st at end of next row (neck edge), then at neck edge on every foll 3rd row 12[13:14] times in all.
Work without shaping until there are same number of rows as first side, ending with a WS row.
Cast (bind) off rem 12[13:14] sts.

NECKBAND

Press pieces lightly on WS with a warm iron over a damp cloth, omitting ribbing.
Join shoulder seams using a small neat backstitch on very edge of work.
Using set of 4 double-pointed needles and A and with RS facing, beg at left shoulder seam and pick up and k39[41:45] sts down left front neck, k centre st from front neck st holder, pick up and k39[41:45] sts up right front neck, 3 sts down right back neck, k19[21:23] sts from back neck st holder, pick up and k3 sts up left back neck. 104[110:120] sts.
Beg working in rounds (RS always facing) of bicolour k1, p1 rib as foll:
Rib round 1 (RS) *Using B k1, using A p1*, rep from * to * until 3 sts before centre front st, using B k1, sl 1-k1A-psso, using B k centre st, using A k2tog, rep from * to * to end of round.
Cont in this way working bicolour k1, p1 rib, dec one st at each side of centre front st on every row and keeping centre front st in B, until 5 bicolour-rib rounds have been completed.
Break off B.
Using A, cast (bind) off loosely in rib.

ARMBANDS

Using smaller needles and A and with RS facing, pick up and k98[104:110] sts evenly around one armhole.
Work 5 rows in bicolour rib as for back ribbing.
Break off B.
Using A, cast (bind) off in rib.
Work 2nd armband in same way as first armband.

FINISHING

Join side seams using a small neat overstitch (overcast st).
Press seams lightly on WS.

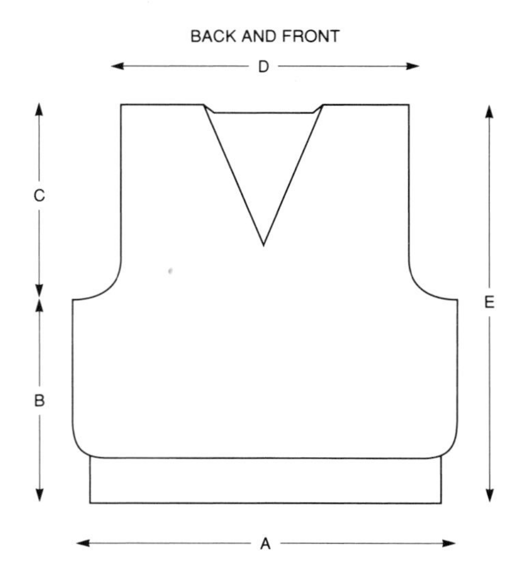

KEY
A = 36.5[39.5:42.5]cm (14½[15¾:17]in)
B = 22[23:24]cm (8½[9:9½]in)
C = 19[20.5:22]cm (7½[8:8½]in)
D = 26[28:30]cm (10¼[11¼:12]in)
E = 41[43.5:46]cm (16[17:18]in)

PATTERN CHART

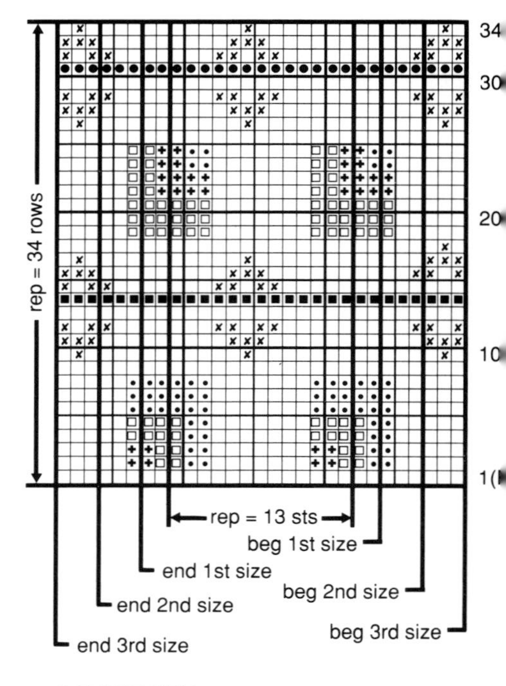

COLOUR KEY
☐ = A in st st
⊡ = B in st st
● = B in rev st st
▫ = C in st st
■ = C in rev st st
✚ = D in st st
☒ = E in st st

Chatsworth

There's lots of stitch interest in this tunic dress which harks back to the Seventies for its source. I chose the beautiful cabled mercerized cotton for the wonderful way it drapes and moves with the body. For a more contemporary look, wear it with trousers or leggings.

SIZES

To fit 81–86[91–96]cm/ 32–34[36–38]in bust

Figures for larger size are given in brackets [ ]; where there is only one set of figures, it applies to both sizes.

See diagram for finished knitted measurements.

MATERIALS

Rowan *Cabled Mercerised Cotton* (no.314: furnace) 13[16] x 50g/1¾oz balls

One pair each of 2¼mm (US size 1) and 3¼mm (US size 3) knitting needles

One 2¼mm (US size 1) and 3¼mm (US size 3) long circular knitting needle

Set of four 2¼mm (US size 1) double-pointed knitting needles for collar

8 stitch markers

2.5mm (US size C) crochet hook for buttonhole band

Four 1cm/⅜in buttons

ALTERNATIVE COLOURWAY

This sweater can also be worked in Rowan *Cabled Mercerised Cotton* in the colour shown on the right, which is no.306: blue scan.

TENSION (GAUGE)

29 sts and 35 rows to 10cm/4in measured over st st worked on 3¼mm (US size 3) needles

Please check your tension (gauge) carefully and change knitting needle size if necessary

NOTES

The lower part of the skirt and the cuffs are flared as a result of the wedge-shaped moss (seed) stitch inserts along the edge. Instructions are given for placing st markers on either side of each insert. These st markers are slipped in each row so that they are always positioned on the needles in the same place. This serves as a guide for the knitter as the wedges are shaped.

Read chart from right to left for the RS (odd-numbered) rows and from left to right for the WS (even-numbered) rows.

BACK

Using smaller circular needle, cast on 294[306] sts.

Working back and forth in rows throughout, k 2 rows.

Change to larger circular needle and beg skirt patt as foll:

Row 1 (RS) K19[25]; *slip a st marker onto RH needle, then over next 37 sts work k3, p1, (k1, p1) 15 times, k3, slip a st marker onto RH needle*; **k36; rep from * to * once**; rep from ** to ** twice more; k19[25].

Row 2 P8[14], k1, p10; *slip st marker, then over next 37 sts work p4, k1, (p1, k1) 14 times, p4, slip st marker*; **p10, k1, p14, k1, p10; rep from * to * once**; rep from ** to ** twice more; p10, k1, p8[14].

Rows 3–6 Rep rows 1 and 2 twice more, but slipping st markers already in place on every row.

Keeping moss (seed) st correct as set, beg shaping moss (seed) st inserts on next row as foll:

Row 7 (RS) K19[25]; *slip st marker, over next 37 sts work sl 1-k1-psso, k2, work in moss (seed) st as set to last 4 sts before next marker, k2, k2tog, slip st marker*; **k36; rep from * to * once**; rep from ** to ** twice more; k19[25]. (There are now 35 sts between each of 4 sets of markers.)

Row 8 P8[14], k1, p10; *slip st marker, p3, work in moss (seed) st to last 3 sts before next marker, p3, slip st marker*; **p10, k1, p14, k1, p10; rep from * to * once**; rep from ** to ** twice more; p10, k1, p8[14].

Row 9 K19[25]; *slip st marker, k3, work in moss (seed) st to last 3 sts before next marker, k3, slip st marker*; **k36; rep from * to * once**; rep from ** to ** twice more; k19[25].

CHAMPAGNE
CHAMPAGNE

Row 10 As row 8.
Rows 11 and 12 Rep rows 9 and 10 once.
Row 13 K2tog, k17[23]; *slip st marker, k3, work in moss (seed) st to last 3 sts before next marker, k3, slip st marker*; **k36; rep from * to * once**; rep from ** to ** twice more; k17[23], k2tog.
Row 14 P7[13], k1, p10; *slip st marker, p2tog, p2, work in moss (seed) st to last 4 sts before next st marker, p2, p2tog tbl, slip st marker*; **p10, k1, p14, k1, p10; rep from * to * once**; rep from ** to ** twice more; p10, k1, p7[13]. (There are now 33 sts between each of 4 sets of markers.)
Row 15 K18[24]; *slip st marker, k3, work in moss (seed) st to last 3 sts before next st marker, k3, slip st marker*; **k36; rep from * to * once**; rep from ** to ** twice more; k18[24].
Row 16 P7[13], k1, p10; *slip st marker, p3, work in moss (seed) st to last 3 sts before next st marker, p3, slip st marker*; **p10, k1, p14, k1, p10; rep from * to * once**; rep from ** to ** twice more; p10, k1, p7[13].
Rows 17–20 Rep rows 15 and 16 twice.
Row 21 K to first marker; *slip st marker, sl 1-k1-psso, k2, work in moss (seed) st to last 4 sts before next st marker, k2, k2tog, slip st marker*; **k36; rep from * to * once**; rep from ** to ** twice more; k to end. (There are now 31 sts between each of 4 sets of markers.)
Row 22 P7[13], k1, p10; *slip st marker, p3, work in moss (seed) st to last 3 sts before next st marker, p3, slip st marker*; **p10, k1, p14, k1, p10; rep from * to * once**; rep from ** to ** twice more; p10, k1, p7[13].
Row 23 K to first marker; *slip st marker, k3, work in moss (seed) st to last 3 sts before next st marker, k3, slip st marker*; **k36; rep from * to * once**; rep from ** to ** twice more; k to end.
Row 24 As row 22.
Row 25 K2tog, k to first marker; *slip st marker, k3, work in moss (seed) st to last 3 sts before next marker, k3, slip st marker*; **k36; rep from * to * once**; rep from ** to ** twice more; k to last 2 sts, k2tog.
Row 26 P6[12], k1, p10; *slip st marker, p3, work in moss (seed) st to last 3 sts before next st marker, p3, slip st marker*; **p10, k1, p14, k1, p10; rep from * to * once**; rep from ** to ** twice more; p10, k1, p6[12].
Row 27 As row 23.
Cont in this way, keeping patt and wedge-shaped inserts correct as set and cont to dec inserts as set by dec one st at each side of each insert on next row and then on every foll 7th row until there are only 7 sts between each set of 4 st markers, *and at the same time* cont dec one st at each end of row on every 12th row as set (so decreasing at sides on 37th, 49th, 61st, 73rd, 85th and 97th rows), and so ending with a RS row (row 105). 158[170] sts.
Row 106 (WS) P0[6], k1, p10, *remove st marker, p3, k1, p3, remove st marker*, **p10, k1, p14, k1, p10, rep from * to * once**, rep from ** to ** twice more, p10, k1, p0[6].
Row 107 K to end.
Row 108 P0[6], k1, *p13, k1, p13, k1, p14, k1*, rep from * to * twice more, p13, k1, p13, k1, p0[6].
Row 109 K to end, dec one st at each end of row. 156[168] sts.

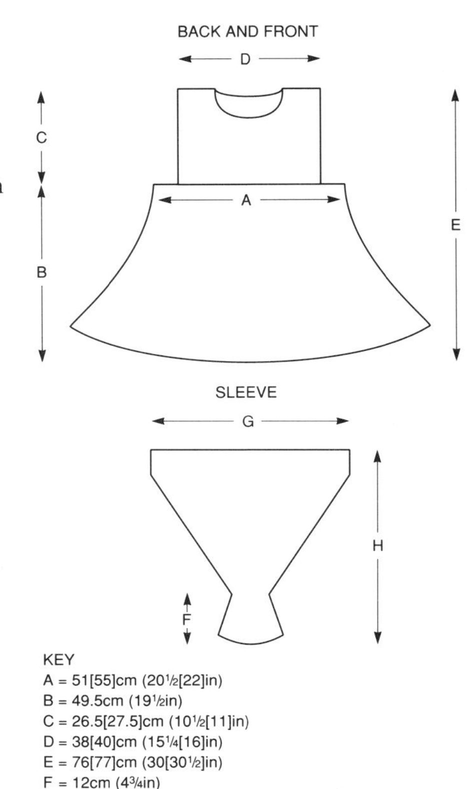

Row 110 P0[5], k0[1], *p13, k1, p13, k1, p14, k1*, rep from * to * twice more, p13, k1, p13, k0[1], p0[5].
Row 111 K to end.
Last 2 rows set patt for remainder of skirt.
Keeping patt correct as set, cont in patt *and at the same time* cont to dec one st at each end of every 12th row as set until there are 148[160] sts, so ending with a RS row.
Work in patt without shaping until skirt measures 49.5cm/19½in from cast-on edge, ending with a WS row.

Armhole shaping

Keeping patt correct, cast (bind) off 19[22] sts at beg of next 2 rows, so ending with a WS row. 110[116] sts.

Yoke

Beg with chart row 1, foll chart for yoke pattern until chart row 12 has been completed, so ending with a WS row.
Cont in patt, rep chart rows 11 and

12 only for patt for remainder of yoke, until yoke measures 24.5[25.5]cm/9¾[10¼]in from armhole shaping, ending with a WS row.

Neck shaping

Keeping patt correct as set throughout, beg neck shaping on next row as foll:

Next row (RS) Work first 36[39] sts in patt, turn leaving rem sts on a spare needle.

Working on first side of neck only, dec one st at beg of next row (neck edge), then at neck edge on every foll row 5 times in all, so ending with a WS row.

Cast (bind) off rem 31[34] sts in patt.

Return to rem sts and with RS facing, slip centre 38 sts onto a st holder, rejoin yarn to rem sts and work in patt to end of row.

Complete 2nd side of neck to match first side, reversing shaping.

FRONT

Work as for back until yoke measures 19[20]cm/7½[8]in from armhole shaping, ending with a WS row.

Neck shaping

Keeping patt correct as set throughout, beg neck shaping on next row as foll:

Next row (RS) Work first 45[48] sts in patt, turn leaving rem sts on a spare needle.

Working on first side of neck only, dec one st at beg of next row (neck edge) and at neck edge on every foll row 11 times in all, then on every alt row 3 times, so ending with a WS row. 31[34] sts.

Work in patt without shaping until there are same number of rows as back to shoulder.

Cast (bind) off in patt.

Return to rem sts and with RS facing, slip centre 20 sts onto a st holder, rejoin yarn to rem sts and work in patt to end of row.

Complete 2nd side of neck to match first side, reversing shaping.

SLEEVES

Using smaller needles, cast on 93 sts.

K 2 rows.

Change to larger needles and beg cuff patt as foll:

Row 1 (RS) K7; *slip a st marker onto RH needle, then over next 21 sts work k3, p1, (k1, p1) 7 times, k3, slip a st marker onto RH needle*; **k8; rep from * to * once**; rep from ** to ** once more; k7.

Row 2 P7; *slip st marker, then over next 21 sts work p4, k1, (p1, k1) 6 times, p4, slip st marker*; **p8; rep from * to * once**; rep from ** to ** once more; p7.

Rows 3 and 4 As rows 1 and 2.

Keeping moss (seed) st correct as set, beg shaping moss (seed) st inserts on next row as foll:

Row 5 (RS) K7; *slip st marker, over next 21 sts work sl 1-k1-psso, k2, work in moss (seed) st as set to last 4 sts before next marker, k2, k2tog, slip st marker*; **k8; rep from * to * once**; rep from ** to ** once more; k7. (There are now 19 sts between each of 3 sets of markers.)

Row 6 P7; *slip st marker, p3, work in moss (seed) st to last 3 sts before next marker, p3, slip st marker*; **p8; rep from * to * once**; rep from ** to ** once more; p7.

Row 7 K7; *slip st marker, k3, work in moss (seed) st to last 3 sts before next marker, k3, slip st marker*; **k8; rep from * to * once**; rep from ** to ** once

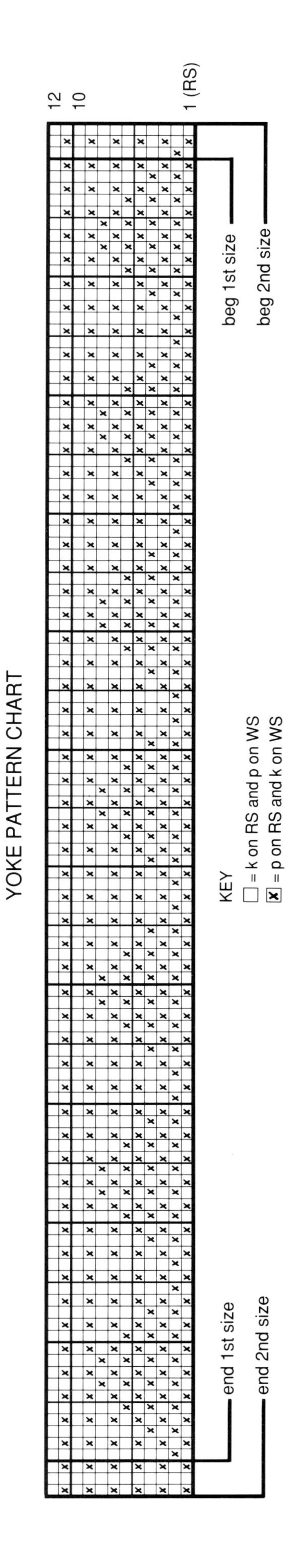

more; k7.
Rows 8 and 9 As rows 6 and 7.
Row 10 P7; *slip st marker, p2tog, p2, work in moss (seed) st to last 4 sts before next st marker, p2, p2tog tbl, slip st marker*; **p8; rep from * to * once**; rep from ** to ** once more; p7. (There are now 17 sts between each of 3 sets of markers.)
Row 11 As row 7.
Rows 12 and 13 As rows 6 and 7.
Row 14 As row 6.
Row 15 K to first marker; *slip st marker, sl 1-k1-psso, k2, work in moss (seed) st to last 4 sts before next st marker, k2, k2tog, slip st marker*; **k8; rep from * to * once**; rep from ** to ** once more; k to end. (There are now 15 sts between each of 3 sets of markers.)
Rows 16–19 Rep rows 6 and 7 twice.
Cont in this way, keeping patt and wedge-shaped inserts correct as set and cont to dec inserts as set by dec one st at each side of each insert on next row and then on every foll 5th row until there are only 7 sts between each set of 3 st markers, so ending with a RS row (row 35). 51 sts.
Row 36 (WS) P7, *remove st marker, p3, k1, p3, remove st marker*, **p8, rep from * to * once**, rep from ** to ** once more, p7.
Row 37 K to end.
Row 38 P10, k1, *p14, k1*, rep from * to * once more, p10.
Last 2 rows set patt for remainder of sleeve.
Keeping patt correct as set throughout, work 2 rows without shaping, then inc one st at each end of next row and every foll alt row 43[48] times in all (137[147] sts), then at each end of every foll alt 3rd row 8[6] times, working increased sts into patt. 153[159] sts.
Note: When working increased sts into patt, k all sts in every RS row as set; but on WS rows k single st in each stripe as set, and introduce new single st stripes as sts are increased so that there is a stripe after every group of 14 plain sts.
Work in patt without shaping until sleeve measures 54[55]cm/21[21½]in from cast-on edge, ending with a WS row.
Cast (bind) off in patt.
Make 2nd sleeve in same way.

COLLAR

Do not press pieces.
Join shoulder seams, using a small neat backstitch on edge of work.
Using set of 4 double-pointed needles and with RS facing, beg halfway down shaped edge of left front neck and pick up and k12 sts down left front neck to centre front st holder, k20 sts from front st holder, pick up and k24 sts up right front neck, 6 sts down right back neck, k38 sts from back neck st holder, pick up and k6 sts up left back neck and 12 sts down left front neck, ending next to first st picked up; then cast on 8 sts at end of last needle (these sts will be stitched to WS behind sts of beg of row as button band). 126 sts.
Turn so that WS is facing and beg with sts just cast on, work back and forth in rows on 126 sts in moss st rib as foll:
Rib row 1 (WS) K1, (p1, k1) twice, p2, *k1, p2, k1, p1, k1, p2, rep from *, ending last rep p1 instead of p2.
Rib row 2 *K1, p1, rep from * to end.
Rep last 2 rows until collar measures 7.5cm/3in, ending with a WS row.
Cast (bind) off in rib.

FINISHING

Using one strand of yarn, embroider in chain st along top edge of triangles at bottom of yoke, working outline 3 rows above moss (seed) st.

Join seams using a small neat backstitch.

Placing centre of top of sleeve at shoulder seam, sew cast (bound) off edge of sleeves to vertical edge of armhole, then sew cast (bound) off armhole edge to side of sleeves.

Join side and sleeve seams.

Buttonhole band

Sew cast-on edge of button band (8 cast-on sts at end of collar) to WS behind beg of collar.

Using crochet hook and with RS facing, work a row of dc (US sc) evenly along row ends of beg of collar. Fasten off.

Then with RS facing, rejoin yarn and work a row of tr (US dc) along the row of dc (US sc) just worked. Fasten off.

Sew 4 buttons to button band, evenly spaced apart. Buttons are buttoned through corresponding spaces between tr (US dc) of the buttonhole band.

Birthday

This is my feast of a Fair Isle for your baby's first birthday! I've knitted it in wool and silk to create a special sweater which, I hope, will become a family heirloom. For a more practical version, knit it in wool and cotton. For a personal touch add your baby's initial, or choose a teddybear or some other favourite motif for the back.

SIZE

One size only to fit 12–18 months or 48–51cm/19–20in chest

See diagram for finished knitted measurements.

MATERIALS

Rowan *Silk and Wool* 20g/¾oz balls as foll:

A (no.851: camel) 6 balls
B (no.857: ecru) 1 ball
C (no.855: coral) 1 ball

Rowan *Wool and Cotton* 40g/1½ oz balls as foll:

D (no.920: hazelnut) 1 ball
E (no.923: wedgewood) 1 ball
F (no.910: kashmir) 1 ball
G (no.912: sage) 1 ball
H (no.913: musk) 1 ball

Rowan *Soft Cotton* 50g/1¾oz balls as foll:

J (no.527: smoke) 1 ball
L (no.555: shrimp) 1 ball
M (no.528: raincloud) 1 ball

One pair each of 2¾mm (US size 2) and 3¼mm (US size 3) knitting needles

Six 12mm/½in buttons

ALTERNATIVE COLOURWAY

This sweater can also be worked in the colourway shown below, where:

A = *Silk and Wool* no.848: rapid blue
B = *Soft Cotton* no.560: bronze
C = *Soft Cotton* no.552: rosehip
D = *Silk and Wool* no.841: purple
E = *Silk and Wool* no.843: fuchsia
F = *Wool and Cotton* no.922: rosemary
G = *Wool and Cotton* no.912: sage
H = *Wool and Cotton* no.913: musk
J = *Wool and Cotton* no.921: chocolate
L = *Nice Cotton* no.433: parakeet
M = *Silk and Wool* no.856: donkey

Note: All colours other than A require less than 20g/¾ oz of yarn.

TENSION (GAUGE)

30 sts and 32 rows to 10cm/4in measured over patt worked on 3¼mm (US size 3) needles

PLEASE CHECK YOUR TENSION (GAUGE) CAREFULLY AND CHANGE KNITTING NEEDLE SIZE IF NECESSARY

NOTES

When working with only two colours in a row, strand colour not in use loosely across the back of work, weaving it around other colour every fourth stitch to avoid long loose strands.

When working with more than two colours in a row, strand the background colour and use the intarsia method for the remaining colours, using a separate length of yarn for each isolated area of colour and twisting yarns together when changing colours to avoid making a hole. Use the intarsia method for the back motif as well.

Read charts from right to left for the RS (odd-numbered) rows and from left to right for the WS (even-numbered) rows.

BACK

Using smaller needles and A, cast on 92 sts and beg k1, p1 rib for hem as foll:

Rib row 1 (RS) *K1, p1, rep from * to end.

Rep last row 11 times more, so ending with a WS row.

Change to larger needles and work in st st foll chart from row 1 until chart row 53 has been completed, so ending with a RS row.

Place back motif

Beg teddy bear or heart motif on next row (foll back motif chart 1 or 2) as foll:

Chart row 54 (WS) Using A p32, using B p28, using A p32.

Cont foll main chart and motif chart until row 83 has been completed, then cont working from main chart only until chart row 92 has been completed, so ending with a WS row.

Neck shaping

Cont to foll chart throughout, beg neck shaping as foll:

Chart row 93 (RS) Work first 32 sts in patt, turn leaving rem sts

on a spare needle.
Working first side of neck only, dec one st at beg of next row (neck edge), then at neck edge on foll row. 30 sts.
Work one row without shaping.
Cast (bind) off.
Return to rem sts and with RS facing, slip centre 28 sts onto a st holder, rejoin yarn to rem sts and work in patt to end of row.
Complete 2nd side of neck to match first side, reversing shaping.

LEFT FRONT

Using smaller needles and A, cast on 44 sts and work 12 rows in k1, p1 rib for hem as for back.
Change to larger needles and work in st st foll chart from row 1 until chart row 79 has been completed (omitting back motif), so ending with a RS row.

Neck shaping

Cont to foll chart throughout, cast (bind) off 6 sts at beg of next row, then dec one st at neck edge on next row and every foll row 8 times in all. 30 sts.
Work without shaping until chart row 96 has been completed.
Cast (bind) off.

RIGHT FRONT

Work as for left front, foll chart for right front and reversing all shaping.

SLEEVES

Using smaller needles and A, cast on 50 sts and work 14 rows in k1, p1 rib for hem as for back, so ending with a WS row.
Change to larger needles and work in st st foll chart from row 1 *and at the same time* shape sleeve by inc one st at each end of 11th row and then at each end of every foll alt row 25 times in all. 100 sts.
Work in patt without shaping until chart row 68 has been completed.
Cast (bind) off all sts.

BUTTON BAND

Press pieces lightly on WS with a warm iron over a damp cloth, omitting ribbing.
Join seams using a small neat backstitch on very edge of work.
Join shoulder seams.
Placing centre of top of sleeve at shoulder seam, sew cast (bound) off edge of sleeves to back and fronts.
Join side and sleeve seams.
Turn hem on back and fronts to WS along last row of rib and slip stitch in place. Turn hem on sleeves to WS in same way and stitch in place.

Button band for boy's version

Using smaller needles and A and with RS facing, pick up and k80 sts evenly up right front from hemline to neck shaping.
****Row 1** (WS) *Using E p2, using D p2, rep from * to end.
Row 2 *Using D k2, using E k2, rep from * to end.
Row 3 (WS) *Using D p2, using E p2, rep from * to end.
Row 4 *Using E k2, using D k2, rep from * to end.
Using A only, work 4 rows in k1, p1 rib as for back.
Cast (bind) off in rib.

Button band for girl's version

Using smaller needles and A and with RS facing, pick up and k80 sts evenly down left front from neck shaping to hemline. Then work as for boy's version from **

Both versions

Mark positions for 6 buttonholes, the first to beg 1.5cm/½in from lower edge, the last to come 1cm/¼in *above* neck shaping (to be worked horizontally in neckband) and the rem 4 evenly spaced between, with each buttonhole to be worked over 3 sts.

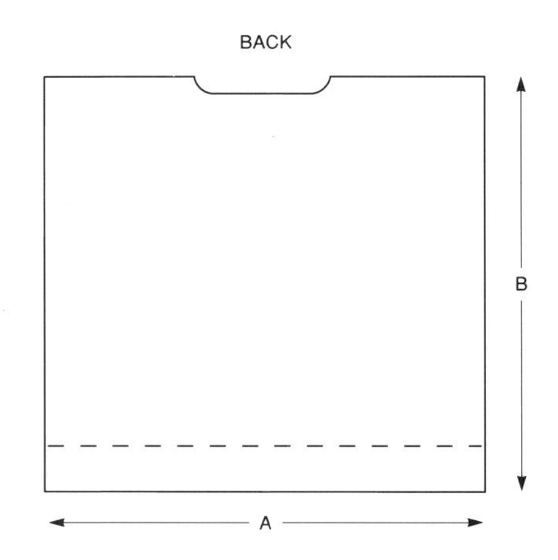

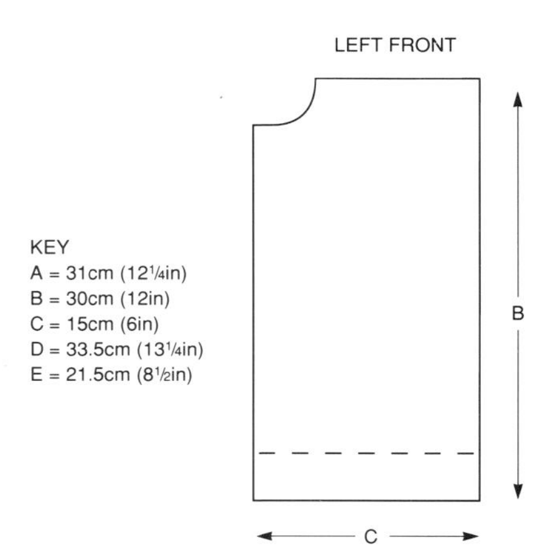

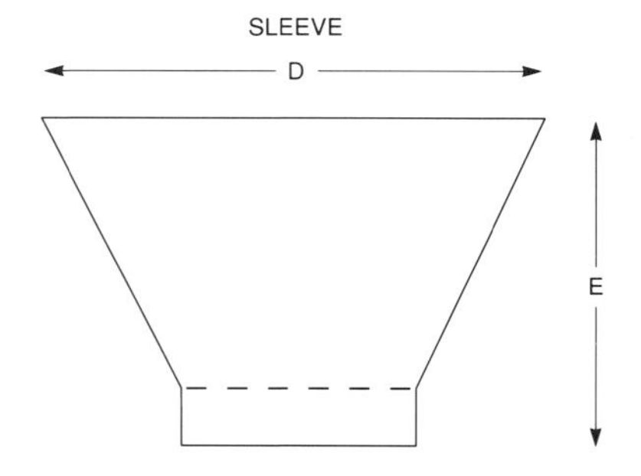

BUTTONHOLE BAND

Boy's version

Pick up sts down left front as for girl's version button band.
***Then work as for button band, but using D for E and E for D, *and at the same time* work buttonholes on row 2 by casting (binding) off 3 sts when position of each 5 buttonholes is reached, then in foll row cast on 3 sts over those cast (bound) off in

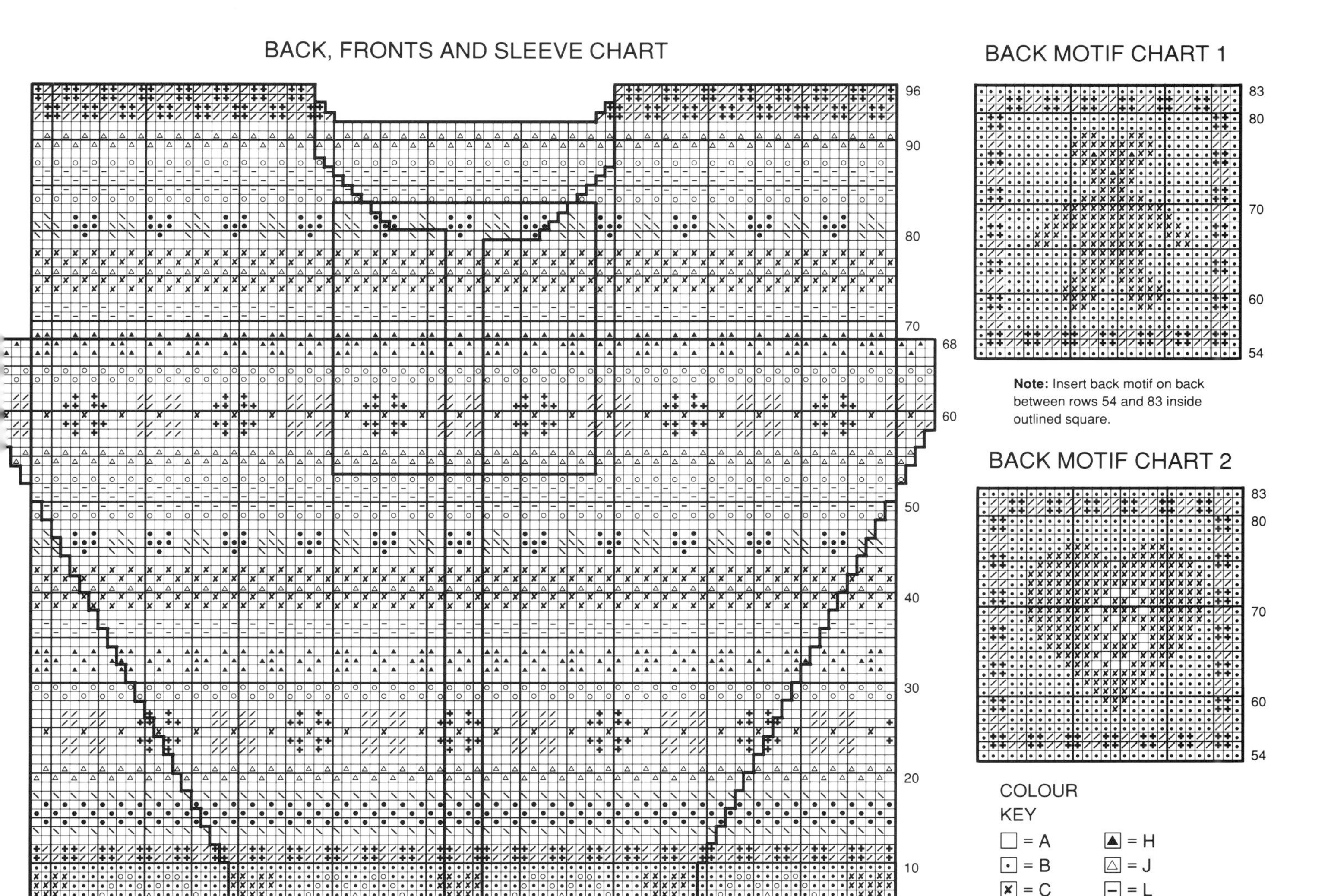

last row, then work buttonholes over 2nd and 3rd rib rows in same positions.

Girl's version

Pick up sts up right front as for boy's version button band. Then work as for boy's version from ***.

Both versions

Turn front bands to WS along first rib row and slip stitch in place.

NECKBAND

Using smaller needles and A and with RS facing, beg at centre front edge of right front neck edge, pick up and k10 sts evenly along top of band and horizontal neck edge, 20 sts up right front neck, 5 sts down left back neck, k28 sts from back neck st holder, pick up and k5 sts up right back neck, 20 sts down left front neck and 10 sts along horizontal neck edge and top of band. 98 sts.

Row 1 (WS) *Using E p2, using D p2, rep from * to last 2 sts, using E p2.

Row 2 Using D for all D sts and E for all E sts, k across row casting (binding) off 3 sts (3 sts from edge) at end of row for boy's version and at beg of row for girl's version to form buttonhole.

Row 3 (WS) *Using D p2, using E p2, rep from * to last 2 sts, using D p2, *and at the same time* cast on 3 sts over those cast (bound) off.

Row 4 *Using D k2, using E k2, rep from * to last 2 sts, using D k2.

Using A only, work 4 rows in k1, p1 rib as for back *and at the same time* work buttonhole over 2nd and 3rd rib rows in same position as first buttonhole.

Cast (bind) off in rib.

FINISHING

Turn neckband to WS along first rib row and slip stitch in place.

Sew 2 layers of each buttonhole tog. Press seams lightly on WS.

Sew buttons to button band and neckband in positions corresponding to buttonholes.

DITTISHAM

BLUE AND WHITE IS AN ENDURING FASHION THEME AND DENIM IS ALWAYS AN IMPORTANT PART OF THIS STORY. HERE IS A HARD-WEARING WORK SWEATER, INSPIRED BY THOSE OF THE FISHERFOLK OF NORTHERN BRITAIN. THE ALL-OVER WOODGRAIN PATTERN IS SURPRISINGLY SIMPLE TO KNIT. TRY WORKING IT WITHOUT THE BUTTONS FOR A WARMER WINTER VERSION.

SIZE

One size only to fit 101–122cm/ 40–48in chest

See diagram for finished knitted measurements.

MATERIALS

Rowan *Den-m-nit Indigo Dyed Cotton DK* (no.225: Nashville) 27 x 50g/1¾oz balls

One pair each of 3mm (US size 3) and 3¾mm (US size 5) knitting needles

One 3mm (US size 3) circular needle for neckband

Cable needle (cn)

2 stitch markers

Three 18mm/⅝in buttons

ALTERNATIVE COLOURWAY

This sweater can also be worked in the colour shown on the right, which is no.230: Tennessee.

TENSION (GAUGE)

29 sts and 34 rows to 10cm/4in measured over honeycomb cable patt after washing (see *Notes*) worked on 3¾mm (US size 5) needles

PLEASE CHECK YOUR TENSION (GAUGE) CAREFULLY AND CHANGE KNITTING NEEDLE SIZE IF NECESSARY

NOTES

Den-m-nit yarn shrinks when washed, so the lengths called for in the instructions are longer than the finished lengths when washed. The width of the garment is unaffected by washing. The measurement diagram gives the finished measurements after washing. All pieces must be washed in hot water and tumble dried before they are sewn together.

Read motif charts from right to left for the RS (odd-numbered) rows and from left to right for the WS (even-numbered) rows.

HONEYCOMB CABLE PATTERN

This pattern is worked over a multiple of 14 sts plus 14 extra.

Row 1 (RS) P4, *k6, p8, rep from *, ending last rep p4 instead of p8.

Row 2 K4, *p6, k8, rep from *, ending last rep k4 instead of k8.

Row 3 P4, *slip next 3 sts onto a cn and hold at back of work, k3, then k3 from cn – called *cable 6 right* or *C6R* –, p8, rep from *, ending last rep p4 instead of p8.

Row 4 As row 2.

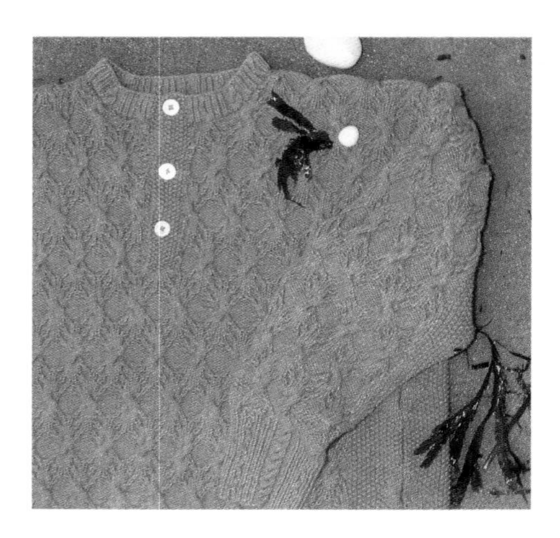

Rows 5 and 6 As rows 1 and 2.

Row 7 P2, *slip next 2 sts onto a cn and hold at back of work, k1, then p2 from cn – called *cable 3 right* or *C3R* –, k4, slip next st onto a cn and hold at front of work, p2, then k1 from cn – called *cable 3 left* or *C3L* –, p4, rep from *, ending last rep p2 instead of p4.

Row 8 K2, *p1, k2, p4, k2, p1, k4, rep from *, ending last rep k2 instead of k4.

Row 9 *C3R, p2, k4, p2, C3L, rep from * to end.

Row 10 P1, *k4, p4, k4, p2, rep from *, ending last rep p1 instead of p2.

Row 11 K1, *p2, C3R, k2, C3L, p2, k2, rep from *, ending last rep k1 instead of k2.

Row 12 P1, *k2, p1, k2, p2, k2, p1, k2, p2, rep from *, ending last rep p1 instead of p2.

Row 13 K1, *C3R, p2, k2, p2, C3L, k2, rep from *, ending k1 instead of k2.

Row 14 P2, *k4, p2, k4, p4, rep from *, ending last rep p2 instead of p4.

Row 15 K2, *p2, C3R, C3L, p2, k4, rep from * ending last rep k2 instead of k4.

Row 16 P2, *k2, p1, k4, p1, k2, p4, rep from *, ending last rep p2 instead of p4.

Row 17 K2, *C3R, p4, C3L, k4, rep from *, ending last rep k2 instead of k4.

Row 18 P3, *k8, p6, rep from *, ending last rep p3 instead of p6.

Row 19 K3, *p8, k6, rep from *, ending last rep k3 instead of k6.

Row 20 As row 18.

Row 21 K3, *p8, slip next 3 sts onto a cn and hold at front of work, k3, then k3 from cn – called *cable 6 left* or *C6L* –, rep from *, ending last rep k3 instead of C6L.
Rows 22 and 23 As row 18 and row 19.
Row 24 As row 18.
Row 25 K2, *C3L, p4, C3R, k4, rep from *, ending last rep k2 instead of k4.
Row 26 As row 16.
Row 27 K2, *p2, C3L, C3R, p2, k4, rep from *, ending last rep k2 instead of k4.
Row 28 As row 14.
Row 29 K1, *C3L, p2, k2, p2, C3R, k2, rep from *, ending last rep k1 instead of k2.
Row 30 As row 12.
Row 31 K1, *p2, C3L, k2, C3R, p2, k2, rep from *, ending last rep k1 instead of k2.
Row 32 As row 10.
Row 33 *C3L, p2, k4, p2, C3R, rep from * to end.
Row 34 As row 8.
Row 35 P2, *C3L, k4, C3R, p4, rep from *, ending last rep p2 instead of p4.
Row 36 As row 2.
Rep rows 1–36 to form honeycomb cable patt.

BACK
Using smaller needles, cast on 147 sts and beg cable rib patt as foll:
Rib row 1 (RS) *(K1, p1) twice, k2, p2, k1, (p1, k1) twice, p2, k4, p2, rep from * to end.
Rib row 2 *K2, p4, k2, p1, (k1, p1) twice, k2, p2, (k1, p1) twice, rep from * to end.
Rib row 3 *(K1, p1) twice, k1, slip next st onto a cn and hold at front of work, p1, then k1 tbl from cn – called *left twist* or *LT* –, (p1, k1) 3 times, p2, slip next 2 sts onto a cn and hold at back of work, k2, then k2 from cn – called *cable 4 back* or *C4B* –, p2, rep from * to end.
Rib row 4 *K2, p4, k2, p1, (k1, p1) 6 times, rep from * to end.
Rib row 5 *(K1, p1) 3 times, LT, k1, (p1, k1) twice, p2, k4, p2, rep from * to end.
Rib row 6 *K2, p4, k2, (p1, k1) twice, p2, k2, p1, (k1, p1) twice, rep from * to end.
Rib row 7 *(K1, p1) 3 times, slip next st onto a cn and hold at back of work, k1 tbl, then p1 from cn – called *right twist* or *RT* –, k1, (p1, k1) twice, p2, C4B, p2, rep from * to end.
Rib row 8 As row 4.
Rib row 9 *(K1, p1) twice, k1, RT, (p1, k1) 3 times, p2, k4, p2, rep from * to end.
Rep rib rows 2–9 until ribbing measures 9.5cm/3¾in from cast-on edge, ending with a WS row.
Change to larger needles and beg zigzag patt as foll:
Row 1 (RS) Purl.
Row 2 P1, k1, *p1, k2, p1, (k1, p1) twice, k2, p1, k1, rep from * to last st, p1.
Row 3 P2, *LT, p2, k1, p1, k1, p2, RT, p1, rep from * to last st, p1.
Row 4 K3, *(p1, k3) 3 times, rep from * to end.
Row 5 P3, *LT, p5, RT, p3, rep from * to end.
Row 6 K4, *p1, k5, p1, k5, rep from *, ending last rep k4, instead of k5.
Row 7 P4, *LT, p3, RT, p5, rep from *, ending last rep p4, instead of p5.
Row 8 K1, p1, *(k3, p1) 3 times, rep from * to last st, k1.
Row 9 K1, *p1, k1, p2, LT, p1, RT, p2, k1, rep from * to last 2 sts, p1, k1.

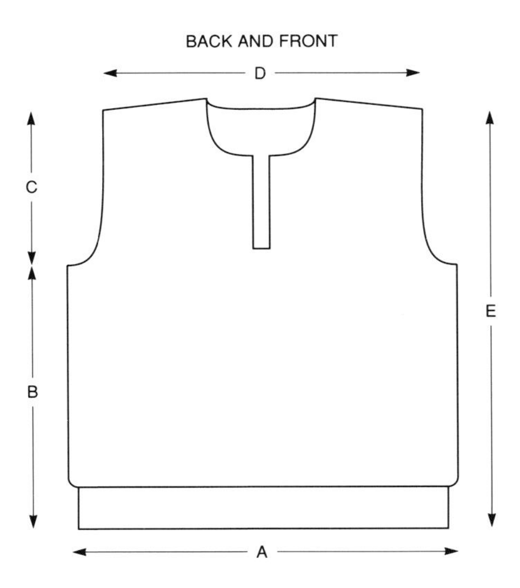

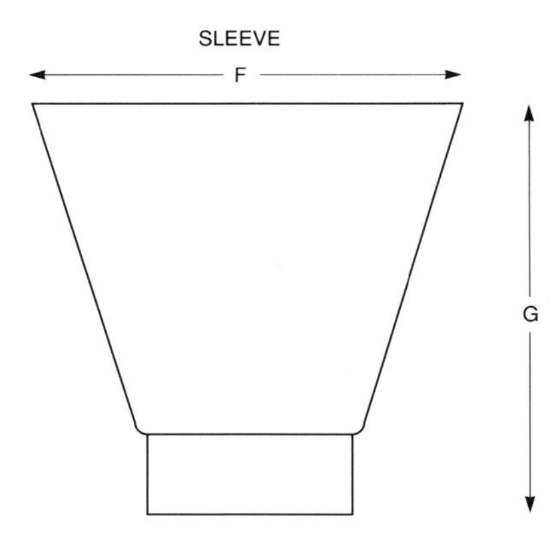

KEY
A = 66cm (26¼in)
B = 47cm (18½in)
C = 26.5cm (10½in)
D = 53cm (21¼in)
E = 73.5cm (29in)
F = 55.5cm (22in)
G = 54.5cm (21½in)

Row 10 K1, p1, *k1, p1, k2, p1, k1, p1, k2, p1, k1, p1, rep from * to last st, k1.
Purl one row.
Inc 35 sts evenly across next row as foll:
Next row (inc row) (WS) P5, *p into front and back of next st – called *inc 1* –, p3*, rep from * to * 33 times more, inc 1 into next st, p5. 182 sts.
Beg honeycomb cable patt on next row as foll:
Patt row 1 (RS) (P1, k1) 7 times and slip a st marker onto RH needle; work first row of honeycomb cable patt over next 154 sts and slip a st marker onto RH needle; (k1, p1) 7 times.

BORDER CHART B

26
20
10
1(RS)
rep = 14 sts

BORDER CHART A

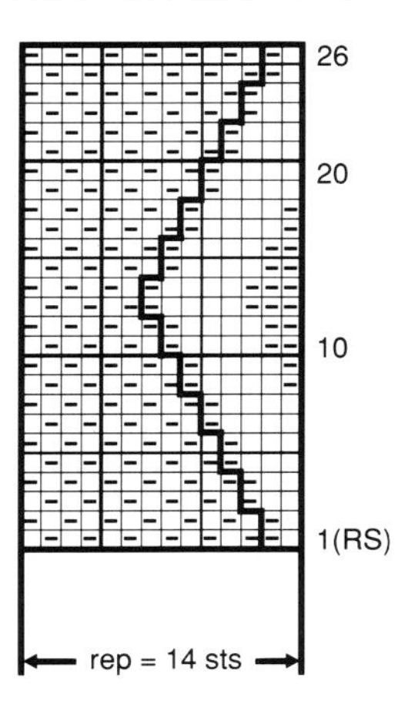

KEY
☐ = k on RS and p on WS
⊟ = p on RS and k on WS

Patt row 2 (P1, k1) 7 times and slip st marker; work 2nd row of honeycomb cable patt over next 154 sts and slip st marker; (k1, p1) 7 times.
Cont in this way working honeycomb cable patt over 154 sts between markers and moss (seed) st outside markers *and at the same time* when back measures 15cm/6in, 28cm/11in and 41cm/16in from cast-on edge (ending with a WS row) beg working the 26 rows of Border Chart A instead of 14 moss (seed) sts at beg of row and Border Chart B instead of 14 moss (seed) sts at end of row, working 14 edge sts in moss (seed st) only in rows where chart patts are not worked.
Cont in patt as set until back measures 54.5cm/21½in from cast-on edge, ending with a WS row.**

Armhole shaping
Keeping patt correct throughout, dec one st at each end of next row and then every foll alt row 14 times in all. 154 sts.
Work without shaping in honeycomb cable patt throughout, until back measures 85cm/33½in from cast-on edge, ending with a WS row.

Neck and shoulder shaping
Next row (RS) Cast (bind) off first 18 sts, work next 39 sts in patt (including st already on needle after cast (bind) off), turn leaving rem 97 sts on a spare needle.
Working first side of neck only, work as foll:
Next row Dec one st at beg of row and work in patt to end.
Next row Cast (bind) off 18 sts, work in patt to end, dec one st at end of row.
Next row Dec one st at beg of row and work in patt to end.
Cast (bind) off rem 18 sts.
Return to rem sts and with RS facing, slip centre 40 sts onto a st holder, rejoin yarn to rem sts and work in patt to end of row.
Next row Cast (bind) off 18 sts, work in patt to end, dec one st at end of row.
Next row Dec one st at beg of row and work in patt to end.
Next row Cast (bind) off 18 sts, work in patt to end, dec one st at end of row.
Work one row without shaping.
Cast (bind) off rem 18 sts.

FRONT
Work as for back to **.

Armhole shaping
Keeping patt correct throughout, dec one st at each end of next row and then every foll alt row 14 times in all *and at the same time* when front measures 58cm/22¾in from cast-on edge, ending with a WS row, mark position of centre 8 sts.

Divide for neck
Then divide for neck (cont to work armhole decs as set) as foll:
Next row (RS) Work in patt to centre 8 sts, turn, slip centre sts onto a st holder, leaving rem sts on a spare needle.
Working first side of neck only, cont in patt keeping centre edge straight and working armhole decs as set until armhole shaping has been completed. 73 sts.
Work without shaping in honeycomb cable patt throughout, until front measures 77cm/30¼in from cast-on edge, ending with a RS row.

Neck shaping
Next row (WS) Work first 7 sts in patt and slip these sts onto a st holder (neck edge), work in patt to end.
Dec one st at neck edge on next and every foll row 8 times in all, then every foll alt row 4 times. 54 sts.
Work without shaping until there are same number of rows as back to shoulder, so ending with a WS row.
Cast (bind) off 18 sts at beg of next row and foll alt row.
Work one row without shaping.
Cast (bind) off rem 18 sts.
Return to rem sts and with RS facing, leaving centre 8 sts on st holder, rejoin yarn to rem sts and work in patt to end of row.
Cont in patt keeping centre edge straight and working armhole decs as set until armhole shaping has been completed. 73 sts.
Work without shaping in honeycomb cable patt throughout, until there is one more row than first side of neck to beg of neck shaping, so ending with a WS row.

Neck shaping
Next row (RS) Work first 7 sts in patt and slip these sts onto a st holder (neck edge), work in patt to end.
Dec one st at neck edge on next and every foll row 8 times in all, then every foll alt row 4 times. 54 sts.
Work without shaping until there are same number of rows as back to shoulder, so ending with a RS row.
Cast (bind) off 18 sts at beg of next row and foll alt row.
Work one row without shaping.
Cast (bind) off rem 18 sts.

SLEEVES
Using smaller needles, cast on 63 sts.
Work in cable rib patt as for back until ribbing measures 13.5cm/5¼in from cast-on edge, ending with a RS row.
Keeping rib patt correct, inc 9 sts evenly across next row as foll:
Next row (inc row) (WS) Rib 3, work into front and back of next st – called *inc 1* –, *rib 6, inc 1 into next st*, rep from * to * 7 times more, rib 3. 72 sts.
Change to larger needles and beg zigzag patt as foll:
Row 1 (RS) Purl.
Row 2 *P1, k2, (p1, k1) twice, p1, k2, p1, k1, rep from * to end.
Row 3 P into front and back of first st, *LT, p2, k1, p1, k1, p2, RT, p1, rep from *, ending last rep RT, instead of RT, p1, and p into front and back of last st of RT. 74 sts.
Row 4 K2, *p1, k3, rep from * to end.
Row 5 P3, *LT, p5, RT, p3, rep from *, ending last rep p2, instead of p3.
Row 6 K3, *p1, k5, rep from *, ending last rep k4, instead of k5.
Row 7 P into front and back of first st, p3, *LT, p3, RT, p5, rep from *, ending last rep p2, p into front and back of last st, instead of p5. 76 sts.
Row 8 K1, p1, *k3, p1, rep from * to last 2 sts, k2.
Row 9 P1, k1, *p1, k1, p2, LT, p1, RT, p2, k1, rep from * to last 2 sts, p1, k1.
Row 10 K1, p1, *(k1, p1, k2, p1) twice, k1, p1, rep from * to last 2 sts, k1, p1.
Purl one row, inc one st at each end of row. 78 sts.
Inc 12 sts evenly across next row as foll:
Next row (inc row) (WS) P into front and back of first st – called *inc 1* –, *p6, inc 1 into next st, rep from * to * 10 times more. 90 sts.
Beg honeycomb cable patt on next row as foll:
Patt row 1 (RS) K1, p1, k1 and slip a st marker onto RH needle; work first row of honeycomb cable patt over next 84 sts and slip a st marker onto RH needle; k1, p1, k1.
Patt row 2 (RS) K1, p1, k1 and slip st marker; work 2nd row of honeycomb cable patt over next 84 sts and slip st marker; k1, p1, k1.
Cont in this way working honeycomb cable patt over 84 sts between markers and moss (seed) st outside markers *and at the same time* inc one st at each end of next row and every foll 5th row 26 times in all, working all inc sts into moss (seed) st patt. 142 sts.
Work in patt as set without shaping until sleeve measures 62cm/24½in from cast-on edge, ending with a WS row.
Cast (bind) off.
Make 2nd sleeve in same way.

BUTTON BAND
Do not press.
Using smaller needles, cast on 8 sts.
Work in moss (seed) st as foll:
Row 1 (RS) *K1, p1, rep from * to end.
Row 2 *P1, k1, rep from * to end.
Rep last 2 rows until band fits from neck divide to beg of neck shaping, ending with a WS row.
Do not break off yarn, but slip sts onto a st holder.
Mark positions of two 4-row vertical buttonholes on button band, with a third buttonhole (horizontal) to be positioned 1.5cm/½in above the top of the band in the neckband, the last vertical buttonhole 4cm/1½in from cast-on edge of band and the other vertical buttonhole evenly spaced between.

BUTTONHOLE BAND
Using smaller needles and with RS facing, work in moss (seed) st, as for button band, across 8 sts on st holder at neck divide.
Keeping moss (seed) st correct throughout, work as for button band, but working buttonholes over 4 rows when position for buttonhole is reached as foll:
Next row Work 4 sts in patt, turn leaving rem 4 sts unworked.
Work 3 rows more on these 4 sts.
Do not break off yarn.
Using a separate length of yarn, work 4 rows on 4 sts left unworked and break off yarn.
Return to first set of sts and work in patt across all 8 sts.
When band has been completed, break off yarn and slip sts onto a st holder.

NECKBAND
Join shoulder seams using a small neat backstitch on very edge of work so that the cast (bound) off edge does not show.
Keeping top of buttonhole band on

st holder and using a small overstitch (overcast st), join band to left side of neck opening so that top of band is even with beg of neck shaping. Then join cast-on edge of button band to WS at beg of neck opening *behind* buttonhole band and stitch side of band to rem right side of neck opening, keeping top of band on st holder.

Using circular needle and with RS facing, work across 8 sts from button band st holder in moss (seed) st, k7 sts from right front neck st holder, then pick up and k26 sts up right front neck, 4 sts down right back neck, k40 sts from back neck st holder, pick up and k4 sts up left back neck, 26 sts down left front neck, k7 sts from left front neck st holder and work across 8 sts from buttonhole band st holder in moss (seed) st. 130 sts.

Working back and forth on neckband sts in rows and keeping first 8 sts and last 8 sts in moss (seed) st, purl one row.

Beg cable rib patt as foll:

Rib row 1 (RS) Work first 8 sts in moss (seed) st, *k1, p1, k2, p2, k1, (p1, k1) twice, p2, k4, p2, k1, p1*, rep from * to * 4 times more, k1, p1, k2, p2, k1, p1, k1, work last 8 sts in moss (seed) st.

Rib row 2 Work first 8 sts in moss (seed) st, p1, k1, p1, k2, p2, k1, p1, *k1, p1, k2, p4, k2, p1, (k1, p1) twice, k2, p2, k1, p1*, rep from * to * 4 times more, work last 8 sts in moss (seed) st.

Rib row 3 Work first 8 sts in moss (seed) st, *k1, p1, k1, LT, (p1, k1) 3 times, p2, C4B, p2, k1, p1*, rep from * to * 4 times more, k1, p1, k1, LT, (p1, k1) twice, work last 8 sts in moss (seed) st.

Rib row 4 Work first 3 sts in moss (seed) st, cast (bind) off 3 sts, work next 2 sts in moss (seed) st (including st already on needle after cast (bind) off), p1, (k1, p1) 4 times, *k1, p1, k2, p4, k2, p1, (k1, p1) 5 times*, rep from * to * 4 times more, work last 8 sts in moss (seed) st.

Rib row 5 Work first 8 sts in moss (seed) st, *(k1, p1) twice, LT, k1, (p1, k1) twice, p2, k4, p2, k1, p1*, rep from * to * 4 times more, (k1, p1) twice, LT, k1, p1, k1, work next 2 sts in moss (seed) st, cast on 3 sts over those cast (bound) off in last row, work last 3 sts in moss (seed) st.

Rib row 6 Work first 8 sts in moss (seed) st, p1, k1, p2, k2, p1, k1, p1, *k1, p1, k2, p4, k2, (p1, k1) twice, p2, k2, p1, k1, p1*, rep from * to * 4 times more, work last 8 sts in moss (seed) st.

Rib row 7 Work first 8 sts in moss (seed) st, *(k1, p1) twice, RT, k1, (p1, k1) twice, p2, C4B, p2, k1, p1*, rep from * to * 4 times more, (k1, p1) twice, RT, k1, p1, k1, work last 8 sts in moss (seed) st.

Rib row 8 Work first 8 sts in moss (seed) st, p1, (k1, p1) 4 times, *k1, p1, k2, p4, k2, p1, (k1, p1) 5 times*, rep from * to * 4 times more, then work last 8 sts in moss (seed) st.

Rib row 9 Work first 8 sts in moss (seed) st, *k1, p1, k1, RT, (p1, k1) 3 times, p2, k4, p2, k1, p1*, rep from * to * 4 times more, work last 8 sts in moss (seed) st.

Knitting all k sts and purling all p sts, cast (bind) off.

FINISHING

Wash and tumble dry pieces before sewing tog.

Join seams using a small neat backstitch on very edge of work, except for the ribbing where an invisible overstitch (overcast st) should be used.

Placing centre of top of sleeve at shoulder seam, sew cast (bound) off edge of sleeves to armhole edge (including decreased edge).

Join side and sleeve seams, matching up diamond motifs on back and front.

Sew the buttons to the button band in positions corresponding to the buttonholes.

SALTWICK

THIS SWEATER TAKES ITS INSPIRATION FROM THE MYSTERIOUS LABYRINTHS OF THE JACOBEAN MAZE GARDEN. I'VE USED THE BLUE AND WHITE THEME ONCE AGAIN, REVERSED OUT FOR THE ALTERNATIVE COLOURWAY, BUT FOR A MORE DRAMATIC EFFECT, WHY NOT PUT THE RED ON MAIN STAGE?

SIZES

To fit 81–86[91–96]cm/ 32–34[36–38]in chest

Figures for larger size are given in brackets [ ]; where there is only one set of figures, it applies to both sizes.

See diagram for finished knitted measurements.

MATERIALS

Rowan *Handknit DK Cotton* 50g/1¾oz balls as foll:

A (no.277: Turkish plum) 11[12] balls

B (no.251: ecru) 9[10] balls

Rowan *Cotton Glacé* 50g/1¾oz balls as foll:

C (no.742: matador) 4[5] balls

One pair each of 3¼mm (US size 3) and 4½mm (US size 7) knitting needles

Set of four 3¼mm (US size 3) double-pointed needles for collar

ALTERNATIVE COLOURWAY

This sweater can also be worked in the colourway shown on the right, where:

A = *Handknit DK Cotton* no.251: ecru

B = *Handknit DK Cotton* no.244: true navy

C = *Cotton Glacé* no.741: poppy

TENSION (GAUGE)

22 sts and 22 rows to 10cm/4in measured over colourwork patt worked on 4½mm (US size 7) needles

PLEASE CHECK YOUR TENSION (GAUGE) CAREFULLY AND CHANGE KNITTING NEEDLE SIZE IF NECESSARY

NOTES

Use *Cotton Glacé* double throughout. When working the border patt (chart rows 4–28) strand A and C loosely across back of work in the Fair Isle method. But use a separate length of B for each isolated st in the intarsia method, twisting yarns together at WS when changing colours to avoid making a hole.

When working remaining colourwork patt (chart rows 31–102) use a separate length of C for each isolated square of colour, and strand A and B.

Read pattern chart from right to left for the RS (odd-numbered) rows and from left to right for the WS (even-numbered) rows.

The collar chart is worked in the round and all rows are RS and are all read from right to left.

BACK

Using smaller needles and A, cast on 110[120] sts and beg moss (seed) st as foll:

Row 1 (RS) *K1, p1, rep from * to end.

Row 2 *P1, k1, rep from * to end.

Rep last 2 rows until back measures 4cm/1½in from cast-on edge, ending with a RS row.

Keeping moss (seed) st patt correct, inc 10 sts evenly as foll:

Next row (inc row) (WS) Work 5 sts in patt, work into front and back of next st – called *inc 1* –, *work 10[11] sts in patt, inc 1 into next st*, rep from * to * 8 times more, work 5[6] sts in patt. 120[130] sts.

Change to larger needles, and beg with chart row 1, foll pattern chart until chart row 30 has been completed.

Cont foll chart (rep chart rows 31–102 for patt throughout) until back measures 42[44]cm/16½[17¼]in from cast-on edge, ending with a WS row.

Armhole shaping

Keeping patt correct throughout, beg armhole shaping as foll:

Next row (dec row) (RS) K2, sl 1-k1-psso, work in patt to last 4 sts, k2tog, k2.

Work one row without shaping. Rep dec row once.

Rep from ** to ** 6 times more. 104[114] sts.***

Cont without shaping until back measures 64.5[68.5]cm/25½[27]in from cast-on edge, ending with a WS row.

Neck shaping

Next row (RS) Work first 39[44]

sts in patt, then turn leaving rem sts on a spare needle.
Working on first side of neck only, dec one st at beg of next row (neck edge), then at neck edge on every foll row 4 times in all.
Slip rem 35[40] sts onto a st holder.
Return to rem sts and with RS facing, slip centre 26 sts onto a st holder, rejoin yarn to rem sts and work in patt to end of row.
Complete 2nd side of neck to match first side, reversing shaping.

FRONT

Work as for back to ***.
Cont without shaping until back measures 59[63]cm/23½[25]in from cast-on edge, ending with a WS row.

Neck shaping

Next row (RS) Work first 46[51] sts in patt, then turn leaving rem sts on a spare needle.
Working on first side of neck only, dec one st at beg of next row (neck edge), then at neck edge on every foll row 11 times in all. 35[40] sts.
Work without shaping until there are same number of rows as back to shoulder.
Slip these sts onto a st holder.
Return to rem sts and with RS facing, slip centre 12 sts onto a st holder, rejoin yarn to rem sts and work in patt to end of row.
Complete 2nd side of neck to match first side, reversing shaping.

SLEEVES

Using smaller needles and A, cast on 39 sts and beg rib patt as foll:
Rib row 1 (RS)*P1, k1, p1, k2, p2, k2, rep from * to last 3 sts, p1, k1, p1.
Rib row 2 *K1, p1, k1, p2, k2, p2, rep from * to last 3 sts, k1, p1, k1.
Rib row 3 K1, *p1, k3, p2, k3, rep from * to last 2 sts, p1, k1.
Rib row 4 P1, *k1, p3, k2, p3, rep from * to last 2 sts, k1, p1.
Rep last 4 rows 6 times more, so ending with a WS row.
Keeping rib patt correct, inc 11 sts evenly across next row as foll:
Next row (inc row) (RS) Rib 1, inc 1 into next st, *rib 2, inc 1 into next st, rib 3, inc 1 into next st*, rep from * to * 4 times more, rib 2. 50 sts.
Change to larger needles and beg with 14th chart row (as indicated on patt chart), foll chart for patt throughout (beg again with row 31 after row 102 has been completed) *and at the same time* shape sleeve by inc one st at each end of 2nd row and then at each end of every foll alt row 22 times in all (94 sts), then every foll 3rd row 11[15] times, working all inc sts into patt foll chart. 116[124] sts.
Work in patt without shaping until sleeve measures 51[53.5]cm/20[21]in from cast-on edge, or desired length, ending with a WS row.
Using A only, cast (bind) off all sts.
Make 2nd sleeve in same way.

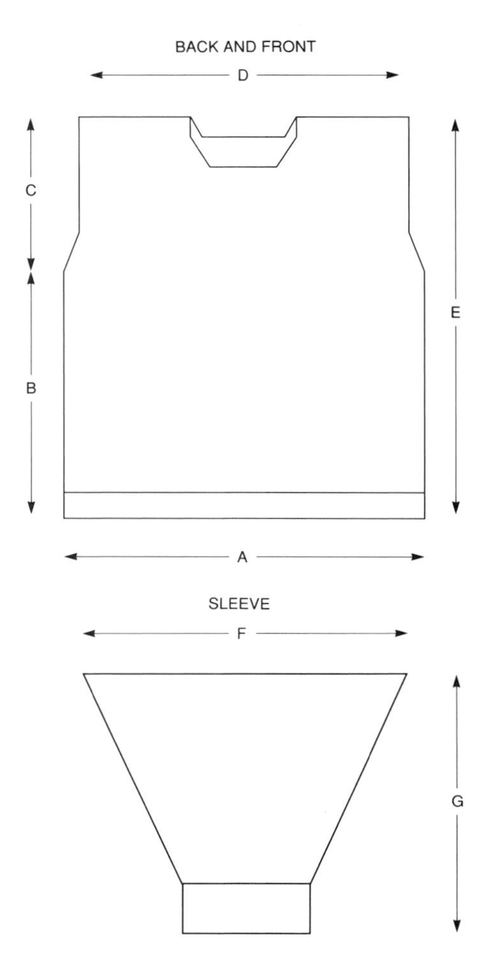

KEY
A = 54.5[59]cm (21¾[23¾]in)
B = 42[44]cm (16½[17¼]in)
C = 25[27]cm (10[10¾]in)
D = 47.5[52]cm (19[20¾]in)
E = 67[71]cm (26½[28]in)
F = 52.5[56.5]cm (21[22½]in)
G = 51[53.5]cm (20[21]in)

COLLAR

Press pieces lightly on WS with a warm iron over a damp cloth, omitting ribbing.
Using larger needles and A, join left shoulder seam by placing WS of back and front tog, then with back facing, knit through both layers along the 35[40] shoulder sts, taking one st from back st holder tog with one st from front st holder with each st and casting (binding) off as the row is worked. This forms a decorative seam on the RS.
Join the right shoulder seam in the same way, working the cast (bind) off with the back facing.
Using set of 4 double-pointed needles and A and with RS of front facing, beg at left shoulder and pick up and k29 sts down left front neck, k12 sts from centre neck st holder, pick up and k29 sts up right front neck, 6 sts down right back neck, k26 sts from back neck st holder and pick up and k6 sts up left back neck. 108 sts.
Working in rounds (RS always facing), beg collar chart as foll:
Chart row 1 Using C only, knit to end.
Chart row 2 *Using A k3, using C k1, using A k5, using C k1, using A k2, rep from * to end.
Cont foll chart from chart row 3, reading all rows from right to left,

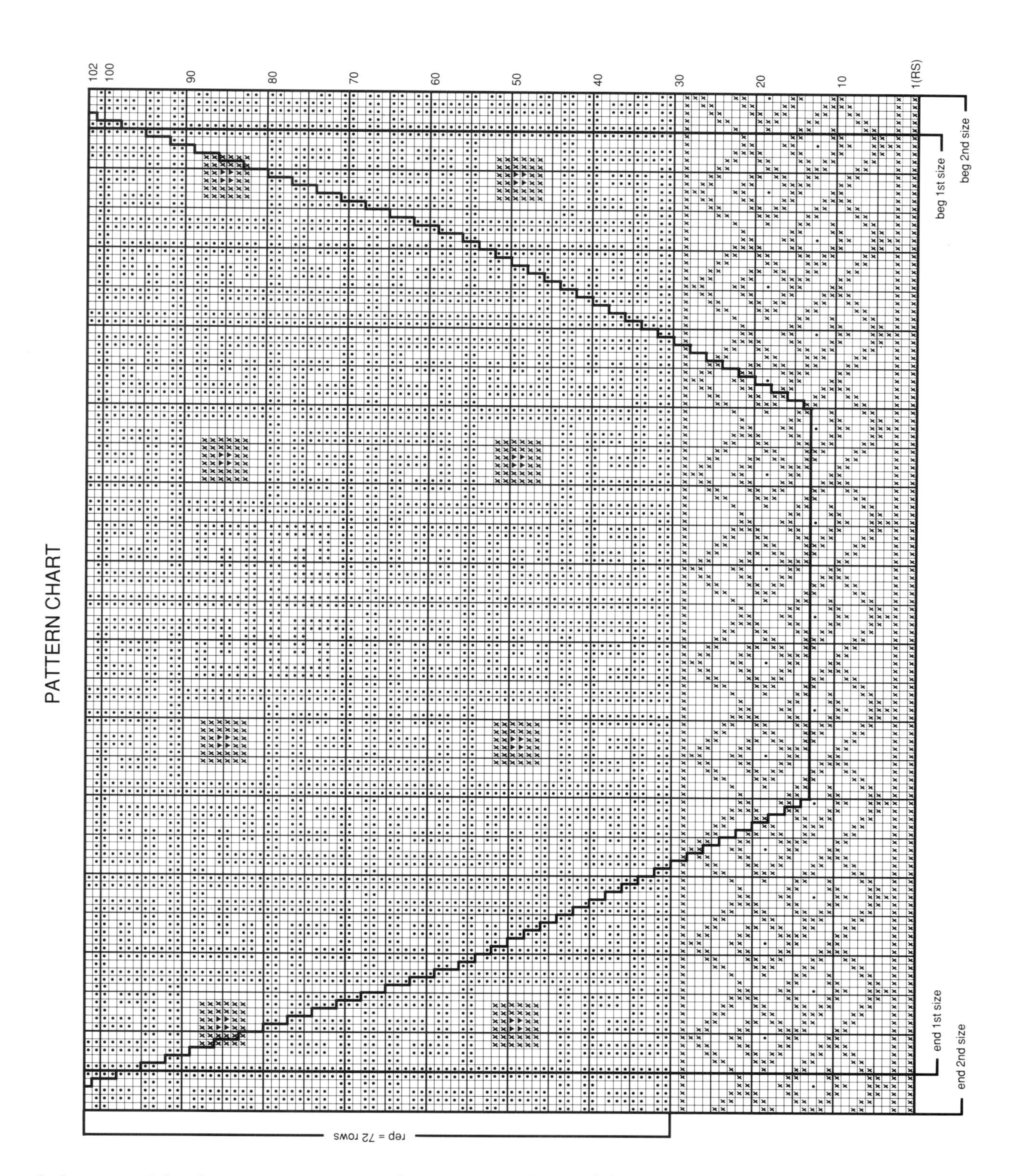

until chart row 9 has been completed.

Using A only, k 11 rounds.

Cast (bind) off loosely.

FINISHING

Join seams using a small neat backstitch on very edge of work, except for ribbing where an invisible slip stitch should be used.

Placing centre of top of sleeve at shoulder seam, sew cast (bound) off edge sleeves to armhole edge (including decreased edge).

Join side and sleeve seams, leaving moss (seed) st borders on back and on front unjoined to form slits at lower edge.

Fold collar in half to WS and sew in place. Press seams lightly on WS.

COLLAR CHART

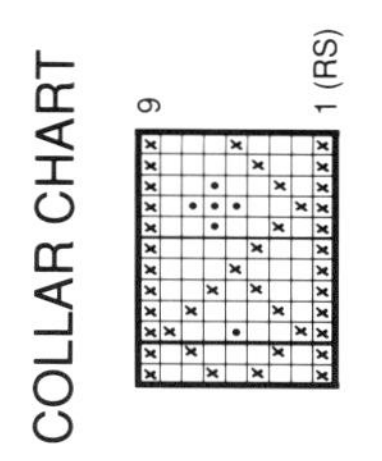

COLOUR KEY

□ = A in st st

⊡ = B in st st

☒ = C in st st

▶ = C in rev st st

A blend of
cool
Spiced

AUTUMN

Autumn

Although each season holds for me its own special treats, Autumn is my favourite. The mellow red and golden sunsets, the giant harvest moons and the mists all contribute to the anticipation of nature's last colourful canvas of the year before the grey days of Winter.

Autumn is a time when there is a glut of everything. The earth yields her *Harvest* to keep us through the coming months, and what a fabulous feast it is! When we lived in the country, we spent many hours picking and preserving the apples and plums from our orchard. Apple chutney, damson jam, quince jelly, elderberry wine, sloe gin ... anything that could be put into a jar or bottle was preserved each Autumn and stored for the coming winter months. In the woods hiding under the beech trees are blewits, chanterelles, ceps and other edible mushrooms. There is nothing I relish more than to harvest the fruits of the woods, hedgerows and garden.

In North Yorkshire, where I live now, a sign that *Halloween* is approaching is the village competition. Who can grow the biggest pumpkin? Well, all I can tell you is that the winner needs a trailer and four men to take it away! Although we have never produced any world-record-breakers, my children have always enjoyed growing pumpkins, watching their golden-skinned flesh swell and ripen over the summer months. We usually throw a Halloween party, when we make our pumpkins into Jack-o'-Lanterns, dress up, paint our faces and try to frighten away the hobgoblins.

As the evenings draw in, my family enjoys making *Bonfires* and sitting around them toasting chestnuts and potatoes and sharing songs. At this time of year there's plenty of dead wood around, which children will enthusiastically collect when they know that there is to be a campfire at the end of the day. We have lots of birthdays in the Autumn, and so what better excuse is there for holding a fireworks party – an explosion of colour before the Winter gloom finally sets in.

PEARMAIN

I LOVE OLD MINTON TILED FLOORS AND THIS SWEATER TAKES THEIR GENERAL DESIGN LAYOUT AND VIVID COLOURS FOR ITS SOURCE. I'VE KEPT THE SCALE OF THE PATTERN SMALL TO COMPLEMENT THE DELICATE SHAPE OF THE SWEATER. THIS IS ONE OF MY AUTUMN FAVOURITES – IT'S SO EASY AND COMFORTABLE TO WEAR.

SIZES

To fit 86[91:96]cm/34[36:38]in bust
Figures for larger sizes are given in brackets [ ]; where there is only one set of figures, it applies to all sizes.
See diagram for finished knitted measurements.

MATERIALS

Rowan *Cotton Glacé* 50g/1¾oz balls as foll:
A (no.730: oyster) 9[10:10] balls
B (no.728: sweet pea) 1 ball
C (no.744: Provence) 1 ball
Rowan *Soft Cotton* 50g/1¾oz balls as foll:
D (no.555: shrimp) 1 ball
E (no.558: truffle) 2 balls
Rowan *Cabled Mercerised Cotton* 50g/1¾oz balls as foll:
F (no.334: speedwell) 1 ball
G (no.337: firethorn) 1 ball
H (no.338: geranium) 1 ball
J (no.339: pippin) 1 ball
One pair each of 3mm (US size 3) and 3¾mm (US size 5) needles
Set of four 3mm (US size 3) double-pointed needles for neckband (or circular needle)
Cable needle (cn)

ALTERNATIVE COLOURWAY

This sweater can also be worked in the colourway shown below, where:
A = *Soft Cotton* no.527: smoke
Note: Because there are more m (yd) per ball of *Soft Cotton*, only 5[6:6] balls are required.
B = *Soft Cotton* no.555: shrimp
C = *Soft Cotton* no.560: bronze
D = *Cabled Mercerised Cotton* no.338: geranium
E = *Cotton Glacé* no.744: Provence
F = *Cabled Mercerised Cotton* no.339: pippin
G = *Cabled Mercerised Cotton* no.315: claret
H = *Cabled Mercerised Cotton* no.337: firethorn
J = *Cabled Mercerised Cotton* no.334: speedwell

TENSION (GAUGE)

29 sts and 34 rows to 10cm/4in measured over patt worked on 3¾mm (US size 5) needles
PLEASE CHECK YOUR TENSION (GAUGE) CAREFULLY AND CHANGE KNITTING NEEDLE SIZE IF NECESSARY

NOTES

When working the colourwork pattern, use the intarsia method, using a separate length of yarn for each isolated area of colour and twisting yarns together when changing colours to avoid making a hole.

Where there are insufficient stitches to complete the cables along side edges of back and front, do not work cables but work in st st only.

Read chart from right to left for the RS (odd-numbered) rows and from left to right for the WS (even-numbered) rows.

CABLES

C4B or *cable 4 back* – slip next 2 sts onto a cn and hold at back of work, k2 from LH needle, then k2 from cn.
C5B or *cable 5 back* – using the colours specified on the pattern chart, slip next 3 sts onto a cn and hold at back of work, k2 from LH needle, then k3 from cn.

BACK

Using smaller needles and A, cast on 122[129:136] sts and cable and eyelet rib as foll:
Rib row 1 (RS) P3, *k4, p3, rep from * to end.
Rib row 2 K1, yarn to front of work between two needles and to back of work over top of RH needle to make a new st – called *yarn over* or *yo* –, k2tog, *p4, k1, yo, k2tog, rep from * to end.
Rib row 3 P3, *C4B, p3, rep from * to end.
Rib row 4 As row 2.
Rib row 5 As row 1.
Rib row 6 As row 2.
Rep last 6 rows until ribbing measures 4cm/1½in from cast-on

edge, ending with a RS row.
Inc 24[25:26] sts evenly across next row as foll:
Next row (inc row) (WS) P3[4:5], p into front and back of next st – called *inc 1* –, *p4, inc 1 into next st*, rep from * to * 22[23:24] times more, p3[4:5]. 146[154:162] sts.
Change to larger needles, and beg with chart row 1, foll pattern chart, rep 48-row repeat, until back measures 28[29:30.5]cm/ 11[11½:12]in from cast-on edge, ending with a WS row.

Armhole shaping

Keeping patt correct throughout, dec one st at each end of next row and then every foll alt row 7 times in all. 132[140:148] sts.***
Work without shaping, until back measures 42[44:46]cm/16½[17¼:18]in from cast-on edge, ending with a WS row.

Neck shaping

Next row (RS) Work first 60[64:68] sts in patt, then turn leaving rem sts on a spare needle.
Working on first side of neck only, *cast (bind) off 2 sts at beg of next row (neck edge), then dec one st at neck edge on next row*, rep from * to * 9 times more. 30[34:38] sts.
Work without shaping until back measures 49[51:53]cm/19¼[20:20¾]in from cast-on edge, ending with a WS row.
Cast (bind) off.
Return to rem sts and with RS facing, slip centre 12 sts onto a st holder, rejoin yarn to rem sts and work in patt to end of row.
Complete 2nd side of neck to match first side, reversing shaping.

FRONT

Work as for back to ***.
Work without shaping, until front measures 39[41:43]cm/15¼[16:16¾]in from cast-on edge, ending with a WS row.

Neck shaping

Next row (RS) Work first 59[63:67] sts in patt, then turn leaving rem sts on a spare needle.
Working on first side of neck only, *cast (bind) off 2 sts at beg of next row (neck edge), then dec one st at neck edge on next row*, rep from * to * twice more.
Dec one st at neck edge on every foll row 20 times more. 30[34:38] sts.
Work without shaping until there are same number of rows as back to shoulder, so ending with a WS row.
Cast (bind) off.
Return to rem sts and with RS facing, slip centre 14 sts onto a st holder, rejoin yarn to rem sts and work in patt to end of row.
Complete 2nd side of neck to match first side, reversing shaping.

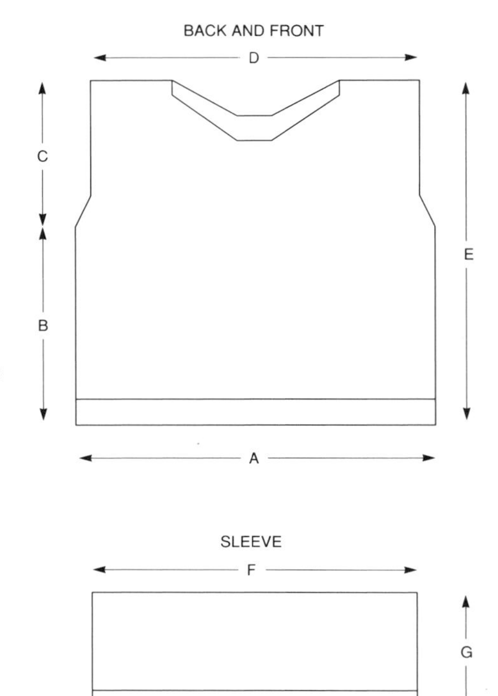

KEY
A = 50.5[53:56]cm (20[21¼:22¼]in)
B = 28[29:30.5]cm (11[11½:12]in)
C = 21[22:22.5]cm (8¼[8½:8¾]in)
D = 45.5[48.5:51]cm (18¼[19½:20½]in)
E = 49[51:53]cm (19¼[20:20¾]in)
F = 43.5[45:46]cm (17½[18:18½]in)
G = 18.5cm (7¼in)

SLEEVES

Using smaller needles and A, cast on 108[108:115] sts.
Work 2cm/¾in in cable and eyelet rib as for back, ending with a RS row.
Inc 18[22:19] sts evenly across next row as foll:
Next row (inc row) (WS) P2[1:3], inc 1 into next st, *p5[4:5], inc 1 into next st*, rep from * to * 16[20:17] times more, p3[1:3]. 126[130:134] sts.
Change to larger needles, and beg with chart row 1, foll pattern chart, rep 48-row repeat, until sleeve measures 18.5cm/7¼in from cast-on edge, ending with a WS row.
Cast (bind) off.
Make 2nd sleeve in same way.

NECKBAND

Press back, front and sleeve pieces lightly on WS with a warm iron over a damp cloth, omitting ribbing and cables.
Join shoulder seams using a small neat backstitch on edge of work.
Using set of 4 double-pointed needles (or circular needle) and A and with RS of front facing, beg at left shoulder and pick up and k49 sts down left front neck, k14 sts from centre front neck st holder, pick up and k49 sts up right front neck, 40 sts down right back neck, k12 sts from centre back neck st holder and pick up and k39 sts up left back neck. 203 sts.
Working in rounds (RS always facing), beg cable and eyelet rib as foll:
Rib round 1 *K4, p3, rep from * to end.
Rib round 2 *K4, p2tog, yarn over top of RH needle and to front again between 2 needles to make a

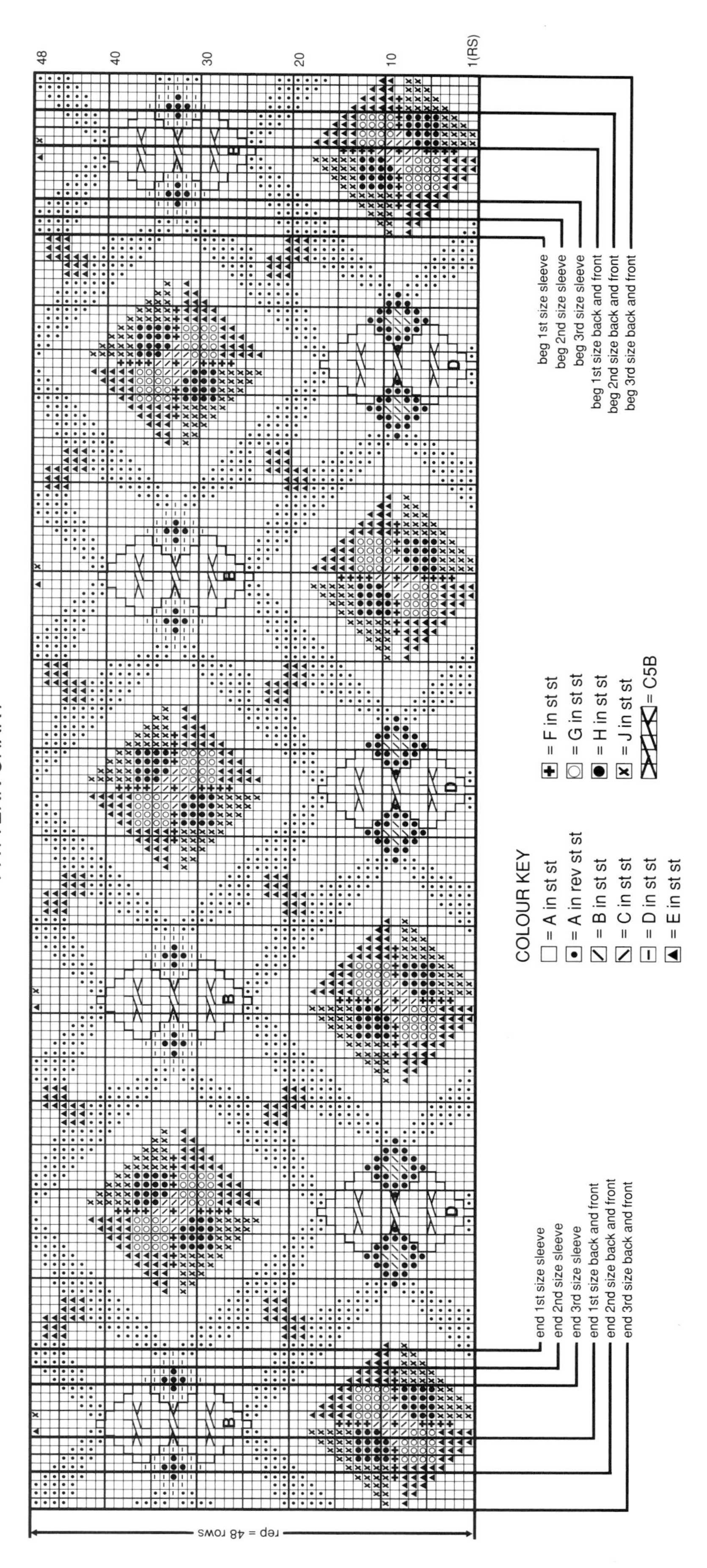

new st – called *yarn over* or *yo* –, p1, rep from * to end.

Rib round 3 *C4B, p3, rep from * to end.

Rib round 4 As round 2.

Rib round 5 As round 1.

Rib round 6 As round 2.

Rep last 6 rounds of cable and eyelet rib pattern until ribbing measures 2cm/¾in from cast-on edge.

Cast (bind) off firmly in patt (as for round 1).

FINISHING

Join seams using a small neat backstitch on very edge of work, except for ribbing where an overstitch (overcast st) should be used.

Placing centre of top of sleeve at shoulder seam, sew cast (bound) off edge of sleeves to armhole edge (including decreased edge).

Join side and sleeve seams.

Press seams lightly on WS.

Newton

I borrowed this design from an old Navajo rug, adding the vertical lines of the cables to bring the eye down and away from the horizontal bands. I feel this gives the sweater a better balance and also offers an opportunity for me to include some stitch interest.

SIZES

To fit 96–106[112–122]cm/ 38–42[44–48]in chest

Figures for larger size are given in brackets [ ]; where there is only one set of figures, it applies to both sizes.

See diagram for finished knitted measurements.

MATERIALS

Rowan *Handknit DK Cotton* 50g/1¾oz balls as foll:

A (no.251: ecru) 18[20] balls

B (no.264: sky blue) 4 balls

C (no.257: bathstone) 2 balls

One pair each of 3mm (US size 3) and 4mm (US size 6) knitting needles

Cable needle (cn)

ALTERNATIVE COLOURWAY

This sweater can also be worked in the colourway shown on the right, where:

A = no.253: tope

B = no.297: nut

C = no.279: bayou

TENSION (GAUGE)

21 sts and 28 rows to 10cm/4in measured over st st worked on 4mm (US size 6) needles

Please check your tension (gauge) carefully and change knitting needle size if necessary

NOTES

When working the colourwork triangle motifs and the zigzags, use the intarsia method, using a separate length of yarn for each isolated area of colour and twisting yarns together at WS when changing colours to avoid making a hole.

Read chart from right to left for the RS (odd-numbered) rows and from left to right for the WS (even-numbered) rows.

BACK

Using smaller needles and A, cast on 120[128] sts and beg bicolour k2, p2 rib as foll:

Rib row 1 (RS) *Using B k2, using A p2, rep from * to end.

Rib row 2 *Using A k2, using B p2, rep from * to end.

Rep last 2 rib rows until ribbing measures 8cm/3in from cast-on edge, ending with a RS row.

Keeping rib patt and colours correct as set, inc 18[20] sts evenly across next row as foll:

Next row (inc row) (WS) Rib 1, (work into front and back of next st – called *inc 1* –, rib 2) once [twice], rib 5, inc 1 into next st, (rib 7, inc 1 into next st) twice, *(rib 3, inc 1 into next st) twice, (rib 7, inc 1 into next st) 3 times*, rep from * to * once more, (rib 3, inc 1 into next st) twice, (rib 7, inc 1 into next st) 2[3] times, rib 6[2]. 138[148] sts.

Change to larger needles, and beg with chart row 1 of pattern chart (on page 131) as foll:

Chart row 1 (RS) Using A k27[32], (p2, k8, p2, k24) twice, p2, k8, p2, k27[32].

Chart row 2 Using A p27[32], (k2, p8, k2, p24) twice, k2, p8, k2, p27[32].

Chart row 3 Using A k9[14], *using C k12, using A k6, p2, k8, p2, k6*, rep from * to * twice more, using C k12, using A k9[14].

Chart row 4 Using A p9[14], *using C p12, using A p6, k2, p8, k2, p6*, rep from * to * twice more, using C p12, using A p9[14].

Chart row 5 Using A k10[15], *using C k10, using A k7, p2, then for cable sl next 2 sts onto a cn and hold at back of work, k2, then k2 from cn – called *cable 4 right* or *C4R* –, sl next 2 sts onto a cn and hold at front of work, k2, then k2 from cn – called *cable 4 left* or *C4L* –, p2, k7*, rep from * to * twice more, using C k10, using A k10[15].

Beg with chart row 6, cont foll chart until chart row 38 has been completed, so ending with a WS row.

Rep chart rows 1–38 for patt throughout, cont in patt until back measures 44.5[46]cm/17½[18]in from cast-on edge, ending with a WS row.

Armhole shaping

Keeping patt correct throughout, beg armhole shaping as foll:

Next row (dec row) (RS) K2, sl 1-k1-psso, work in patt to last 4 sts, k2tog, k2.

Work one row without shaping. Rep dec row once.

Rep from ** to ** 7[9] times more. 120[126] sts.

Cont in patt as set without shaping until back measures 65.5[68.5]cm/25¾[26¾]in from cast-on edge, ending with a WS row.

Neck shaping

Next row (RS) Work first 47[49] sts in patt, then turn leaving rem sts on a spare needle.

Working on first side of neck only, dec one st at beg of next row (neck edge), then at neck edge on every foll row 12 times in all.

Using A only, cast (bind) off rem 35[37] sts.

Return to rem sts and with RS facing, slip centre 26[28] sts onto a st holder, rejoin yarn to rem sts and work in patt to end of row.

Complete 2nd side of neck to match first side, reversing shaping.

FRONT

Work front as for back.

SLEEVES

Using smaller needles and A, cast on 48 sts.

Work 9cm/3½in in bicolour k2, p2 rib as for back, ending with a WS row and inc one st at each end of last row. 50 sts.

Change to larger needles and beg with 7th chart row (as indicated on patt chart), foll chart for patt throughout (beg again with row 1 after row 38 has been completed) *and at the same time* shape sleeve by inc one st at each end of 3rd row and then at each end of every foll 3rd row 15[23] times in all, then every foll 4th row 19[13] times, working all inc sts into patt foll chart. 118[122] sts.

Work in patt without shaping until sleeve measures 58.5cm/23in from cast-on edge, or desired length, ending with a WS row.

Using A only, cast (bind) off all sts.

Make 2nd sleeve in same way as given for first sleeve.

NECKBAND

Press pieces lightly on WS with a warm iron, omitting ribbing and cables.

Using smaller needles and A and with RS of front facing, beg at left shoulder and pick up and k20 sts down left front neck, k26[28] sts from centre neck st holder and pick up and k20 st up right front neck. 66[68] sts.

Beg bicolour k2, p2 rib as foll:

Rib row 1 (WS) Using A k2[1], *using B p2, using A k2, rep from * to last 4[3] sts, using B p2, using A k2[1].

Rib row 2 Using A p2[1], *using B k2, using A p2, rep from * to last 4[3] sts, using B k2, using A p2[1].

Rep last 2 rib rows until ribbing measures 6.5cm/2½in, ending with a WS row.

Using A only, cast (bind) off.

Work neckband ribbing along back neck edge in same way as given for front neckband.

FINISHING

Using smaller needles and A, with WS of back and front tog and with RS of front facing, pick up and k one st for each cast (bound) off st along left shoulder and 3 sts for

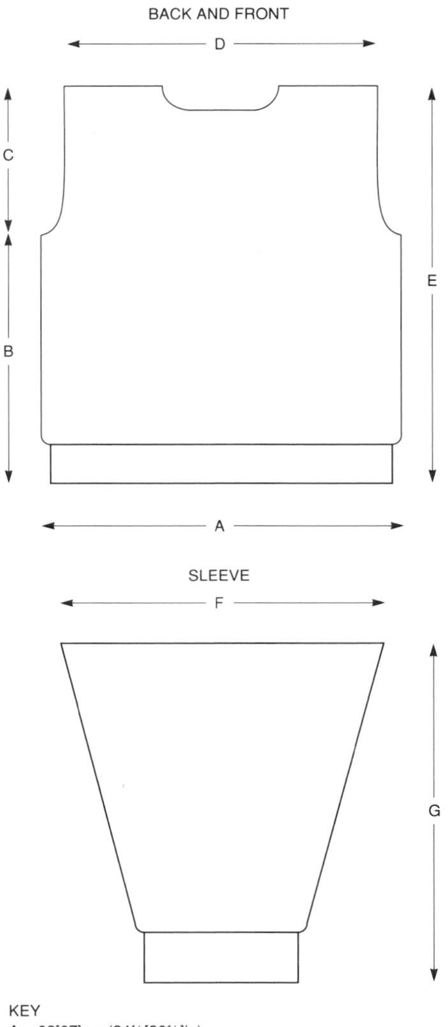

KEY

A = 62[67]cm (24½[26½]in)
B = 44.5[46]cm (17½[18]in)
C = 25.5[27]cm (10[10½]in)
D = 53.5[56.5]cm (21[22¼]in)
E = 70[73]cm (27½[28½]in)
F = 52.5[54.5]cm (20¾[21¾]in)
G = 58.5cm (23in)

every 4 rows of sides of neckband, working through both layers of knitting with each st and casting (binding) off as you knit each time there are 2 sts on needle.

Using smaller needles and A, work right shoulder seam in same way and with RS of front facing while seam is worked.

Placing centre of top of sleeve at shoulder seam, sew cast (bound) off edge of sleeves to armhole edge (including decreased edge).

Join side and sleeve seams, using a small neat backstitch on very edge of work for long seams and a slip stitch for ribbings.

PATTERN CHART

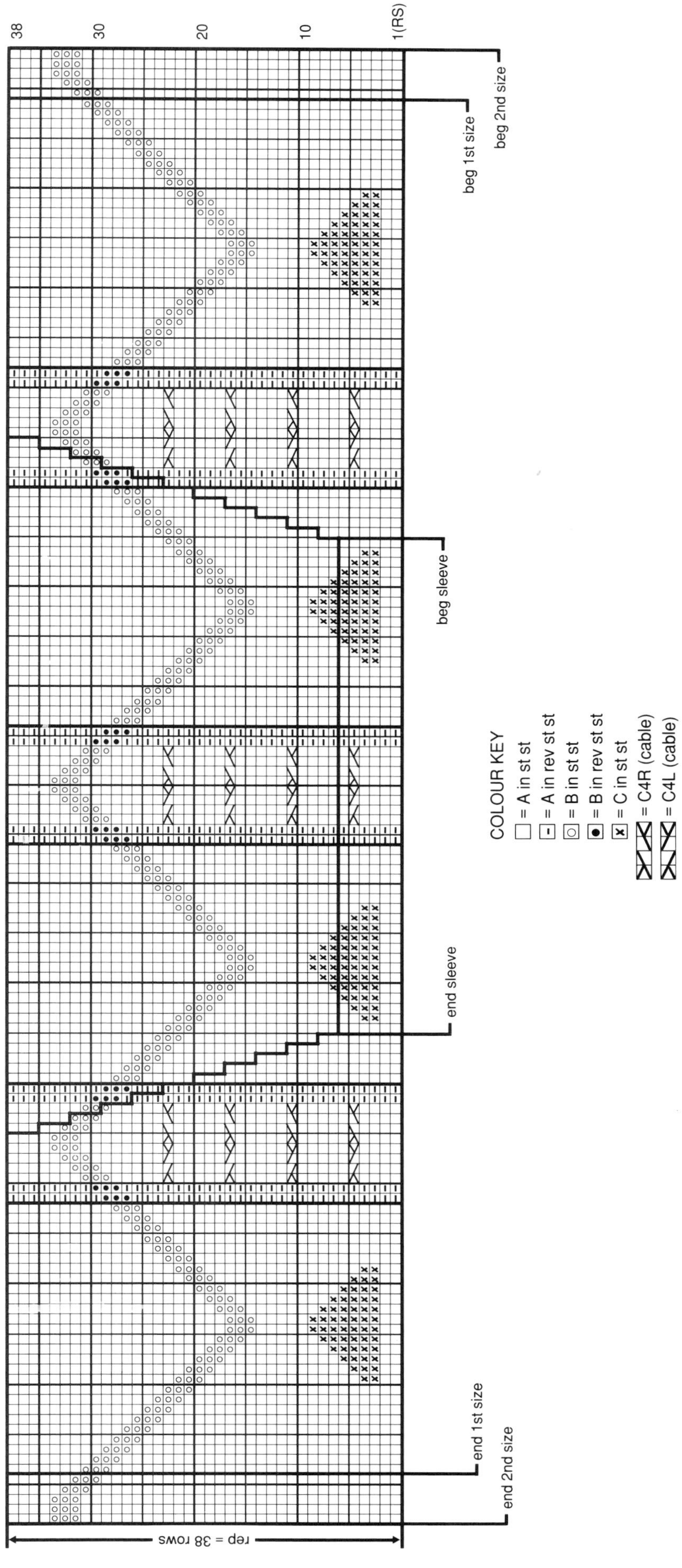

38

30

20

10

1(RS)

rep = 38 rows

end 2nd size

end 1st size

end sleeve

beg sleeve

beg 1st size

beg 2nd size

COLOUR KEY

- ☐ = A in st st
- ⊟ = A in rev st st
- ⊙ = B in st st
- ● = B in rev st st
- ☒ = C in st st
- = C4R (cable)
- = C4L (cable)

CREEPY-CRAWLY

I CAME ACROSS THIS DESIGN ON AN OLD SILK TEXTILE IN THE VICTORIA AND ALBERT MUSEUM. I IMMEDIATELY KNEW THAT I HAD TO MAKE IT INTO A SWEATER AND SET ABOUT IT ON THE TUBE HOME. USING LOTS OF LICENCE, I CHANGED THE COLOURS AND PLAYED AROUND WITH THE FRUITS, AND THEN ADDED MY OWN LEAF BORDER AT THE HEM TO FEED THE CREEPY-CRAWLIES.

SIZE

One size only to fit 10–12 yrs or 71–76cm/28–30in chest

See diagram for finished knitted measurements.

MATERIALS

Rowan *Nice Cotton* 50g/1¾oz balls as foll:

A (no.438: swimming pool) 8 balls
B (no.440: lilac wine) 2 balls
C (no.432: carnival) 1 ball
D (no.435: samba) 1 ball
E (no.445: blood orange) 1 ball
F (no.436: mardi gras) 1 ball
G (no.443: kiwi) 1 ball
H (no.430: parade) 1 ball
I (no.437: fiesta) 1 ball
J (no.444: banana) 1 ball
L (no.431: rio) 1 ball

Rowan *Cotton Glacé* 50g/1¾oz ball as foll:

M (no.737: spice) 1 ball

One pair each of 3mm (US size 2) and 3¼mm (US size 3) knitting needles

ALTERNATIVE COLOURWAY

This sweater can also be worked in the colourway shown on the right, where:

A = *Nice Cotton* no.432: carnival
B = *Nice Cotton* no.440: lilac wine
C = *Nice Cotton* no.443: kiwi
D = *Nice Cotton* no.436: mardi gras
E = *Cotton Glacé* no.737: spice
F = *Nice Cotton* no.438: swim. pool
G = *Nice Cotton* no.430: parade
H = *Nice Cotton* no.434: adobe
I = *Nice Cotton* no.437: fiesta
J = *Nice Cotton* no.444: banana
L = *Nice Cotton* no.431: rio
M = *Nice Cotton* no.435: samba

TENSION (GAUGE)

27 sts and 31 rows to 10cm/4in measured over main colourwork pattern st st worked on 3¼mm (US size 3) needles

PLEASE CHECK YOUR TENSION (GAUGE) CAREFULLY AND CHANGE KNITTING NEEDLE SIZE IF NECESSARY

NOTES

When working the colourwork pattern, use the intarsia method for all colours except A, using a separate length of yarn for each isolated area of colour and twisting yarns together when changing colours to avoid making a hole.

Carry main colour (A) loosely across back of row on chart rows 14–149, twisting it around working yarn every few sts when it is not in use to avoid long loose strands at the back of the work.

Read chart from right to left for the RS (odd-numbered) rows and from left to right for the WS (even-numbered) rows.

BACK

Using larger needles and A, cast on 130 sts.
P one row.
Beg with a k row, work in st st foll chart for back from row 1, until chart row 84 has been completed, so ending with a WS row.

Armhole shaping

Cont in st st foll chart throughout, cast (bind) off 8 sts at beg of next 2 rows. 114 sts.
Work without shaping until chart row 146 has been completed, so ending with a WS row.

Neck shaping

Chart row 147 (RS) Work first 42 sts in patt, turn leaving rem sts on a spare needle.
Working first side of neck only, dec one st at beg of next row (neck edge), then at neck edge on foll row, so ending with a RS row.
Cast (bind) off rem 40 sts.
Return to rem sts and with RS facing, cast (bind) off centre 30 sts, work in patt to end of row.
Complete 2nd side of neck as for first side, reversing shaping.

FRONT

Work as for back until chart row 106 has been completed, so ending with a WS row.

V-neck shaping

Chart row 107 (RS) Work first 55 sts in patt, k2tog, turn leaving rem sts on a spare needle. 56 sts.

Working first side of neck only, work one row without shaping.

Dec one st at end of next row (neck edge) and at neck edge on every foll alt row 13 times in all, then on every foll 3rd row 3 times. 40 sts.

Work without shaping until chart row 149 has been completed.

Cast (bind) off.

Return to rem sts and with RS facing, rejoin yarn to rem sts, k2tog and work in patt to end of row. 56 sts.

Complete 2nd side of neck as for first side, reversing shaping.

SLEEVES

Using smaller needles and A, cast on 44 sts.

Work 2.5cm/1in in garter st (k every row).

Change to larger needles and beg with a k row, work in st st foll chart for sleeve from row 1, inc one st at each end of 3rd row and every foll alt row 27 times in all (98 sts), then every foll 3rd row 8 times. 114 sts.

Work without shaping until chart row 98 has been completed, so ending with a WS row.

Cast (bind) off all sts.

Make 2nd sleeve in same way.

COLLAR

Press pieces lightly on WS with a warm iron over a damp cloth, omitting garter st.

Join shoulder seams, using a small backstitch on very edge of work.

Using smaller needles and A, cast on 9 sts and knit one row.

Beg collar patt as foll:

Row 1 K6, k into front and back of next st – called *inc 1* –, k2.

Row 2 K1, inc 1 into next st, k8.

Row 3 K8, inc 1 into next st, k2.

Row 4 K1, inc 1 into next st, k10.

Row 5 K10, inc 1 into next st, k2.

Row 6 K1, inc 1 into next st, k12.

Row 7 K12, inc 1 into next st, k2.

Row 8 K1, inc 1 into next st, k14.

Row 9 K14, k2tog, k1.

Row 10 K1, k2tog tbl, k13.

Row 11 K12, k2tog, k1.

Row 12 K1, k2tog tbl, k11.

Row 13 K10, k2tog, k1.

Row 14 K1, k2tog tbl, k9.

Row 15 K8, k2tog, k1.

Row 16 K1, k2tog tbl, k7. 9 sts.

Rep rows 1–16 to form collar patt.

Cont in patt until collar fits from centre front neck around neckline and back to centre front, ending with a 16th patt row.

Cast (bind) off.

FINISHING

Join seams using a small neat backstitch, except for cuffs and collar where an invisible overstitch (overcast st) should be used.

Placing centre of top of sleeve at shoulder seam, sew cast (bound) off edge of sleeves to vertical armhole edge and sew cast (bound) off edge of armhole to side of sleeve.

Join side and sleeve seams.

Press seams lightly on WS.

Sew straight edge of collar to neck edge, beg and ending collar at centre front and leaving cast on and cast (bound) off edges of collar open to form collar points.

FRONT AND BACK BORDER

Using smaller needles and A, cast on 8 sts and beg leaf border patt as foll:

Row 1 (RS) K5, yarn to front of work between 2 needles, then over top of RH needle to back of work to make a new st – called *yarn over* or *yo* –, k1, yo, k2.

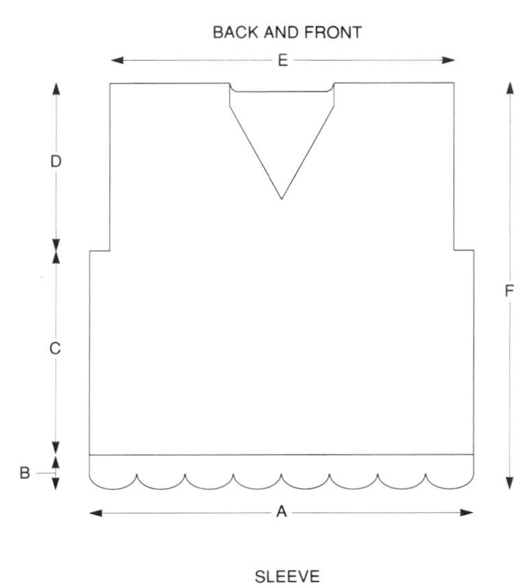

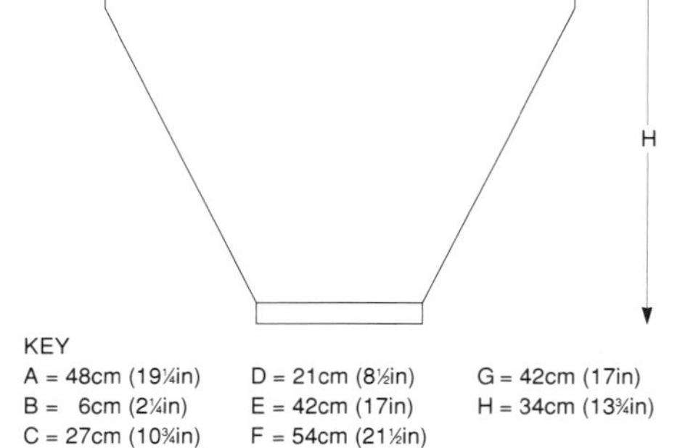

Row 2 P6, inc 1 into next st, k3.

Row 3 K4, p1, k2, yo, k1, yo, k3.

Row 4 P8, inc 1 into next st, k4.

Row 5 K4, p2, k3, yo, k1, yo, k4.

Row 6 P10, inc 1 into next st, k5.

Row 7 K4, p3, k4, yo, k1, yo, k5.

Row 8 P12, inc 1 into next st, k6.

Row 9 K4, p4, yarn to back of work between 2 needles – called *yarn back* or *yb* –, sl 1-k1-psso, k7, k2tog, k1.

Row 10 P10, inc 1 into next st, k7.

Row 11 K4, p5, yb, sl 1–k1-psso, k5, k2tog, k1.

Row 12 P8, inc 1 into next st, k2, p1, k5.

Row 13 K4, p1, k1, p4, yb, sl 1-k1-psso, k3, k2tog, k1.

Row 14 P6, inc 1 into next st, k3, p1, k5.

Row 15 K4, p1, k1, p5, yb, sl 1-k1-psso, k1, k2tog, k1.

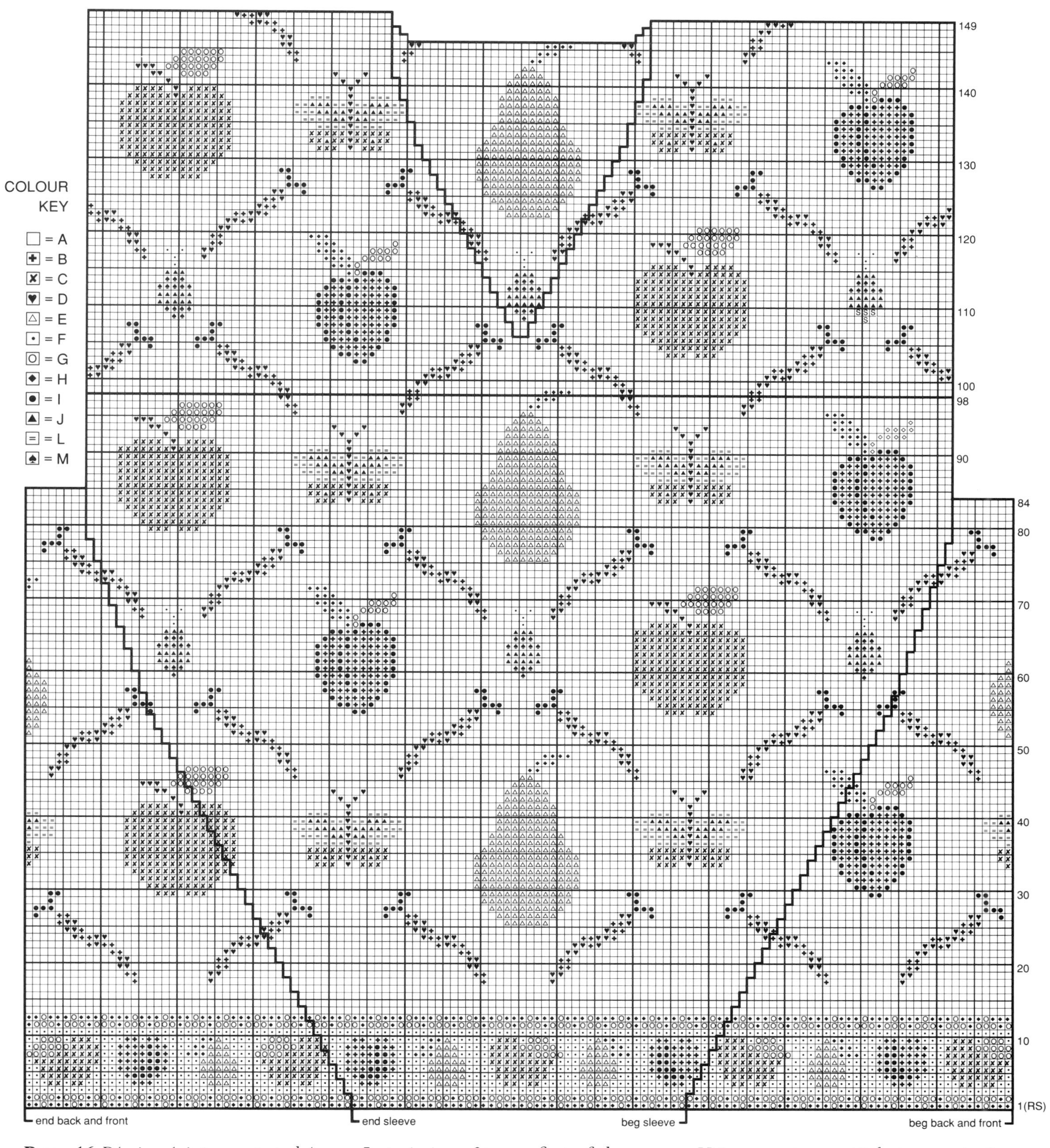

Row 16 P4, inc 1 into next st, k4, p1, k5.
Row 17 K4, p1, k1, p6, yb, sl 1-k2tog-psso, k1.
Row 18 P2tog, cast (bind) off first 5 sts (using p2tog as first of these sts), k1, p1, k5. 8 sts.
Rep rows 1–18 until border fits around lower edge of front and back, ending with an 18th patt row.

Using a neat overstitch (overcast st), sew straight edge of front and back border to lower edge of sweater, beg and ending at left side seam. Join ends of border tog.

Samhain

For many years now I have admired the weavings of the Ewe people of West Africa. I adore their sumptuous use of vibrant gold and red silks, and I wanted to explore and develop this in the jacket here. This design would also make a beautiful pullover – just use the shape given in the Cairngorm pattern.

SIZES

To fit 96–106[112–117]cm/ 38–42[44–46]in chest

Figures for larger size are given in brackets [ ]; where there is only one set of figures, it applies to both sizes.

See diagram for finished knitted measurements.

MATERIALS

Rowan *Rowanspun Tweed* 100g/3½oz hanks as foll:

A (no.759: cedar) 3[3] hanks

B (no.752: tea) 3[3] hanks

C (no.756: one a.m.) 1[2] hanks

Rowan *Lightweight DK* 25g/1oz hanks as foll:

D (no.9: old gold) 7[8] hanks

Rowan *Magpie* 100g/3½oz hanks as foll:

E (no.503: Comanche) 1[1] hank

F (no.505: ginger) 2[2] hanks

One pair each of 3¼mm (US size 3) and 4½mm (US size 7) knitting needles

Five [six] 2.5cm/1in buttons

ALTERNATIVE COLOURWAY

This jacket can also be worked in the colourway shown on the right, where:

A = *Rowanspun Tweed* no.752: tea

B = *Rowanspun Tweed* no.753: cranberry

C = *Magpie* no.505: ginger

D = *Designer DK* no.673: red

E = *Magpie* no.675: butter

F = *Magpie* no.503: Comanche

TENSION (GAUGE)

19 sts and 28 rows to 10cm/4in measured over patt worked on 4½mm (US size 7) needles

Please check your tension (gauge) carefully and change knitting needle size if necessary

NOTES

When working the colourwork pattern, use the intarsia method, using a separate length of yarn for each isolated area of colour and twisting yarns together when changing colours to avoid making a hole.

Read charts from right to left for the RS (odd-numbered) rows and from left to right for the WS (even-numbered) rows.

BACK

Using smaller needles and B, cast on

116[128] sts and beg moss (seed) st as foll:

Row 1 (RS) Using B, *k1, p1, rep from * to end.

Row 2 Using B, *p1, k1, rep from * to end.

Row 3 Using A, as row 1.

Row 4 Using A, as row 2.

Rep last 4 rows once more, so ending with a WS row.

Change to larger needles and beg foll back patt chart as foll:

Chart row 1 (RS) Work first 0[6] sts of chart before patt repeat begins as indicated on chart, rep 58-st repeat twice, work last 0[6] sts of chart as indicated.

Cont foll chart for patt and rep 78-row repeat throughout, until back measures 36.5[39]cm/14½[15½]in from cast-on edge, ending with a WS row.

Armhole shaping

Keeping patt correct throughout, beg armhole shaping as foll:

Next row (dec row) (RS) Work 2 sts in patt, sl 1-k1-psso, work in patt to last 4 sts, k2tog, work 2 sts in patt.

Work one row without shaping. Rep dec row once.

Rep from ** to ** 6 times more. 100[112] sts.

Work without shaping until back measures 62[66]cm/24½[26]in from cast-on edge, ending with a WS row.

Neck shaping

Next row (RS) Work first 38[44] sts in patt, turn leaving rem sts on a spare needle.

Working first side of neck only, dec one st at beg of next row (neck

edge), then at neck edge on every foll row 3 times in all.
Cast (bind) off rem 35[41] sts in patt.
Return to rem sts and with RS facing, slip centre 24 sts onto a st holder, rejoin yarn to rem sts and work in patt to end of row.
Complete 2nd side of neck to match first side, reversing shaping.

LEFT FRONT

Before beg front, work pocket lining.

Pocket lining

Using larger needles and B, cast on 22 sts.
Beg with a k row, work in st st until lining measures 13.5cm/5¼in from cast-on edge, ending with a WS row.
Break off yarn and slip sts onto a st holder.

Begin front

Using smaller needles and B, cast on 62[68] sts and beg moss (seed) st as foll:
Row 1 (RS) Using B, *k1, p1, rep from * to end.
Row 2 Using B, k2tog (centre front edge), *p1, k1, rep from * to end.
Row 3 Using A, *k1, p1, rep from * to last st, k1.
Row 4 Using A, p2tog (centre front edge), *k1, p1, rep from * to last st, k1.
Rep last 4 rows once more, so ending with a WS row. 58[64] sts.
Change to larger needles and beg foll front patt chart as foll:
Chart row 1 (RS) Work first 0[6] sts of chart before patt repeat begins as indicated on chart, work 58-st repeat once.
Cont foll chart for patt and rep 78-row repeat throughout, until chart row 38 has been completed, so ending with a WS row.

Insert pocket lining

Chart row 39 (RS) Work first 18[21] sts in patt, slip next 22 sts onto a st holder, then with RS of pocket lining facing work in patt across 22 sts of pocket lining, work rem 18[21] sts in patt.
Cont in patt until there are same number of rows as back to armhole, ending with a WS row.

Armhole shaping

Keeping patt correct throughout, beg armhole shaping as foll:
Next row (dec row) (RS) Work 2 sts in patt, sl 1-k1-psso, work in patt to end.
**Work one row without shaping.
Rep dec row once.**
Rep from ** to ** 6 times more. 50[56] sts.
Work without shaping until back measures 56[59.5]cm/22[23½]in from cast-on edge, ending with RS row.

Neck shaping

Cast (bind) off 8 sts at beg of next row.
Work one row without shaping.
Dec one st at neck edge on next row and every foll alt row 7 times in all. 35[41] sts.
Work without shaping until there are same number of rows as back to shoulder, ending with a WS row.
Cast (bind) off all sts in patt.

RIGHT FRONT

Work as for left front, but foll chart for right front and reversing all shaping and position of pocket.

SLEEVES

Using smaller needles and B, cast on 50 sts and work 8 rows in moss (seed) st as for back and working in same colours as for back, so ending with a WS row.
Change to larger needles and beg

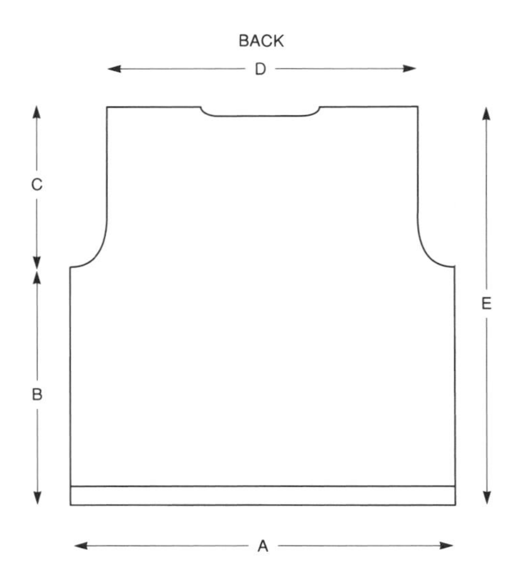

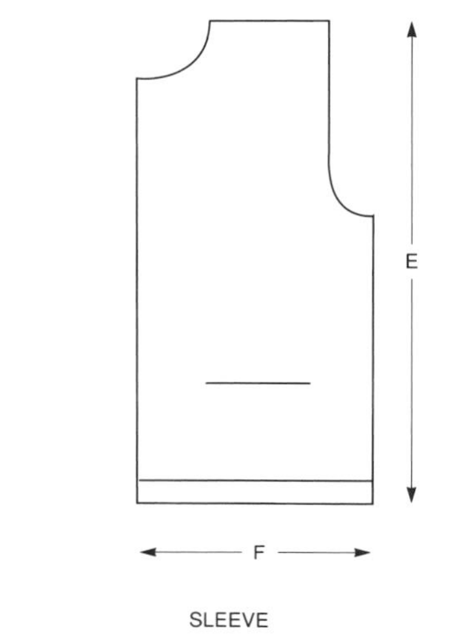

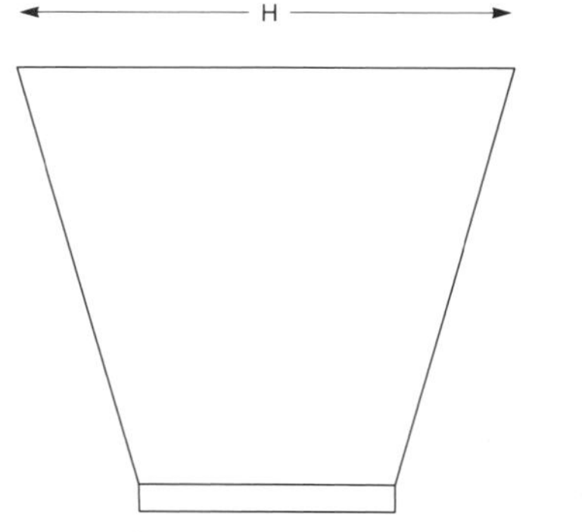

KEY
A = 61[67]cm (24½[27]in)
B = 36.5[39]cm (14½[15½]in)
C = 26.5[28]cm (10½[11]in)
D = 53[59]cm (21[23½]in)
E = 63[67]cm (25[26½]in)
F = 30.5[34]cm (12¼[13½]in)
G = 26.5[29.5]cm (10½[11¾]in)
H = 54[56]cm (21½[22½]in)
I = 51[52]cm (20[20½]in)

foll sleeve patt chart as foll:
Chart row 1 (RS) Skip first 4 sts of chart as indicated on chart, then work next 50 sts, omitting last 4 sts.

BACK AND FRONTS PATTERN

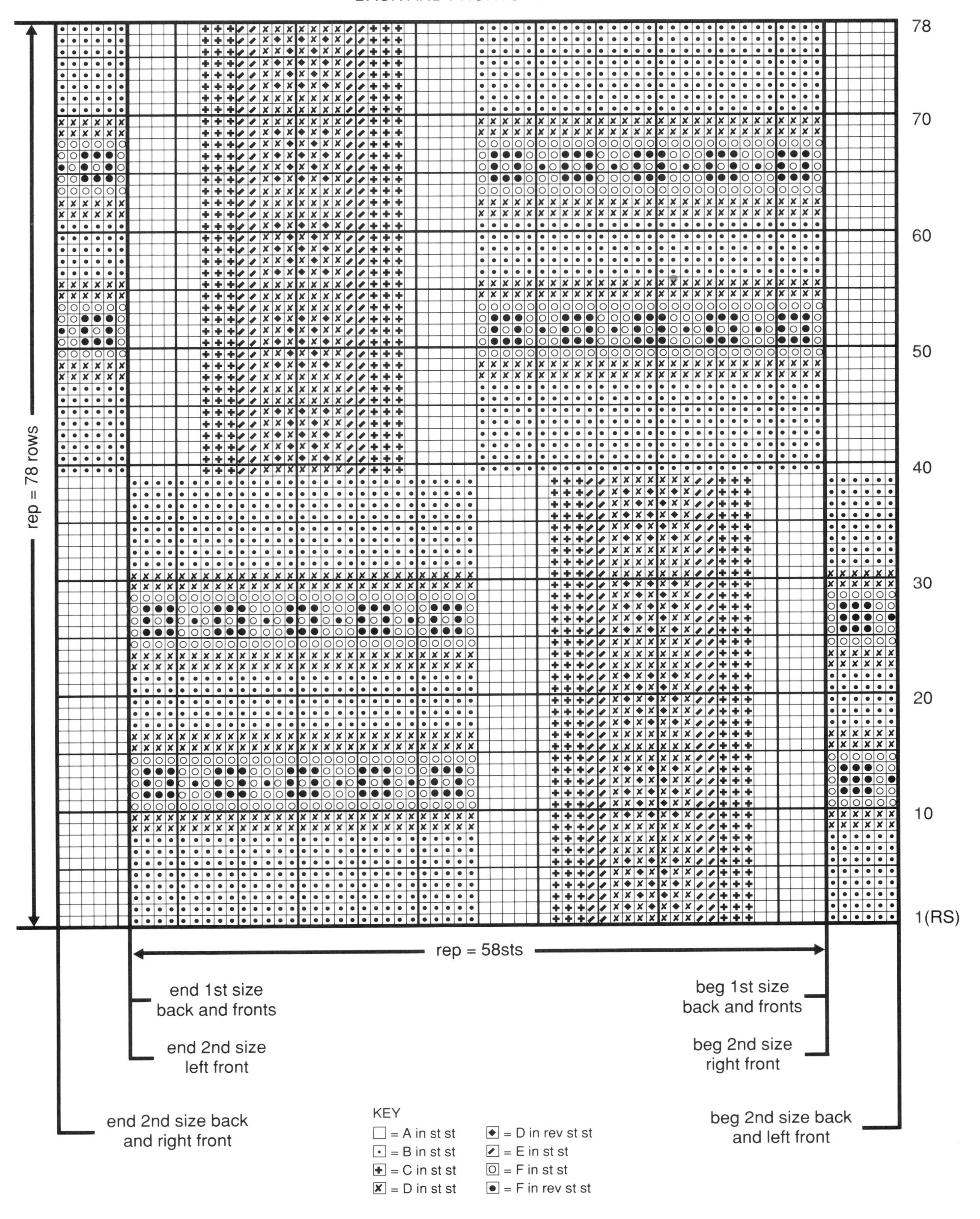

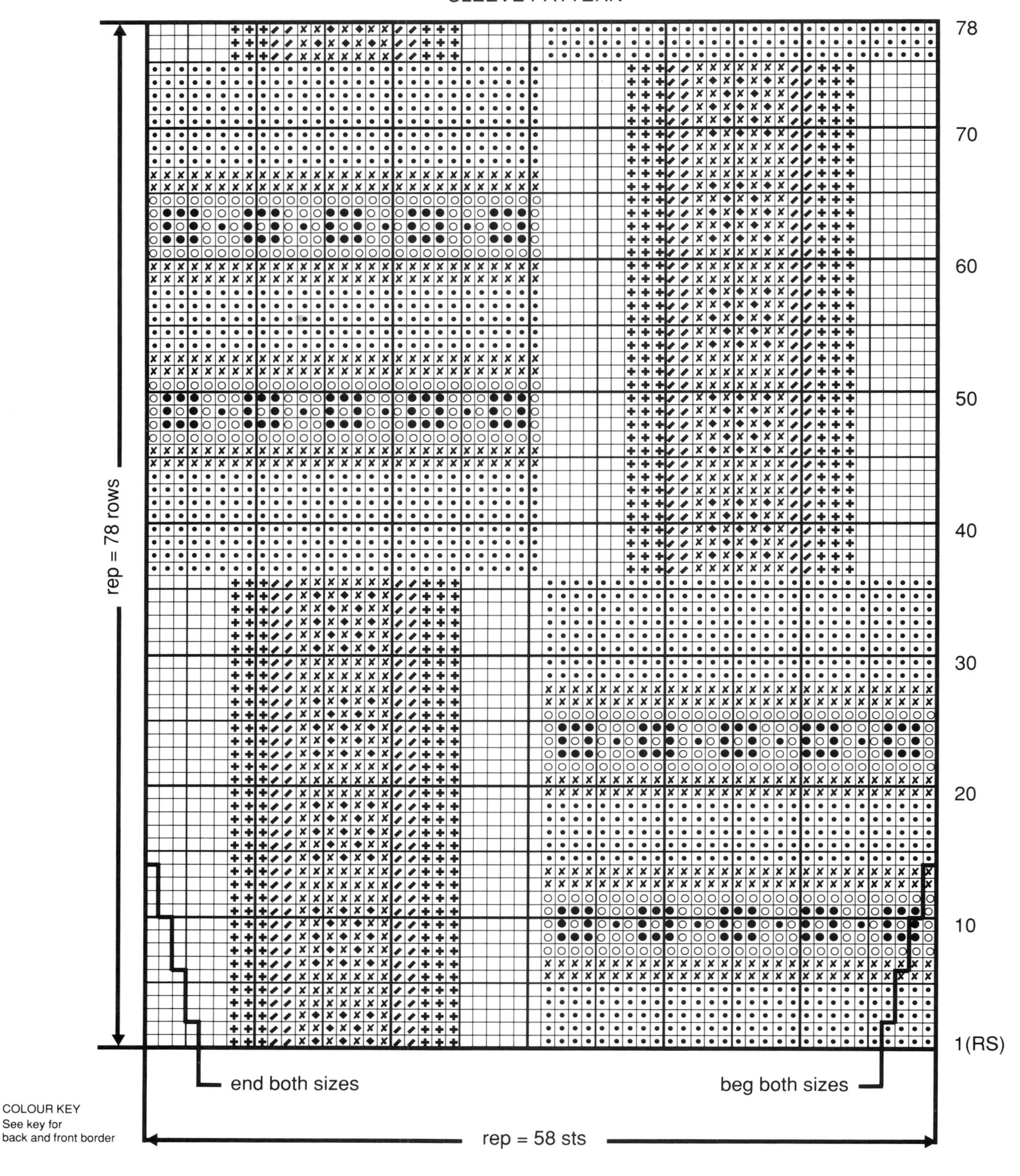

Cont foll chart for patt and rep 78-row repeat throughout *and at the same time* shape sleeve by inc one st at each end of 3rd row and then at each end of every foll 4th row 10[16] times in all, then every foll 5th row 16[12] times, working added sts into patt as set.
102[106] sts.
Work in patt without shaping until sleeve measures 51[52]cm/20[20½]in from cast-on edge, ending with a WS row.
Cast (bind) off all sts in patt.
Make 2nd sleeve in same way.

BUTTON BAND

Press pieces lightly on WS with a warm iron over a damp cloth, omitting moss (seed) st.

Using smaller needles and B and with RS facing, pick up and k94[102] sts evenly up right front from cast-on edge to neck shaping.

Beg moss (seed) st as foll:

Row 1 (WS) Using B, *k1, p1, rep from * to last 2 sts, k1, p into front and back of last st.

Row 2 Using B, *k1, p1, rep from * to last st, k1.

Row 3 Using A, *k1, p1, rep from * to last st, k into front and back of last st.

Row 4 Using A, *p1, k1, rep from * to end.

Rep last 4 rows once more, so ending with a RS row.

Cast (bind) off all 98[106] sts.

Mark positions for 5[6] buttonholes, the first to beg 2.5cm/1in from lower edge, the last to come 1.5cm/½in above neck shaping (to be worked horizontally in neckband) and the rem 3[4] evenly spaced between, with each buttonhole to be worked over 3 sts.

BUTTONHOLE BAND

Using smaller needles and B and with RS facing, pick up and k94[102] sts evenly down left front from neck shaping to cast-on edge.

Beg moss (seed) st as foll:

Row 1 (WS) Using B, k into front and back of first st, *p1, k1, rep from * to last st, p1.

Row 2 Using B, *p1, k1, rep from * to last st, p1.

Row 3 Using A, p into front and back of first st, *k1, p1, rep from * to end.

Row 4 Using A, *p1, k1, rep from * to end *and at the same time* cast (bind) off 3 sts when position of each buttonhole is reached.

Row 5 Using B, k into front and back of first st, *p1, k1, rep from * to last st, p1 *and at the same time* cast on 3 sts over those cast (bound) off in last row.

Rep rows 2–4 once more (omitting buttonholes), so ending with a RS row.

Cast (bind) off all 98[106] sts.

NECKBAND

Using smaller needles and B, with WS of back and left front tog and with RS of left front facing, pick up and k one st for each cast (bound) off st along shoulder, working through both layers with each st and casting (binding) off as you knit each time there are 2 sts on needle.

Work right shoulder seam in same way and with RS of right front facing while seam is worked.

Then using smaller needles and B and with RS facing, beg at centre front edge of right front neck edge, pick up and k25 sts evenly up right front neck, 3 sts down left back neck, k24 sts from back neck st holder, pick up and k3 sts up right back neck and 25 sts down left front neck. 80 sts.

Work 8 rows in moss (seed) st as for back and working in same colours as for back *and at the same time* on row 4 work buttonhole as foll:

Work to last 6 sts, then cast (bind) off 3 sts, work in patt to end; then in next row cast on 3 sts over those cast (bound) off in last row.

When 8th row of moss (seed) st has been completed, cast (bind) off in patt.

FINISHING

Placing centre of top of sleeve at shoulder seam, sew cast (bound) off edge of sleeves to armhole edge (including decreased edge).

Join side and sleeve seams, using a small neat overstitch (overcast st) on very edge of work.

Pocket hems

Using larger needles and with RS facing, p across 22 sts of left front pocket using matching colours. This forms foldline for hem.

Using B, beg with a p row work 4 rows in st st.

Cast (bind) off loosely.

Work hem at top of right front pocket in same way.

Turn pocket hems to WS of fronts and slip stitch in place.

Slip stitch pocket linings to WS of fronts.

Join front bands to lower edges of jacket using slip stitch.

Press seams lightly on WS.

Sew the buttons to the button band in positions corresponding to the buttonholes.

Tamlin

I FIRST KNITTED THIS SWEATER YEARS AGO FROM AN OLD 1940S PATTERN WHICH I ENLARGED ALL ROUND TO GIVE IT A MORE CONTEMPORARY LOOK. SINCE THEN IT HAS BECOME AN OLD FRIEND AND I'M JUST AS THRILLED WITH THIS CHENILLE VERSION AS I WAS WITH THE FIRST ONE. THERE HAVE BEEN MANY IN BETWEEN – IT'S SO EASY TO KNIT AND SUCH A DELIGHT TO WEAR, THIS IS ONE SWEATER I JUST COULDN'T BE WITHOUT.

SIZES

To fit 81–91[96–106]cm/
32–36[38–42]in bust

Figures for larger size are given in brackets [ ]; where there is only one set of figures, it applies to both sizes.

See diagram for finished knitted measurements.

MATERIALS

Rowan *Chunky Cotton Chenille* (no.375: aquamarine) 7[8] x 100g/3½oz balls

One pair each of 4mm (US size 6) and 5½mm (US size 9) knitting needles

Set of four 4mm (US size 6) double-pointed needles for collar

ALTERNATIVE COLOURWAY

This sweater can also be worked in the colour shown right, which is no.374: beech.

TENSION (GAUGE)

14 sts and 24 rows to 10cm/4in measured over st st worked on 5½mm (US size 9) needles

PLEASE CHECK YOUR TENSION (GAUGE) CAREFULLY AND CHANGE KNITTING NEEDLE SIZE IF NECESSARY

NOTE

Read charts from right to left for the RS (odd-numbered) rows and from left to right for the WS (even-numbered) rows.

BACK

Using smaller needles, cast on 64[72] sts and beg k2, p2 rib as foll:

Rib row 1 *K2, p2, rep from * to end.

Rep last row until ribbing measures 18cm/7in from cast-on edge, ending with a RS row.

Next row (inc row) Work in k2, p2 rib and, keeping patt correct, inc 12 sts evenly across row. 76[84] sts.

Change to larger needles and beg with a k row, work in st st without shaping until work measures 45cm/17½in from cast-on edge, ending with a p (WS) row.

Raglan armhole shaping

Beg raglan shaping and moss (seed) st yoke on next row as foll:

Raglan row 1 (RS) K1, sl 1-k1-psso, k34[38]; then to beg moss (seed) st yoke over next 2 sts (the 2 centre sts of the row), work k1, p1; k to last 3 sts, k2tog, k1.

Raglan row 2 (WS) P35[39]; then over next 4 sts, work (k1, p1) twice; p to end.

Beg with chart row 3 of chart for back (see *Note* above), cont raglan shaping and working moss (seed) st yoke as indicated until chart row 30[34] has been completed.

Raglan row 31[35] (RS) K1, sl 1-k1-psso, work in moss (seed) st as set to last 3 sts, k2tog, k1.

Raglan row 32[36] (WS) P2, work in moss (seed) st to last 2 sts, p2.

Foll chart, cont in moss (seed) st only, shaping raglan as set and purling first 2 and last 2 sts of every WS row, until chart row 58[64] has been completed.

Raglan row 59[65] (RS) K2, work in moss (seed) st to last 3 sts, k2.

Raglan row 60[66] (WS) P2, work in moss (seed) st to last 2 sts, p2.

Leave rem 18[20] sts on st holder for back neck.

FRONT

Work as for back until chart row 50[56] has been completed and 26[28] sts rem, so ending with a WS row.

Neck shaping

Raglan row 51[57] (RS) K1, sl 1-k1-psso, work 5 sts in moss (seed) st, slip next 10[12] sts onto st holder for centre front neck, join on a 2nd ball of yarn and work next 5 sts in moss (seed) st, k2tog, k1.

Keeping raglan shaping correct as set, complete neck shaping foll chart.

Note: For neck shaping dec by working k2tog over 2 neck edge sts on RS rows and p2tog on WS rows.

SLEEVES

Using smaller needles, cast on 26 sts and beg k2, p2 rib as foll:

Rib row 1 *K2, p2, rep from * to last 2 sts, k2.

Rib row 2 P2, *k2, p2, rep from * to end.

Rep last 2 rows until ribbing measures 10cm/4in from cast-on edge, ending with a RS row.

Next row (inc row) Work in k2, p2 rib as set and, keeping patt correct, inc 12 sts evenly across row. 38 sts.

Change to larger needles and beg with a k row, work 3 rows in st st without shaping.

Cont in st st, inc one st at each end of next row and then every foll 5th[4th] row 14[18] times more. 68[76] sts.

Work without shaping until work measures 45[46]cm/17½[18]in from cast-on edge, ending with a p (WS) row.

Raglan sleeve-top shaping

Beg raglan shaping on next row as foll:

Raglan row 1 (RS) K1, sl 1-k1-psso, k to last 3 sts, k2tog, k1.

Raglan row 2 (WS) P to end.

Raglan rows 3–6 Rep rows 1 and 2 twice more.

Raglan row 7 (RS) K1, sl 1-k1-psso, k27[31]; then to beg moss (seed) st yoke over next 2 sts (the 2 centre sts of the row), work k1, p1; k to last 3 sts, k2tog, k1.

Raglan row 8 (WS) P28[32]; then over next 4 sts, work (k1, p1) twice; p to end.

Beg with chart row 9 of chart for sleeve, cont raglan shaping and moss (seed) st yoke as indicated until chart row 30[34] has been completed.

Foll sleeve chart, cont in moss (seed) st only, shaping raglan as set and purling first 2 and last 2 sts of every WS row, until chart row 58[64] has been completed.

Raglan row 59[65] (RS) K2, work in moss (seed) st to last 3 sts, k2.

Raglan row 60[66] (WS) P2, work in moss (seed) st to last 2 sts, p2.

Leave rem 10[12] sts on st holder.

Make 2nd sleeve in same way.

COLLAR

Join two front raglan edges and two back raglan edges to raglan edges of sleeves, using a small neat overstitch (overcast stitch) on WS.

Using 4 double-pointed needles and with RS facing, k18[20] sts from back-neck st holder, k10[12] sts from top-of-sleeve st holder, then pick up and k4 sts down left front neck, k10[12] sts from centre-front-neck st holder, pick up and k4 sts up right front neck and k10[12] sts from rem top-of-sleeve st holder. 56[64] sts.

Working in rounds (RS always facing), work in k2, p2 rib as for back for 5cm/2in.

Cast (bind) off *loosely* in rib.

FINISHING

Join side and sleeve seams, using a small neat overstitch (overcast stitch). Do not press.

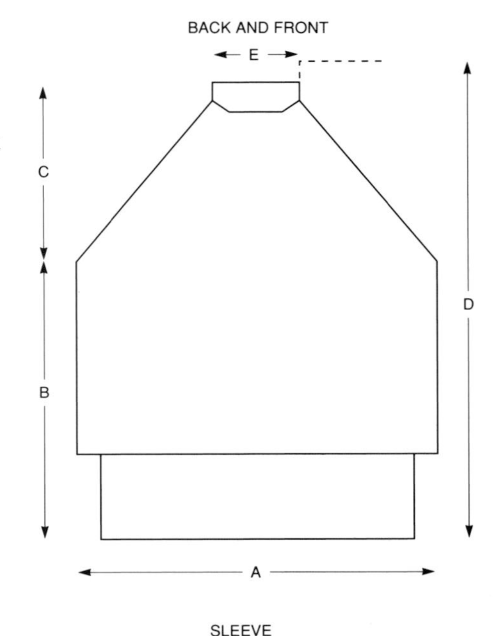

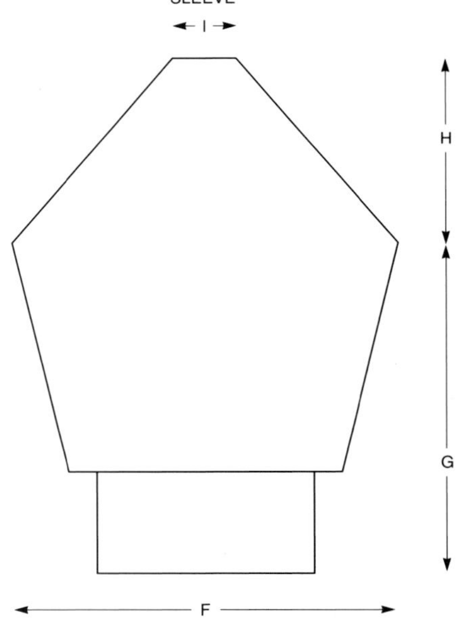

KEY
A = 54[60]cm (21¾[24]in)
B = 45cm (17½in)
C = 25[27.5]cm (10[11]in)
D = 74[76.5]cm (29[30]in)
E = 13[14]cm (5¼[5¾]in)
F = 48.5[54]cm (19½[21½]in)
G = 45[46]cm (17½[18]in)
H = 25[27.5]cm (10[11]in)
I = 7[8.5]cm (3[3½]in)

BACK AND FRONT RAGLAN CHART

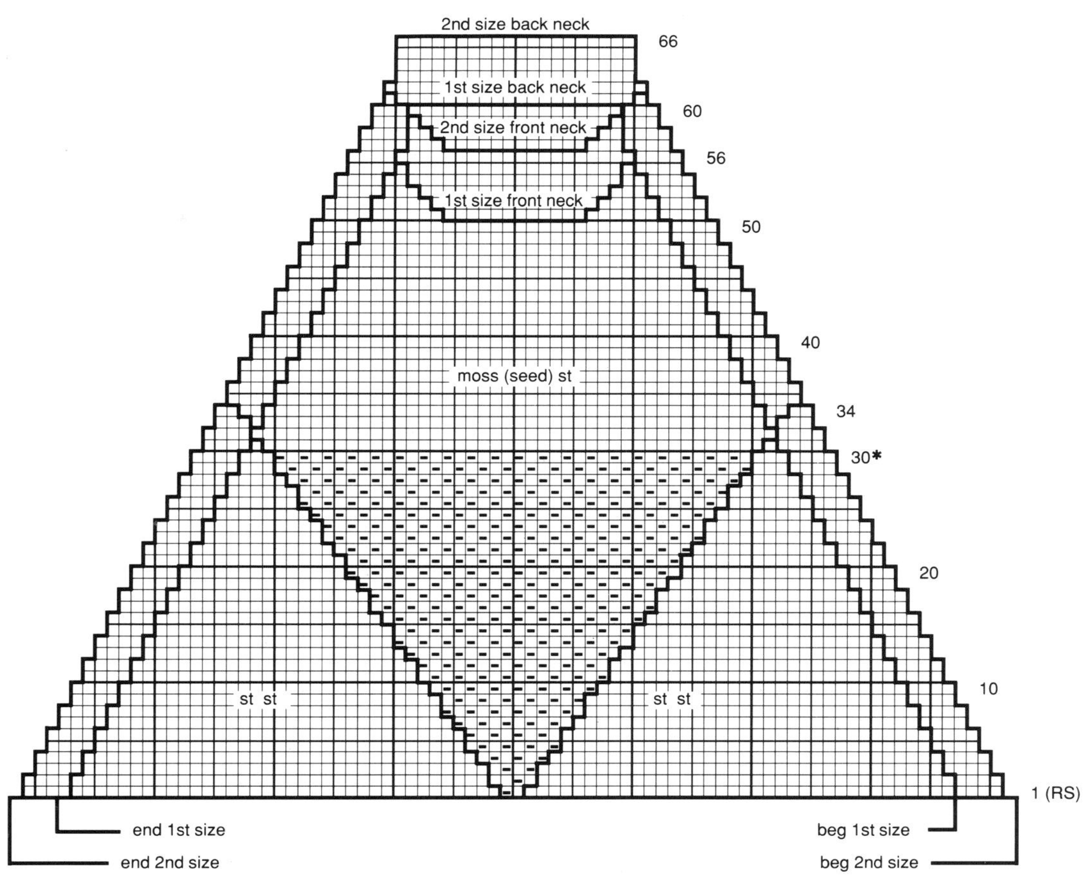

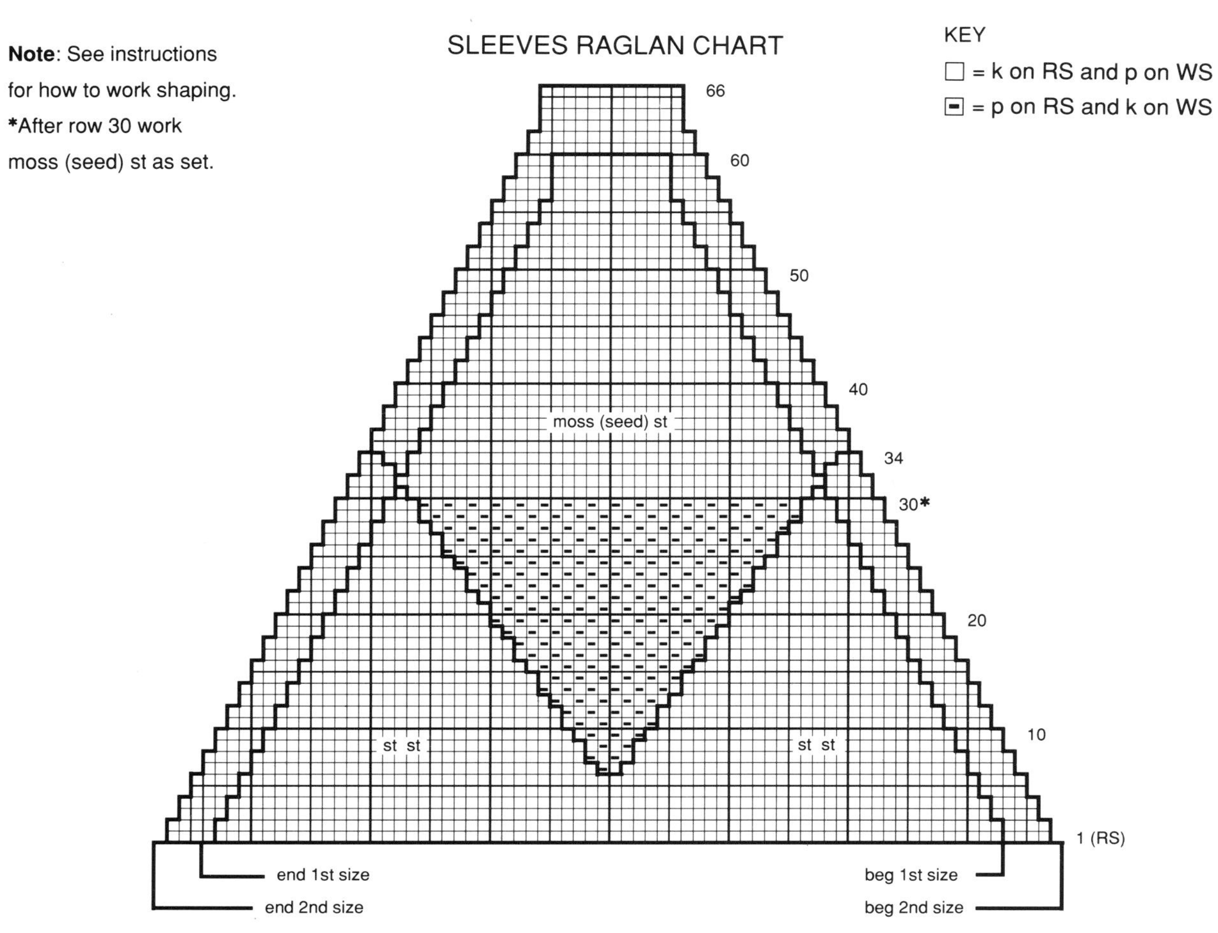

POOKA

LAST HALLOWEEN I WANTED TO DESIGN A NOT-TOO-DEMANDING BUT INTERESTING-TO-KNIT SWEATER FOR MY SIX-YEAR-OLD SON. SINCE THE SHOPS WERE FULL OF PUMPKINS OF ALL SHAPES AND SIZES, I SET ABOUT MAKING A PUMPKIN-COLOURED SWEATER FOR HIM. THE FAIR ISLE BAND IS NOT DIFFICULT, BUT FOR THOSE OF YOU WHO DON'T LIKE KNITTING FAIR ISLE, THE SWEATER ALSO LOOKS BEAUTIFUL WITHOUT IT.

SIZES

To fit 6[8:10] yrs or 61[66:71]cm/24[26:28]in chest

Figures for larger sizes are given in brackets [ ]; where there is only one set of figures, it applies to all sizes.

See diagram for finished knitted measurements.

MATERIALS

Rowan *Handknit DK* Cotton 50g/1¾oz balls as foll:

A (no.246: mustard) 9[10:11] balls

B (no.279: bayou) 1 ball

C (no.254: flame) 1 ball

D (no.251: ecru) 1 ball

One pair each of 3¼mm (US size 3) and 4½mm (US size 7) knitting needles

Set of four 3¼mm (US size 3) double-pointed needles

Three 12mm/½in buttons

ALTERNATIVE COLOURWAY

This sweater can also be worked in the colourway shown on the right, where:

A = no.248: azure

B = no.262: mango

C = no.261: sunflower

D = no.251: ecru

TENSION (GAUGE)

21 sts and 30 rows to 10cm/4in measured over heraldic patt worked on 4½mm (US size 7) needles

PLEASE CHECK YOUR TENSION (GAUGE) CAREFULLY AND CHANGE KNITTING NEEDLE SIZE IF NECESSARY

NOTES

Work the Fair Isle borders using the intarsia method, using a separate length of yarn for each isolated area of colour and twisting yarns tog at WS when changing colours to avoid making a hole.

Read charts from right to left for the RS (odd-numbered) rows and from left to right for the WS (even-numbered) rows.

RIGHT AND LEFT TWISTS

The right and left twists are used in the heraldic pattern and are worked as foll:

RT or *right twist* – k next 2 sts tog leaving sts on LH needle, then insert RH needle from the front between the 2 sts just knitted tog and k the first st again, then slip both sts off needle tog.

LT or *left twist* – with RH needle

behind LH needle skip next st and k the 2nd st on LH needle through the back loop, then insert RH needle through backs of both the skipped st and the 2nd st and k2tog through back loops.

BACK

Using smaller needles and A, cast on 72[80:88] sts and beg garter st rib as foll:

Rib row 1 (RS) *K4, (p1, k1) twice, rep from * to end.

Rib row 2 *P1, (k1, p1) twice, k3, rep from * to end.

Rep last 2 rib rows until ribbing measures 6cm/2½in from cast-on edge, ending with a RS row.

Next row (inc row) Work in garter st rib as set and keeping rib correct, inc 12[10:8] sts evenly across row. 84[90:96] sts.

Change to larger needles and beg charted patt (see *Notes*) as foll:

Chart row 1 (RS) Purl.

Chart row 2 P0[0:1] in B, p6[9:11] in A, *p1 in B, p11 in A, rep from *, ending last rep with p5[8:11] A.

Beg with chart row 3 of chart for back, cont foll chart until chart row 15 has been completed, so ending with a RS row.

Using A only for remainder of back, beg heraldic chart patt on next row as foll:

First size only

Chart row 16 (WS) K2, p2, *k4, p2, rep from * to last 2 sts, k2.

Chart row 17 (RS) *K2, RT, k4, LT, k2, rep from * to end.

2nd size only

Chart row 16 (WS) P1, *k4, p2, rep from *, ending last rep p1 instead of p2.

Chart row 17 (RS) K5, *RT, k4, LT, k4, rep from * ending last rep k5, instead of k4.

3rd size only

Chart row 16 (WS) K2, p2, *k4, p2, rep from * to last 2 sts, k2.

Chart row 17 (RS) *K2, LT, k4, RT, k2, rep from * to end.

All sizes

Beg with chart row 18, cont foll chart until chart row 54[58:62] has been completed, so ending with a WS row.

Note: When working RT and LT from chart, ignore twists that are worked closer than one st from the edges.

Armhole shaping

Keeping heraldic patt correct as shown on chart throughout, dec one st at each end of next row and every foll row 1[3:4] times in all.

Work one row without shaping.

Then dec one st at each end of next row and every alt row 6[5:5] times in all. 70[74:78] sts.

Work without shaping until chart row 106[114:122] has been completed, so ending with a WS row.

Neck shaping

Chart row 107[115:123] (RS) Work 23[24:25] sts in patt, then turn leaving rem sts on a spare needle.

Working on first side of neck only, dec one st at neck edge on next row and then dec one st at neck edge on every foll row 3 times in all.

Cast (bind) off rem 20[21:22] sts.

Return to rem sts and with RS facing, slip centre 24[26:28] sts onto a st holder, rejoin yarn to rem sts and work in patt to end of row.

Then complete 2nd side of neck to match first side of neck, reversing the shaping.

FRONT

Work as for back until chart row 70[74:80] has been completed, so ending with a WS row.

Divide for neck

Chart row 71[75:81] (RS) Work 32[34:36] sts in patt foll chart, then turn leaving rem sts on a spare needle.

Working on first side of neck only and cont to foll chart for patt throughout, work without shaping until chart row 95[101:109] has been completed, so ending with a RS row at centre front.

Neck shaping

Chart row 96[102:110] (WS) Cast (bind) off first 5[7:7] sts, then work in patt to end of row.

Dec one st at neck edge on next row and every foll row 7[6:7] times in all. 20[21:22] sts.

Work 7[10:9] rows without shaping, so ending with a WS row (chart row 110[118:126]). Cast (bind) off.

Return to rem sts and with RS facing, slip centre 6 sts onto a st holder, rejoin yarn to rem sts and work in patt to end.

Complete 2nd side of neck to match first side, reversing shaping.

SLEEVES

Using smaller needles and A, cast on 32[32:40] sts and work 7.5cm/3in in garter st rib as for back, ending with a RS row.

Next row (inc row) Work in garter st rib as set and keeping rib correct, inc 12[16:12] sts evenly across row. 44[48:52] sts.

Change to larger needles and beg charted patt as foll:

Chart row 1 (RS) Purl.

Chart row 2 P4[6:8] in A, *p1 in B, p11 in A, rep from *, ending last rep with p3[5:7] A instead of p11 A.

Beg with chart row 3 of chart for

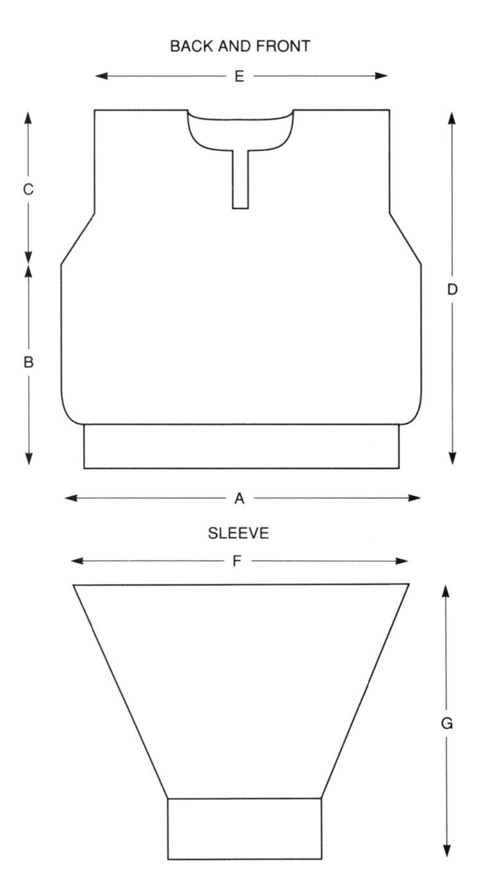

KEY
A = 40[43:46]cm (16[17¼:18¼]in)
B = 24[25:26.5]cm (9¾[10¼:10¾]in)
C = 19[20:21.5]cm (7½[8:8½]in)
D = 43[45:48]cm (17¼[18¼:19¼]in)
E = 33[35:37]cm (13¼[14:14¾]in)
F = 39[41:43]cm (15½[16½:17¼]in)
G = 36[37.5:40]cm (14½[15:16]in)

sleeve, cont foll chart for Fair Isle and then heraldic patt until chart row 86[90:98] has been completed *and at the same time* shape sleeve as indicated by inc one st at each end of next row and every foll 4th row 19[16:12] times in all and then every 5th row 0[3:7] times.

Cast (bind) off all 82[86:90] sts.

Make 2nd sleeve in same way.

BUTTONHOLE BAND

Do not press.

The buttonhole band is attached to right side of front for *girl's version*, and to left side of front for *boy's version*.

Girl's version

First mark positions for 2 buttonholes on right side of front

BACK AND FRONT CHART

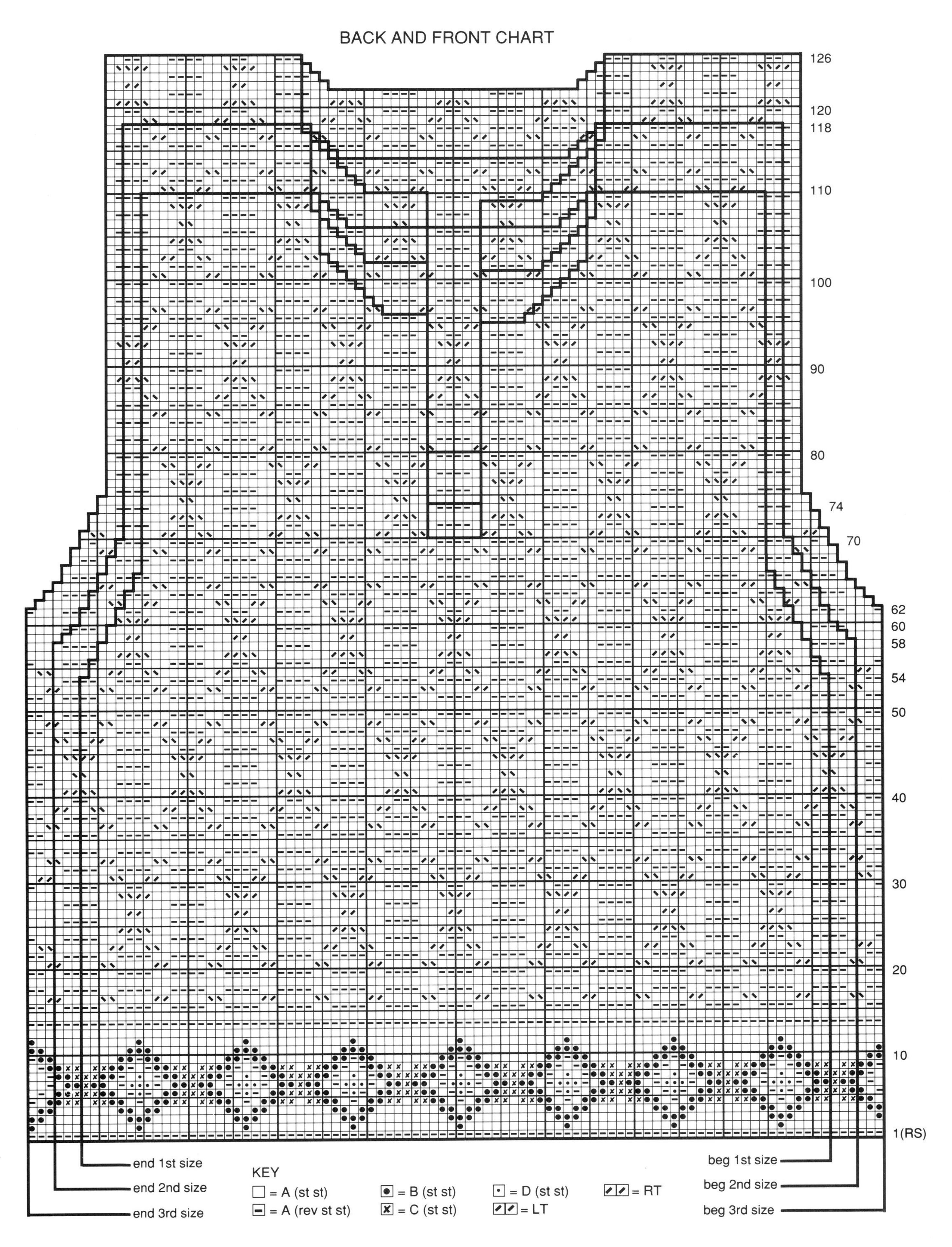

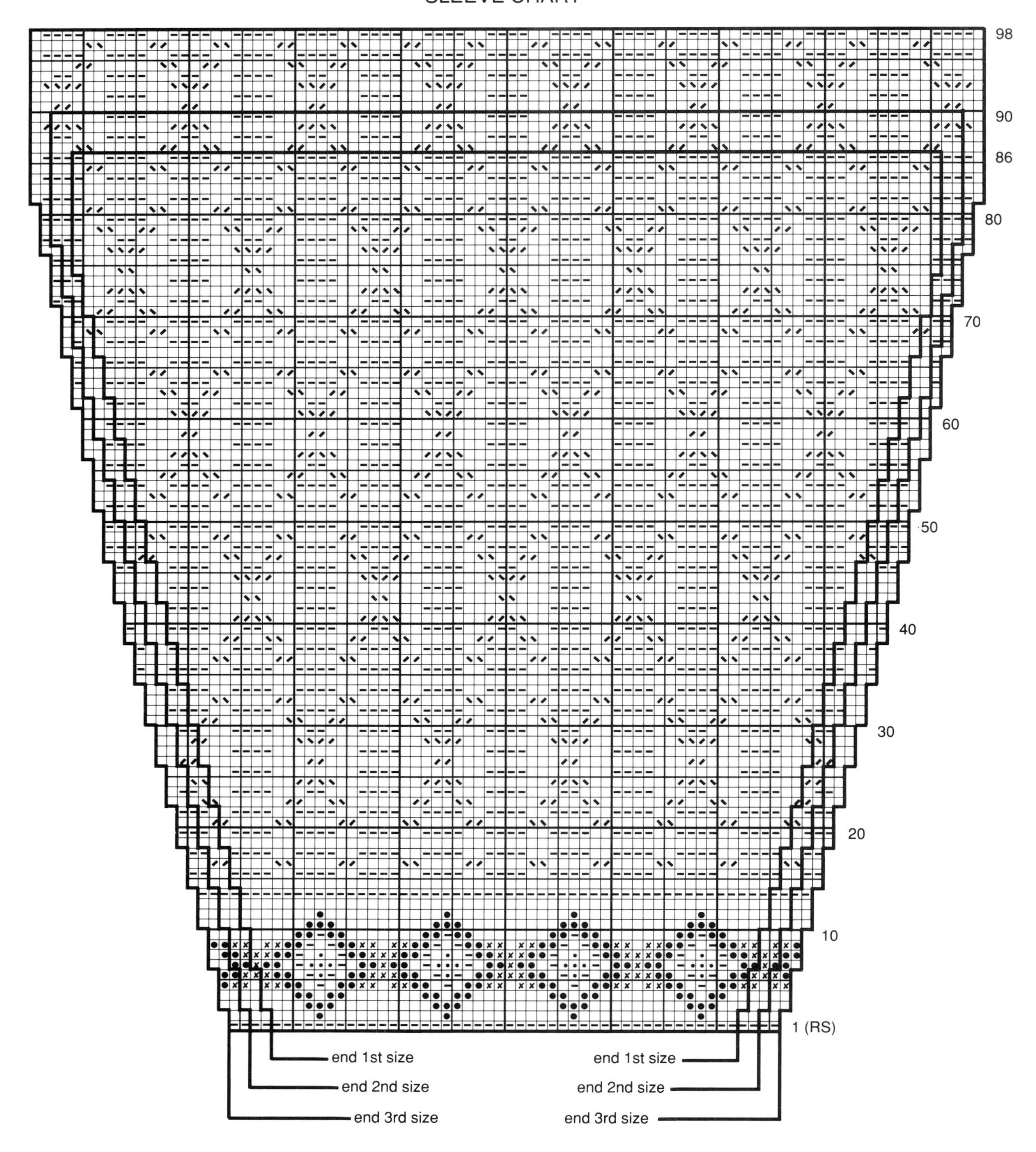

neck opening, the first 3.5cm/1¼in below neck shaping and the 2nd 4cm/1½in below the first.
Using smaller needles and A and with RS facing, work across 6 sts on st holder at neck divide as foll:
Rib row 1 (RS) (K1, p1) twice, k into front and back of next st, k1.
There are now 7 sts for band.
Rib row 2 P1, (k1, p1) 3 times.
Rib row 3 K1, (p1, k1) 3 times.
Rep last 2 rib rows until band fits up neck opening to position of first buttonhole, ending with a WS row.
Then work buttonhole as foll:
Buttonhole row 1 (RS) Rib 3, cast (bind) off next 2 sts, rib to end.
Buttonhole row 2 (WS) Rib, casting on 2 sts over those cast (bound) off in previous row.
**Cont in rib, working 2nd buttonhole when correct position is reached, until buttonhole band fits up neck opening to beg of neck

shaping, ending with a WS row.**
Do not break off yarn, but slip sts onto a st holder.

Boy's version
First mark positions for 2 buttonholes as for girl's version but on left side of front neck opening.
Using smaller needles and A and with RS facing, work across 6 sts on st holder at neck divide as foll:
Rib row 1 (RS) K into front and back of first st, k1, (p1, k1) twice.
There are now 7 sts for band.
Rib row 2 P1, (k1, p1) 3 times.
Rib row 3 K1, (p1, k1) 3 times.
Rep last 2 rib rows until band fits up neck opening to position of first buttonhole, ending with a RS row.
Then work buttonhole over next 2 rows as foll:
Buttonhole row 1 (WS) Rib 3, cast (bind) off next 2 sts, rib to end.
Buttonhole row 2 (RS) Rib, casting on 2 sts over those cast (bound) off in previous row.
Complete as for girl's version from ** to **.
Break off yarn and slip sts onto a st holder.

BUTTON BAND

Using smaller needles and A, cast on 7 sts.
Work in k1, p1 rib as foll:
Rib row 1 (RS) K1, (p1, k1) 3 times.
Rib row 2 P1, (k1, p1) 3 times.
Rep last 2 rib rows until button band is same length as buttonhole band, ending with a WS row.
For girl's version, break off yarn and slip sts onto a st holder.
For boy's version, do not break off yarn, but slip sts onto a st holder.

NECKBAND

Join shoulder seams using a small neat overstitch (overcast st) so that the cast (bound) off edge does not show.
Keeping top of buttonhole band on st holder (or safety pin) and joining the girl's band to the right side of neck opening and boy's to left side of neck opening, join band to neck opening so that top of band is even with cast (bound) off edge at beg of neck shaping.
Then join cast-on edge of button band to WS at beg of neck opening *behind* buttonhole band and stitch side of band to rem edge of neck opening, keeping top of band on st holder (or safety pin).

Girl's version
Using set of four double-pointed needles and A and with RS facing, work in rib across 7 sts from buttonhole band st holder, then pick up and K20[23:22] sts up right front neck, 4 sts down right back neck, K24[26:28] sts from back neck st holder, pick up and K4 sts up left back neck, 19[22:21] sts down left front neck and rib 7 sts from button band st holder. 85[93:93] sts.
Beg garter st rib as foll:
Rib row 1 (WS) P1, (k1, p1) twice, *k3, p1, (k1, p1) twice, rep from * to end.
Work buttonhole on next row as foll:
Rib row 2 (RS) K1, p1, k1, cast (bind) off next 2 sts in rib as set (4 sts now on RH needle), k3, (p1, k1) twice, *k4, (p1, k1) twice, rep from * to end.
Rib row 3 Work as for rib row 1, but casting on 2 sts over those cast (bound) off in last row.
Rib row 4 *(K1, p1) twice, k4, rep from * to last 5 sts, k1, (p1, k1) twice.
Break off A.
Rib row 5 Using C, work as for rib row 1.
Break off C.
Using B, cast (bind) off in garter st rib.

Boy's version
Using set of four double-pointed needles and A and with RS facing, work in rib across 7 sts from button band st holder, then pick up and K19[23:21] sts up right front neck, 4 sts down right back neck, K24[26:28] sts from back neck st holder, pick up and K4 sts up left back neck, 20[22:22] sts down left front neck and rib 7 sts from buttonhole band st holder.
85[93:93] sts.
Beg garter st rib as foll:
Rib row 1 (WS) P1, (k1, p1) twice, *k3, p1, (k1, p1) twice, rep from * to end.
Work buttonhole on the next row as foll:
Rib row 2 (RS) *(K1, p1) twice, k4, rep from * to last 5 sts, cast (bind) off next 2 sts in rib, rib to end as set.
Rib row 3 Work as for rib row 1, but casting on 2 sts over those cast (bound) off in last row.
Rib row 4 *(K1, p1) twice, k4, rep from * to last 5 sts, k1, (p1, k1) twice.
Break off A.
Rib row 5 Using C, work as for rib row 1.
Break off C.
Using B, cast (bind) off in garter st rib.

FINISHING

Placing centre of top of sleeve at shoulder seam, sew cast (bound) off edge of sleeves to armhole edge (including decreased edge).
Join side and sleeve seams.
Sew the buttons to the button band in positions corresponding to the 3 buttonholes.

Chestnut

Every autumn I'm knocked out by the glorious symphony of colour which seems to explode all around us. This sweater is inspired by the sumptuous hues of the fallen leaves that are ankle-deep at this time of year. For a woman's version, omit the bottom rib and work the Creepy-Crawly leaf border instead.

SIZES

One size only to fit 96–117cm/38–46in chest

See diagram for finished knitted measurements.

MATERIALS

Rowan *Designer DK* 50g/1¾oz balls as foll:

A (no.658: dark green) 6 balls
B (no.659: dark plum) 4 balls
C (no.628: French blue) 4 balls
D (no.655: teal) 3 balls
E (no.663: dark rust) 2 balls
F (no.99: purple) 2 balls
G (no.652: lilac) 1 ball
H (no.660: apple green) 1 ball
J (no.627: rust) 1 ball
L (no.407: sage green) 1 ball
M (no.651: burgundy) 1 ball
N (no.65: grey blue) 1 ball

One pair each of 3mm (US size 3) and 4mm (US size 6) knitting needles

Set of four 3mm (US size 3) and 3¾mm (US size 5) double-pointed needles for collar

ALTERNATIVE COLOURWAY

This sweater can also be worked in the colourway shown below, where:

A = no.658: dark green
B = no.628: French blue
C = no.99: purple
D = no.655: teal
E = no.407: sage green
F = no.659: dark plum
G = no.652: lilac
H = no.663: dark rust
J = no.65: grey blue
L = no.660: apple green
M = no.651: burgundy
N = no.627: rust

TENSION (GAUGE)

22 sts and 28 rows to 10cm/4in measured over maple leaf patt worked on 4mm (US size 6) needles

Please check your tension (gauge) carefully and change knitting needle size if necessary

NOTES

When working the bicolour ribbing and the check patt, strand the colour not in use loosely across the WS.

When working maple leaf patt from chart, use the intarsia method, using a separate length of yarn for each isolated area of colour and twisting yarns together at back of work when changing colours to avoid making a hole.

Read chart from right to left for the RS (odd-numbered) rows and from left to right for the WS (even-numbered) rows.

BACK

Using smaller needles and B, cast on 120 sts and beg k2, p2 bicolour rib as foll:

Rib row 1 (RS) *K2 in B, p2 in C, rep from * to end.

Rib row 2 *K2 in C, p2 in B, rep from * to end.

Rep last 2 rows until ribbing measures 5cm/2in from cast-on edge, ending with a WS row.

Change to larger needles and beg check patt in st st as foll:

Row 1 (RS) *K2 in C, k2 in B, rep from * to end.

Row 2 *P2 in B, p2 in C, rep from * to end.

Row 3 As row 1.

Row 4 *P2 in C, p2 in B, rep from * to end.

Row 5 *K2 in B, k2 in C, rep from * to end.

Row 6 As row 4.

Rows 7–9 Rep rows 1–3 once.

Inc 26 sts evenly across next row as foll:

Next row (inc row) (WS) P3, *p into front and back of next st – called *inc 1* –, p4, inc 1 into next st, p3*, rep from * to * 12 times more. 146 sts.

Beg with chart row 1, foll chart for maple leaf patt until chart row 110 has been completed, so ending with a WS row.

Armhole shaping

Cont to foll chart throughout, beg armhole shaping as foll:

Next row (dec row) (RS) K2,

sl 1-k1-psso, work in patt to last 4 sts, k2tog, k2.
Work one row without shaping. Rep dec row once.
Rep from ** to ** 10 times more. 122 sts.***
Work without shaping until chart row 170 has been completed, so ending with a WS row.

Neck shaping

Chart row 171 (RS) Work first 47 sts in patt, then turn leaving rem sts on a spare needle.
Working on first side of neck only, dec one st at beg of next row (neck edge), then at neck edge on every foll row 5 times in all.
Cast (bind) off rem 42 sts.
Return to rem sts and with RS facing, slip centre 28 sts onto a st holder, rejoin yarn to rem sts and work in patt to end of row.
Complete 2nd side of neck to match first side, reversing shaping.

FRONT

Work as for back to ***.
Work without shaping until chart row 156 has been completed, so ending with a WS row.

Neck shaping

Chart row 157 (RS) Work first 52 sts in patt, then turn leaving rem sts on a spare needle.
Working on first side of neck only, dec one st at beg of next row (neck edge), then at neck edge on every foll row 8 times in all, then on every alt row twice. 42 sts.
Work without shaping until chart row 176 has been completed.
Cast (bind) off.
Return to rem sts and with RS facing, slip centre 18 sts onto a st holder, rejoin yarn to rem sts and work in patt to end of row.
Complete 2nd side of neck to match first side, reversing shaping.

SLEEVES

Using smaller needles and B, cast on 52 sts and work 7cm/2¾in in k2, p2 bicolour rib as for back, ending with a WS row.
Change to larger needles and work 9 rows of check patt as for back, so ending with a RS row.
Inc 8 sts across next row as foll:
Next row (inc row) (WS) P4, *inc 1 into next st, p5*, rep from * to * 7 times more. 60 sts.
Beg with chart row 1, foll chart for maple leaf patt throughout, inc one st at each end of 5th row and every foll 4th row 16 times in all (92 sts), then inc one st at each end of every foll 5th row 8 times. 108 sts.
Work without shaping until chart row 114 has been completed.
Using B and C only and still using larger needles, work 10 rows in k2, p2 bicolour rib as for back, working loosely.
Using B, cast (bind) off in rib.
Make 2nd sleeve in same way.

COLLAR

Press pieces lightly on WS with a warm iron over a damp cloth, omitting all ribbing except ribbing at top of sleeves.
Join shoulder seams using a small neat backstitch on edge of work.
Using set of 3mm (US size 3) double-pointed needles and B and with WS facing (so that WS of rib will be on RS of sweater), beg at left shoulder and pick up and k6 sts down left back neck, k28 sts from back neck st holder, pick up and k6 sts up right back neck, 25 sts down right front neck, k18 sts from front neck st holder and pick up and k25 sts up left front neck. 108 sts.
Beg k2, p2 bicolour rib as foll:
Rib round 1 (RS) *K2 in B, p2 in C, rep from * to end.

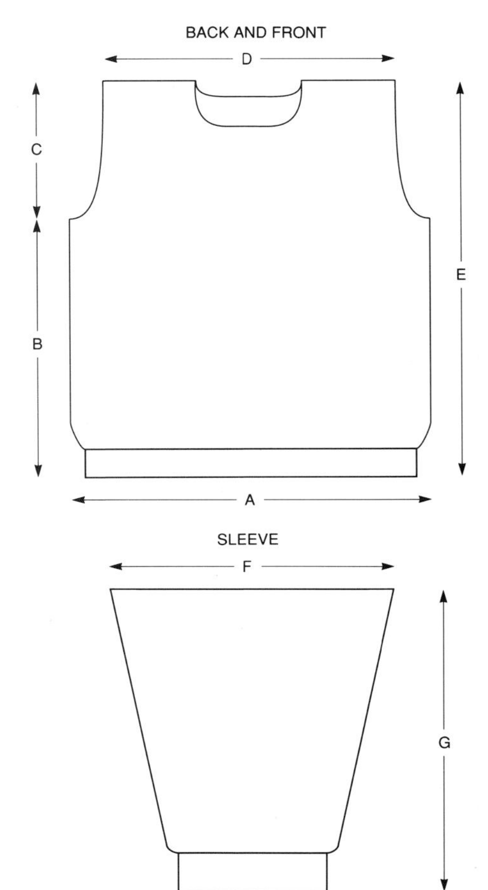

KEY
A = 66.5cm (26½in)
B = 48.5cm (19¼in)
C = 23.5cm (9½in)
D = 55.5cm (22¼in)
E = 72cm (28¾in)
F = 49cm (19½in)
G = 57cm (22½in)

Working in rounds (RS always facing), rep last row until collar measures 7.5cm/3in.
Change to 3¾ mm (US size 5) double-pointed needles and cont in rib as set until collar measures 16.5cm/6½in from beg.
Using B, cast (bind) off in rib.

FINISHING

Join seams using a small neat backstitch on very edge of work, except for ribbing where an invisible slip stitch should be used.

Placing centre of top of sleeve at shoulder seam, sew cast (bound) off edge of sleeves to armhole edge (including decreased edge).

Join side and sleeve seams.

Press seams lightly on WS.

BACK, FRONT AND SLEEVE CHART

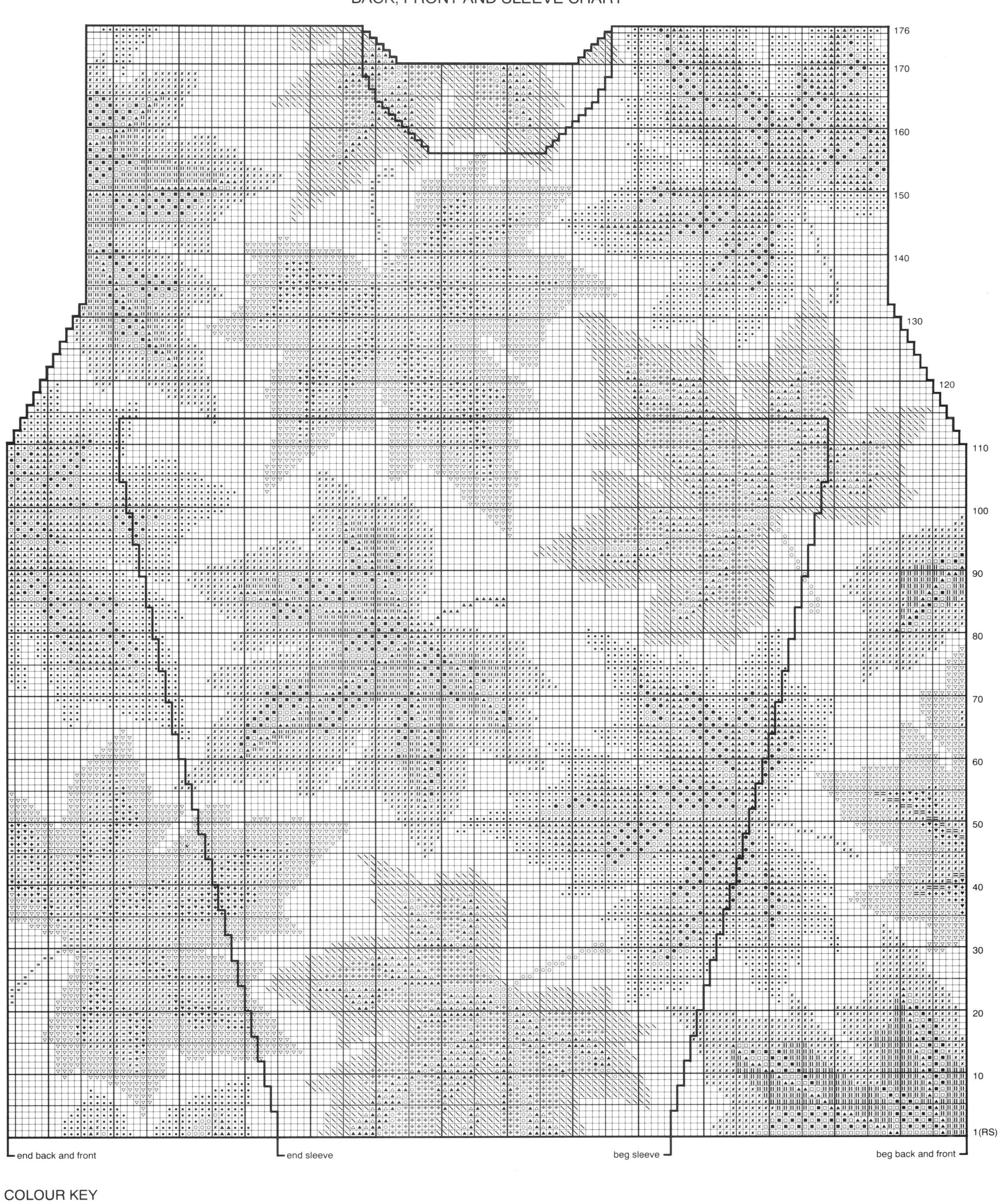

COLOUR KEY

- ☐ = A in st st
- ▽ = B in st st
- ◣ = C in st st
- ☒ = D in st st
- ▲ = E in st st
- △ = E in rev st st
- ⊡ = F in st st
- Ⅲ = G in st st
- ○ = H in st st
- ● = H in rev st st
- ⊞ = J in st st
- □ = L in st st
- ■ = L in rev st st
- ⊟ = M in st st
- ✚ = N in st st
- ♥ = N in rev st st

FIREWORKS

THIS IS A GREAT SWEATER FOR THE CHILD WHO WON'T WEAR A JACKET, AS THE HOT COLOURS AND ARAN-WEIGHT YARN WILL KEEP OUT THE COLDEST OF WINDS. IF YOUR CHILD HAS A FAVOURITE FIREWORK YOU COULD USE THAT ONE INSTEAD – FOR EXAMPLE CATHERINE WHEELS, ROMAN CANDLES, AND GOLDEN RAIN WOULD ALL WORK WELL. IF YOU'RE NOT TOO HAPPY KNITTING INTARSIA, TRY WORKING THE SPARKLERS IN A SCULPTURED REVERSE STOCKING STITCH.

SIZES

To fit 6[8:10:12] yrs or 61[66:71:76]cm/24[26:28:30]in chest

Figures for larger sizes are given in brackets [ ]; where there is only one set of figures, it applies to all sizes.

See diagram for finished knitted measurements.

MATERIALS

Rowan *Magpie Tweed* 100g/3½oz hanks as foll:

A (no.769: punch) 4[4:5:5] hanks
B (no.766: stinger) 1 hank
C (no.767: Zsa Zsa) 1 hank
D (no.768: ringo) 1 hank

Rowan *Magpie* 100g/3½oz hanks as foll:

E (no.114: hunting pink) 1 hank
F (no.503: Comanche) 1 hank
G (no.307: heather) 1 hank
H (no.305: ocean) 1 hank

One pair each of 3¾mm (US size 5) and 5mm (US size 8) knitting needles

Set of four 3¾mm (US size 5) double-pointed needles for neckband

ALTERNATIVE COLOURWAY

This sweater can also be worked in the colourway shown below, where:

A = *Magpie* no.114: hunting pink
B = *Magpie* no.307: heather
C = *Magpie* no.305: ocean
D = *Magpie Tweed* no.767: Zsa Zsa
E = *Magpie Tweed* no.769: punch
F = *Magpie Tweed* no.768: ringo
G = *Magpie Tweed* no.766: stinger
H = *Magpie* no.503: Comanche

TENSION (GAUGE)

17 sts and 22 rows to 10cm/4in measured over patt worked on 5mm (US size 8) needles

PLEASE CHECK YOUR TENSION (GAUGE) CAREFULLY AND CHANGE KNITTING NEEDLE SIZE IF NECESSARY

NOTES

When working the colourwork patt, use the intarsia method, using a separate length of yarn for each isolated area of colour and twisting yarns together at the back of the work when changing colours to avoid making a hole.

When working patt on back, front and sleeves, where there are insufficient sts for CL3 at side edges, omit CL3 and work in st st.

Read the Fireworks pattern chart on page 159 chart from right to left for the RS (odd-numbered) rows and from left to right for the WS (even-numbered) rows.

BACK

Using smaller needles and A, cast on 75[78:81:87] sts and rib patt as foll:

Row 1 (RS) *Using E, *(p3tog, k3tog, p3tog) all into next 3 sts – called *cluster 3* or *CL3* –, rep from * to end.

Row 2 Using E, purl to end.

Break off E.

Using D, rep last 2 rows once more, dec one st at end of last row on first and 4th sizes and inc one st on 3rd size. 74[78:82:86] sts.

Break off D.

Using A, beg k1, p1 rib as foll:

Next row (RS) *K1, p1, rep from * to end.

Rep last row until back measures 6.5cm/2½in from cast-on edge, ending with a WS row.

Change to larger needles, and using A, k one row.

Then beg foll patt chart as foll:

Chart row 2 (WS) Foll chart from left to right, work 3[5:7:9] sts before patt repeat begins as indicated, rep 34-st patt repeat twice, work last 3[5:7:9] sts after patt rep as indicated.

Cont in st st foll chart for patt and rep 40-row repeat throughout, until back measures 28[29.5:30:31]cm/11[11½:11¾:12]in from cast-on edge, ending with a WS row.

Armhole shaping

Keeping patt correct throughout,

beg armhole shaping as foll:
Next row (dec row) (RS) K2, sl 1-k1-psso, work in patt to last 4 sts, k2tog, k2.
**Work one row without shaping.
Rep dec row once.**
Rep from ** to ** 5 times more. 60[64:68:72] sts.***
Work without shaping until back measures 45[47.5:49.5:51.5]cm/ 17¾[18¾:19½:20¼]in from cast-on edge, ending with a WS row.

Neck shaping

Next row (RS) Work first 20[22:23:25] sts in patt, then turn leaving rem sts on a spare needle.
Working on first side of neck only, dec one st at beg of next row (neck edge), then at neck edge on every foll row 4 times in all.
Cast (bind) off rem 16[18:19:21] sts.
Return to rem sts and with RS facing, slip centre 20[20:22:22] sts onto a st holder, rejoin yarn to rem sts and work in patt to end of row.
Complete 2nd side of neck to match first side, reversing shaping.

FRONT

Work as for back to ***.
Work without shaping until front measures 39[41.5:43.5:45.5]cm/ 15½[16½:17¼:18]in from cast-on edge, ending with a WS row.

Neck shaping

Next row (RS) Work first 23[25:26:28] sts in patt, then turn leaving rem sts on a spare needle.
Working on first side of neck only, dec one st at beg of next row (neck edge), then at neck edge on every foll alt row 7 times in all. 16[18:19:21] sts.
Work without shaping until there are same number of rows as back to shoulder.
Cast (bind) off.
Return to rem sts and with RS facing, slip centre 14[14:16:16] sts onto a st holder, rejoin yarn to rem sts and work in patt to end of row.
Complete 2nd side of neck to match first side, reversing shaping.

SLEEVES

Using smaller needles and A, cast on 36[39:39:39] sts.
Using E, work rows 1 and 2 of back.
Using D, rep last 2 rows.
Using A, work in k1, p1 rib as for back until sleeve measures 6.5cm/ 2½in from cast-on edge, ending with a WS row and inc one st at each end of last row on first size, one st only at end last row on 2nd, 3rd and 4th sizes. 38[40:40:40] sts.
Change to larger needles and beg with 19th chart row (as indicated on patt chart), foll chart for patt throughout (beg again with row 1 after row 40 has been completed) *and at the same time* shape sleeve by inc one st at each end of 3rd row and then at each end of every foll 3rd row 3[3:6:10] times in all, then every foll 4th row 12[13:12:10] times, working all inc sts into patt foll chart. 68[72:76:80] sts.
Work in patt without shaping until sleeve measures 36[37:39.5:42]cm/ 14[14½:15½:16½]in from cast-on edge, or desired length, ending with a WS row.
Cast (bind) off all sts.
Make 2nd sleeve in same way.

NECKBAND

Press pieces lightly on WS with a warm iron over a damp cloth, omitting ribbing.
Join shoulder seams using a small neat backstitch on very edge of work.
Using set of 4 double-pointed needles and A and with RS of front facing, beg at left shoulder and pick up and k19 sts down left front neck, k14[14:16:16] sts from front neck st holder, pick up and k19 sts up right front neck, 3[3:4:4] sts down right back neck, k20[20:22:22] sts from back neck st holder and pick up and k3[3:4:4] sts up left back neck. 78[78:84:84] sts.
Working in rounds (RS always facing), beg ribbing as foll:
Round 1 Using C, *(p3tog, k3tog, p3tog) all into next 3 sts, rep from * to end.
Round 2 Using C, knit to end.
Break off C.
Complete neckband using A only.
Round 3 *K1, p1, rep from * to end.
Rep last round once more.
Cast (bind) off in rib.

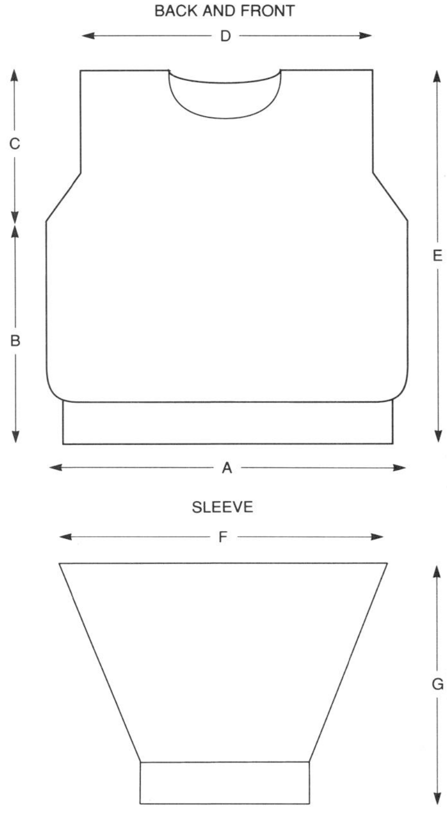

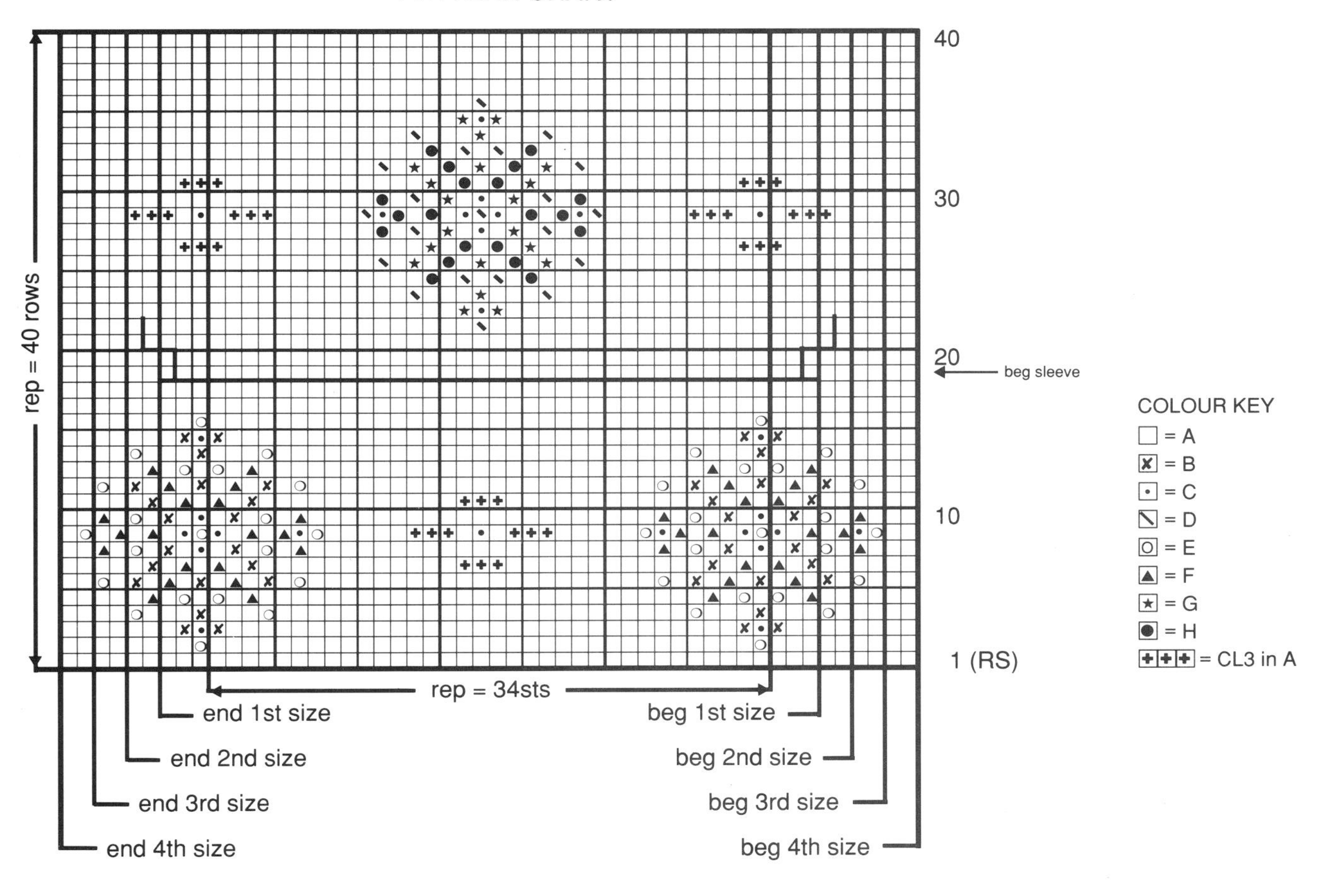

FINISHING

Join seams using a small neat backstitch on very edge of work, except for ribbing where a flat overstitch (overcast st) should be used.

Placing centre of top of sleeve at shoulder seam, sew cast (bound) off edge of sleeves to armhole edge (including decreased edge).

Join side and sleeve seams.

Press seams lightly on WS.

ACKNOWLEDGEMENTS

The author and publishers would like to thank the following for kindly providing clothes, shoes, jewellery and accessories for photography:

BALLY, 246 Oxford St, London W1. BROWNS, 18 South Molton St, London W1. BUTLER AND WILSON, 20 South Molton St, London W1. CAPTAIN WATTS, 49 Albermarle St, London W1. DICKINS AND JONES, 224 Regent St, London W1. DU DU, 171a Finchley Road, London NW3. EARLY CLOTHING, 79 Fortis Green Road, London N10. FARLOW'S, 5 Pall Mall, London SW1. FENWICK, 63 New Bond St, London W1. FRED BARE, 118 Columbia Rd, London E2. FRONTIER, 39 Pembridge Rd, London W11. GRIP, 27 Gt Marlborough St, London W1. JANET FITCH, 2 Percy St, London W1. KANGOL, 50 Duke St, London W1. LIBERTY, 210-220 Regent St, London W1. LUNN ANTIQUES, 86 New King's Rd, London SW6. OILILY, 10 Sloane St, London SW1. PATRIZIA WIGAN, 72 New King's Road, London SW6. PAUL SMITH, 41 Floral St, London WC2. SUN AND SNOW, 229 Brompton Rd, London SW3. THE HAT SHOP, 58 Neal St, London WC2.

BETTYS AND TAYLORS OF HARROGATE, 1 Parliament St, Harrogate supplied the birthday cake.
DUTTONS FOR BUTTONS, 32 Coppergate, York, supplied the buttons for the *Snowdon* (boy's version), *Chatsworth* and *Birthday* knits.
THE BUTTON QUEEN 19 Marylebone Lane, London W1 provided the buttons for the following: *Choo Choo* Unusual English laminated wood green buttons; *Heartstrings* Austrian metal heart buttons with antique finish in bronze/silver; *Equinox* (cream colourway) Handmade Nepalese metal sun buttons, (pink colourway) Swiss bronze knot buttons with polished rim and matt plastic centre; *Samhain* (red colourway) English bark horn button.

YARN INFORMATION

When possible, use the yarn recommended in the knitting pattern instructions. If you want to use a substitute yarn, choose one of the same type and weight as the recommended yarn. Use the descriptions (below) of the various Rowan yarns as a guide to the yarn weight and type (i.e. cotton, mohair, wool, etc.). To calculate the amount needed, determine the number of metres (yards) required rather than the number of grammes (ounces). Your yarn shop will be able to assist you if you have difficulty in choosing a suitable substitute.

Rowan *Botany* (100% pure new wool). Approx 115m (125yd) per 25g (1oz) hank. A 4-ply (US fingering) weight yarn.
Rowan *Cabled Mercerized Cotton* (100% cotton). Approx 185m (203yd) per 50g (1¾oz) ball. A lightweight cotton yarn.
Rowan *Chunky Cotton Chenille* (100% cotton). Approx 140m (153yd) per 100g (3½oz) hank. A chunky (US bulky) weight yarn.
Rowan *Chunky Fox Tweed* (100% pure new wool). Approx 100m (109yd) per 100g (3½oz) hank. A chunky (US bulky) weight yarn.
Rowan *Cotton Glacé* (100% cotton). Approx 112m (123yd) per 50g (1¾oz) ball. A lightweight cotton yarn.
Rowan *Den-m-nit Indigo Dyed Cotton DK* (100% cotton). Approx 93m (102yd) per 50g (1¾oz) ball. A medium weight cotton yarn.
Rowan *Designer DK* (100% pure new wool). Approx 115m (125yd) per 50g (1¾oz) hank. A double knitting (US worsted) weight yarn.
Rowan *Donegal Lambswool Tweed* (100% pure new wool). Approx 100m (109yd) per 25g (1oz) hank. A 4-ply (US sport) weight yarn.
Rowan *Handknit DK Cotton* (100% cotton). Approx 85m (90yd) per 50g (1¾oz) ball. A medium weight cotton yarn.
Rowan *Lightweight DK* (100% pure new wool). Approx 67m (73yd) per 25g (1oz) hank. A lightweight double knitting (US sport) weight yarn.
Rowan *Magpie* (100% pure new wool. Approx 150m (164yd) per 100g (3½oz) hank. An Aran weight yarn.
Rowan *Nice Cotton* (100% cotton). Approx 110m (120yd) per 50g (1¾oz) ball. A lightweight cotton yarn.
Rowan *Rowanspun Tweed* (100% pure new wool). Approx 170m (186yd) per 100g (3½oz) hank. A chunky (US bulky) weight yarn.
Rowan *Silk and Wool* (50% mulberry silk/50% superfine botany wool). Approx 75m (82yd) per 20g (¾oz) ball. A lightweight double knitting (US sport) weight yarn.
Rowan *Silkstones* (52% silk/48% wool). Approx 200m (219yd) per 50g (1¾oz) hank. A lightweight double knitting (US sport) weight yarn.
Rowan *Soft Cotton* (100% cotton). Approx 198m (217yd) per 50g (1¾oz) ball. A lightweight cotton yarn.
Rowan *Wool and Cotton* (50% superfine botany wool/50% Egyptian cotton). Approx 120m (131yd) per 40g (1½oz) ball. A lightweight double knitting (US sport) weight yarn.

AUTHOR'S ACKNOWLEDGEMENTS

There are many people who have contributed to the making of this book and I'd like to thank everyone, even though space prevents me from naming them all. In particular, and most importantly, I'd like to express my warmest appreciation to and admiration of the women who have spent countless hours patiently and skilfully knitting every stitch in this book. To Anne Banks, Anne Heyward-Upton, Sheelagh Shorttle, Rosalind North, Mrs Charlotte Stammers, Miss E. Atkins, Denise Andrews, Mrs J. Clare, Mrs Coe, Mrs Garnett and Mrs Miller goes a huge thank you for your craft. Rowan Yarns generously provided the yarn: a big thank you to Elizabeth and Louisa for sending it to the knitters so efficiently and cheerfully. A special mention goes to Martyn Frith at the Button Queen for his beautiful buttons and also for his thoughtful and creative suggestions. And thanks to Duttons for Buttons for providing some last minute additions.

It was a great thrill to have friends and family wearing the sweaters in the book. Thanks to all the models, but especially to Felix, Philip, James, Rebecca, Rosie, Todd, Nicola, Katy, Bob, Gabriel, Thomas, Stefan, Tom, Nick, Natalie, Ianthe, Simona and Emily.

We spent a wonderful day at the Northern Shire Horse Centre in Market Weighton, courtesy of William and Dorothy Cammidge. My warmest thanks to them, their magnificent horse Captain, and Denis Fairweather, who produced Captain. Angela Williams and the Upper Poppleton County Junior School Maypole Team generously gave up their lunch-hour to dance their whole routine many times on the village green. Unfortunately, the photographs are not in the book but their tireless efforts were much enjoyed by all. Bettys & Taylors of Harrogate kindly donated the beautiful birthday cake for our summer birthday party. It was duly salivated over, and disappeared amazingly quickly after the shoot! Thanks to Pia Tryde for her splendid photography and also for lending her home and garden many times. And thanks to Tessa Codrington, who came in at such short notice and took some beautiful pictures. Thanks to Alex Anderson for styling the clothes and for hosting a weekend shoot at her Dorset home. And thank you to Jane Newdick, who also lent her home, as well as contributing some wonderfully creative props styling. Thanks to Monica Gripaios and Bob Mowbray for the use of their lovely country garden and for the loan of Monica's old family toboggan. A big thank you to Kate Lofthouse for driving us around Yorkshire and feeding the many mouths with her incredible vegan picnic feasts. Her aunt's china tea cups were perfect. No list of acknowledgements would be complete without my saying how much I've appreciated the loyal support and continuous belief in my book which I've received from Sally Harding. Her meticulous editing is so consistent that it gets taken for granted, but her friendship will never be.

And lastly I must acknowledge the important part that Philip Mercer has contributed. He has been an uncomplaining Jack-of-all-trades throughout. For his impromptu catering, tireless driving, photography, creative suggestions and immeasurable practical and emotional support, I owe a great debt, and I extend my gratitude and love as always.

ROWAN YARNS ADDRESSES

Rowan Yarns are widely available in yarn shops. For details of stockists and mail order sources of Rowan yarns, please write or contact the distributors listed below.
For advice on how to use a substitute yarn, see left.

Australia: Rowan (Australia), 191 Canterbury Road, Canterbury, Victoria 3126. Tel. (03) 830 1609
Canada: Estelle Designs & Sales Ltd, Units 65/67, 2220 Midland Avenue, Scarborough, Ontario M1P 3E6. Tel. (416) 298 9922
New Zealand: John Q Goldingham Ltd, PO Box 45083, Epuni Railway, Lower Hutt. Tel. (04) 5674 085
United Kingdom: Rowan Yarns, Green Lane Mill, Holmfirth, West Yorkshire HD7 1RE, England. Tel. (0484) 681881
USA: Westminster Trading Corporation, 5 Northern Boulevard, Amherst, New Hampshire. Tel. (603) 886 5041/5043